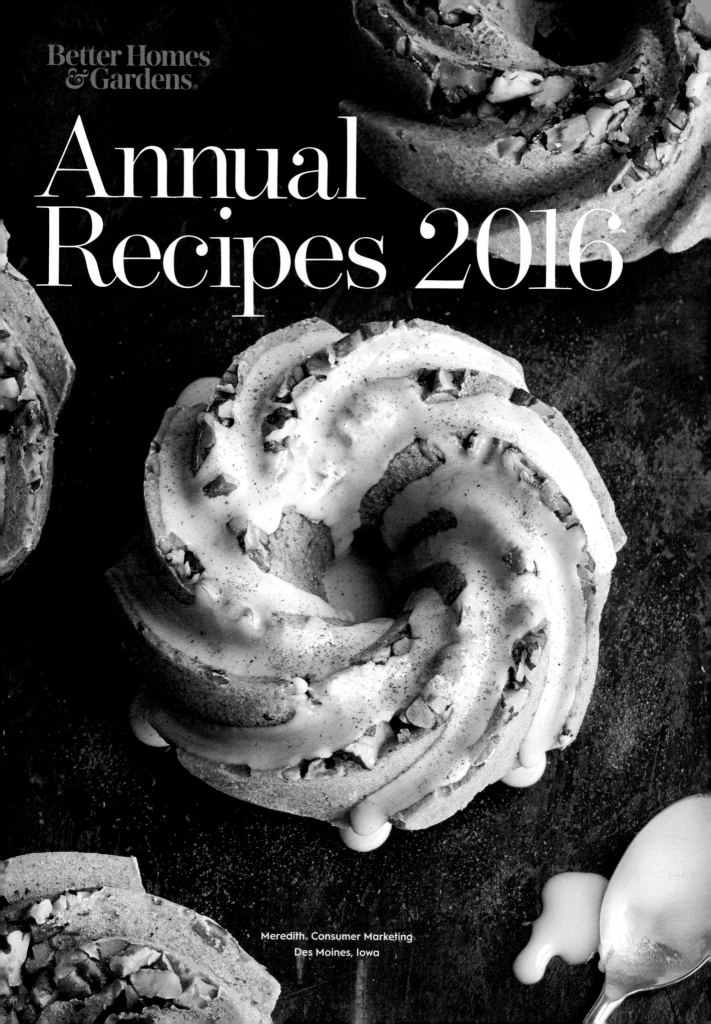

Better Homes
& Gardens®

Annual
Recipes 2016

Meredith. Consumer Marketing
Des Moines, Iowa

PAVLOVA
Recipe on page 110

from the editor

At *Better Homes and Gardens*® we want to inspire your cooking—whether it's a 30-minute weeknight meal or something special for a celebration.

When I look through this book—a collection of all the recipes published in *Better Homes and Gardens* throughout the year—I am so proud of the beauty of the food featured in our magazine. In January we shared nutritious (and flavorful!) recipes with winter greens. In March—our color issue—purple potato soup and a gratin made with violet-tinged cauliflower showed us a new shade of vegetables. In April, fresh garden peas—a sweet but fleeting treat each spring—pop off the page. In July there are blueberries and sunny yellow sweet corn, and in October, a velvety squash soup. The diversity of our recipes represents our tagline—"Life in Color"—in edible form. As a devoted gardener who loves to cook, I am constantly inspired by the seasonal variety of fruits and vegetables featured in our recipes.

We all know that first and foremost food is fuel. But food (and cooking) is pure pleasure as well. That's the mission of our culinary staff—to help you feed your family delicious, nutritious food that you look forward to making. That was just one of the things that came out of ongoing discussions amongst our editors about what our readers want. In fact, we spent a lot of time this year talking about dinner (see "The Dinner Report," starting on page 99). Dinner has much to live up to these days. It needs to both nourish and entertain us—and if it's a weeknight, it needs to be on the table in less than an hour. Most importantly, eating around a table with friends or family bonds us together.

Food is also the centerpiece of most celebrations. It's something we share with family and friends to mark a special occasion or time of year. One of our regular contributors—cookbook author Gesine Bullock-Prado—invites us to her Vermont home to toast the end of the harvest season with an autumnal party inspired by her German roots (see page 233). Food is an edible art form as well. We can challenge ourselves to perfect certain dishes when our days are more

leisurely than harried. Our "How to Cook" section feeds this need, featuring hearty Bolognese sauce in February (page 34), buttery lemon brioche in March (page 53), and ethereal pavlova meringues in May (pictured opposite; see the recipe on page 110).

We want to help and inspire you. The delicious food we share with you in these pages offers a taste of the vast diversity of American cooking—the tried-and-true favorites, the classics with a twist, and the latest trends from every corner of the country and every ethnic group that populates it. I hope as you read our book, you will see, like I have, many things that capture your attention and inspire you to spend time in the kitchen. These days, with so many options for prepared food at our fingertips, we don't cook because we have to. We cook because we want to. Enjoy!

Stephen Orr

Stephen Orr, Editor in Chief
Better Homes and Gardens. magazine

Better Homes & Gardens.

Annual Recipes 2016

TEST KITCHEN

Our seal assures you that every recipe in *Better Homes and Gardens. Annual Recipes 2016* has been tested in the Better Homes and Gardens. Test Kitchen. This means that each recipe is practical and reliable, and it meets our high standards of taste appeal. We guarantee your satisfaction with this book for as long as you own it.

All of us at Meredith Consumer Marketing are dedicated to providing you with information and ideas to enhance your home. We welcome your comments and suggestions. Write to us at: Meredith Consumer Marketing, 1716 Locust St., Des Moines, IA 50309-3023.

Pictured on front cover:
Tiny Tomato Pie, recipe on page 83.

MEREDITH CONSUMER MARKETING
Consumer Marketing Product Director: Heather Sorensen
Consumer Marketing Product Manager: Wendy Merical
Consumer Marketing Billing/Renewal Manager: Tami Beachem
Business Director: Ron Clingman
Senior Production Manager: Al Rodruck

WATERBURY PUBLICATIONS, INC.
Editorial Director: Lisa Kingsley
Associate Editor: Tricia Bergman
Associate Editor/Food Stylist: Annie Peterson
Assistant Food Stylist: Skyler Myers
Creative Director: Ken Carlson
Associate Design Director: Doug Samuelson
Production Assistant: Mindy Samuelson
Contributing Copy Editors: Terri Fredrickson, Peg Smith
Contributing Indexer: Mary Williams

BETTER HOMES AND GARDENS® MAGAZINE
Editor in Chief: Stephen Orr
Senior Deputy Editor: Nancy Wall Hopkins

MEREDITH NATIONAL MEDIA GROUP
President: Tom Harty

MEREDITH CORPORATION
Chairman and Chief Executive Officer: Stephen M. Lacy

In Memoriam: E.T. Meredith III (1933–2003)

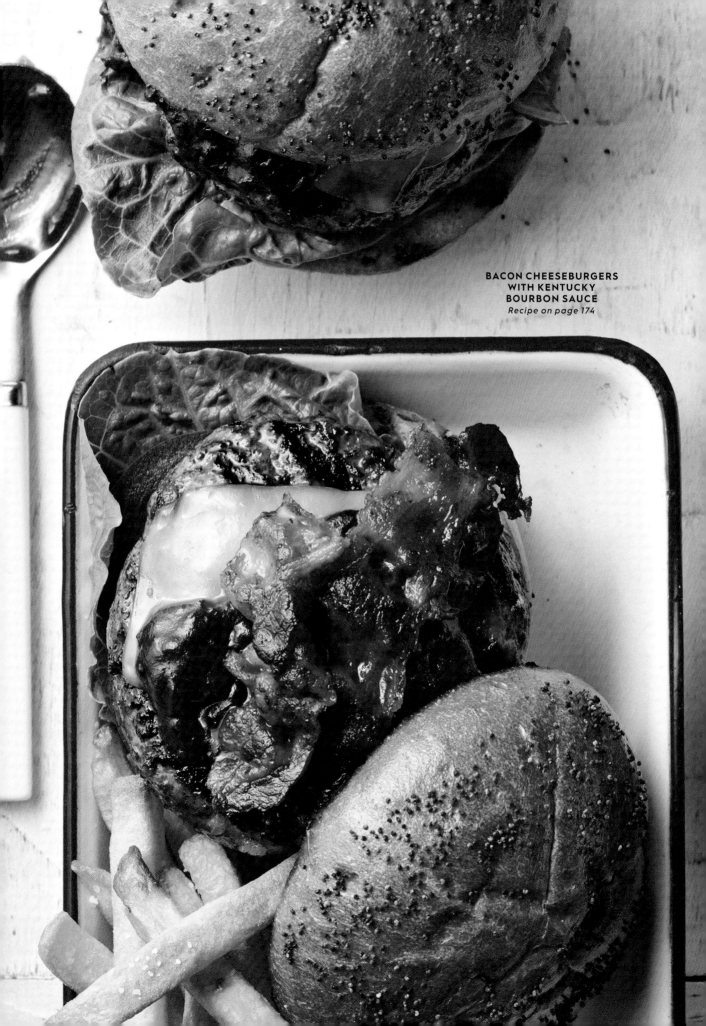

**BACON CHEESEBURGERS
WITH KENTUCKY
BOURBON SAUCE**
Recipe on page 174

PADMA'S
GRILLED CORN
Recipe on page 210

SIMPLICITY Fresh ingredients shine in their own glory—you don't need complicated recipes to create dishes to impress. And the smile on the faces of friends and family with their first bite is the ultimate reward for your effort. In *Better Homes and Gardens Annual Recipes 2016* you'll find traditional recipes refreshed for today's palates, easy-to-follow lessons from recognized chefs, and inspiring features on how to entertain with ease. The focus is on seasonal foods and taking the guesswork out of how to best showcase their flavor. From a fire-roasted menu for a backyard barbecue to weeknight meals, this book is filled with a year's worth of practical how-tos and mouthwatering recipes you'll reach for again and again.

LOOK FOR

MONTHLY FEATURES Winter greens—Swiss chard, mustard greens, chicories, and spinach—start the new year off healthfully in salads, savory tarts, and crackers. With a focus on fresh ingredients and scrumptious recipes, the most senior test kitchen in America—*Better Homes and Gardens* Test Kitchen®—shares seasonal recipes and tips for successful cooking. Culinary legend Jacques Pépin keeps food deliciously simple with recipes for last-of-summer produce. For Top Chef host Padma Lakshmi every meal is a celebration; her recipes reflect her childhood in India and bring exciting flavor to the table. These features and more will inspire confidence in cooking.

HOW TO COOK Cooking class in your own kitchen? Yes, please! Learn the ins and outs of making brioche, the buttery classic French yeast bread as well as versatile bolognese—a complex meat sauce that benefits from low and slow simmering. If you think the restaurant fave steamed dumplings are too difficult to make at home, think again. Invite friends into your kitchen for a class on quick-to-make pesto and the best-ever grilled burgers—all courtesy of grilling pro Jamie Purviance. And if you've dreamed of making pavlova but were intimidated, here's the step-by-step you've waited for.

NEW WAYS This collection of recipes has fresh approaches to common ingredients. Stunning ruby-red beets become noodles for a salad topped with ricotta salata, toasted almonds, and bright balsamic dressing. Featured are enticing summer recipes for bountiful fresh green beans and sweet corn that are anything but ho-hum (Sesame Green Bean Tart and Bucatii Corn-Bonara). Cheesy Hasselback New Potatoes are but one of several that showcase freshly harvested new potatoes. Plus, nature's beautiful eggplant prepared as Greek Eggplant Fries.

FAST & FRESH Need ideas for weeknight dinners? These recipes will spark your creative juices, featuring uber-nutritious leafy greens, garden-fresh fruits and vegetables, lean protein, and cooking techniques to get dinner on the table quickly. From veg-centric Watermelon-Tomato Gazpacho and Root Vegetable & Pomegranate Couscous to savory Thai Rice Noodles & Grilled Steak Salad and Chorizo & Squash Quesadillas you'll have tasty recipes to choose from that your family will love—and you will too because you know they will work every time.

ASIAN BLUEBERRY
COLESLAW
Recipe on page 158.

contents

34

127

168

BARELY ROASTED
PURPLE
VEGETABLES
Recipe on page 60

BASIL PESTO
Recipe on page 77

SPINACH & FETA TART
Recipe on page 21

january

From morning to night, get a healthy start to the new year with dressed-up steel-cut oats, whole food juices and smoothies, über-nutritious leafy green salads, savory tarts, and crisp crackers.

18

22

28

WINTER GREENS

Vibrant, fresh, and totally in season. Conquer the wintertime blues with something green, leafy, and delicious.

PECAN & COLLARD CHICKEN SALAD

This is a hearty salad for a cold winter day. Collard greens are cut into long strands—chiffonade—and tossed with roasted chicken, crispy bacon, and a nutty maple-Dijon dressing. Citrus keeps things tasting bright.

TOTAL TIME 30 min.

- 12 oz. tender young collard greens, washed and dried
- 3   oranges
- 1   cup coarsely chopped toasted pecans
- 2   Tbsp. sherry vinegar
- 2   tsp. maple syrup
- ½   tsp. Dijon-style mustard
- ½   tsp. salt
- ½   tsp. black pepper
     Bottled hot pepper sauce
- 6   Tbsp. extra-virgin olive oil
- 2   cups sliced rotisserie chicken
- 4   slices cooked thick-cut bacon, crumbled

1. Remove ribs from collard leaves; discard. Stack leaves and roll into a cylinder. Slice crosswise into thin ribbons; set aside.

2. Juice one of the oranges. Peel remaining oranges and slice; set aside. Place about ⅓ cup of the pecans into a food processor. Add 2 Tbsp. orange juice, vinegar, syrup, mustard, salt, pepper, and a few dashes of hot sauce. Process until combined. With processor running, drizzle in oil.

3. In an extra-large bowl toss greens, chicken, and dressing. Top with orange slices, remaining pecans, and bacon. Makes 6 servings.

EACH SERVING *595 cal, 50 g fat, 89 mg chol, 781 mg sodium, 15 g carb, 5 g fiber, 28 g pro.*

A GREENS GLOSSARY

CHARD With tender stems and glossy leaves, there's little flavor difference among Swiss, rainbow, and green chard. Use young chard in salads, or slice the thicker stems thinly and cook as you would celery in a soup or stir-fry.

CHICORIES Belgian endive stays pale white and creamy yellow because it's grown in complete darkness. Radicchio, whether ball-shape Chioggia or pointed and narrow Treviso, has a slightly bitter edge.

COLLARDS Part of the cabbage family and just as versatile, use small tender leaves in salads, and large leaves as a wrap (first cut out the tough stem).

KALE Russian red kale is tender and mild. Curly kale has frilly ends that hold on to dressing in salads. Heirloom Tuscan kale (also known as dinosaur, black, and Lacinato) is the heartiest and best for long-cooking soups or in pesto.

SPINACH This versatile green lends itself to smoothies, sandwiches and more. Buy it by the bunch for the freshest option.

TURN TO GREENS FOR FRESH AND SATISFYING EATING ALL WINTER— SAVOR THE TEXTURES THAT RESULT FROM FOLDING HEARTY RAW GREENS INTO A WARM DISH.

MUSTARD GREENS ON TOAST
Recipe on page 18

GREENS CRACKER
Recipe on page 18

MUSTARD GREENS ON TOAST

Photo on page 16.

Mustard greens, like arugula and watercress, are known for their pungent bite. The heat mellows once they're cooked, but a peppery edge lingers. Echo their spiciness with a shower of red pepper flakes and serve with a drizzle of good olive oil.

TOTAL TIME 35 min.

- 6 to 8 Tbsp. extra-virgin olive oil
- 3 cloves garlic, sliced
- 1 medium red sweet pepper, cut into strips
- 1 12- to 14-oz. bunch mustard greens, cut into 4-inch-long pieces
- 1 tsp. finely grated lemon zest
- 1 Tbsp. lemon juice
  Kosher salt
  Black pepper
- 4 thick slices country bread
- 4 eggs
- ½ cup shredded Parmigiano-Reggiano cheese

1. In a large skillet heat ¼ cup of the olive oil over medium heat. Add garlic; cook 1 minute or until fragrant (do not brown). Add sweet pepper; cook and stir 4 minutes or until tender. Gradually add greens, tossing until wilted. Add a splash of water. Cover and cook 4 minutes or until tender. Uncover; cook to reduce any liquid in skillet. Add lemon zest and juice. Season to taste with kosher salt and pepper. Toss well. Cover and keep warm.
2. Brush bread with some of the remaining oil. Broil or grill until toasted; set aside.
3. In a large nonstick skillet heat 1 Tbsp. of the oil over medium heat. Crack eggs into skillet. Season with kosher salt and pepper. Cook 2 to 3 minutes or just until whites are set and yolks are just firm. To serve, top bread slices with greens and any juices. Drizzle with remaining olive oil and top each with an egg. Sprinkle with cheese and additional lemon zest. Makes 4 servings.
EACH SERVING *430 cal, 29 g fat, 193 mg chol, 525 mg sodium, 28 g carb, 3 g fiber, 16 g pro.*

GREENS CRACKER

Photo on page 17.

This take on kale chips is elegantly appealing. Golden, flaky piecrust creates a buttery base for crisp greens. Aromatic rosemary gives the dough a sweet woodsy flavor—a sprinkle of thyme or sage will work as well.

TOTAL TIME 30 min.

- ½ 14.1-oz. pkg. rolled refrigerated unbaked piecrust (1 crust)
- 1 egg yolk
- ½ tsp. snipped fresh rosemary
- 2 to 3 chard or kale leaves with stems
- 1 oz. Gruyère cheese, shredded (½ cup)
  Sea salt

Preheat oven to 400°F. Line a baking sheet with parchment; set aside. On a floured surface, unroll then fold pastry sheet into quarters. Gently roll into a 12×10-inch rectangle. Trim edges. Transfer to prepared baking sheet. Brush with a mixture of egg yolk and 2 tsp. water. Sprinkle with rosemary. Arrange chard on top, pressing lightly. Sprinkle with cheese. Bake 15 minutes or until golden. Remove; cool completely. Sprinkle with sea salt before serving. Makes 8 servings.
EACH SERVING *122 cal, 7 g fat, 29 mg chol, 237 mg sodium, 12 g carb, 0 g fiber, 2 g pro.*

ROASTED CHICORIES WITH BROWN BUTTER

Roasting on high heat mellows the assertive bite of endive and radicchio. They're even better when combined with a silky brown butter sauce and sweet delicata squash that has a skin so tender there's no need to peel.

HANDS-ON TIME 20 min.
TOTAL TIME 50 min.

- 2 oz. focaccia or ciabatta bread, cut into cubes
- ¼ cup extra-virgin olive oil
- 1 Tbsp. grated Parmesan cheese
- 1 Tbsp. finely chopped fresh Italian parsley
- 1 large delicata squash (about 1½ lb.), halved lengthwise, seeded, and sliced
- 2 heads Belgian endive, halved lengthwise
- 1 small head radicchio, cut into sixths
- 3 Tbsp. butter
- 1 Tbsp. lemon juice
- ¼ cup capers

1. Preheat oven to 450°F. In a shallow baking pan toss bread cubes with 1 Tbsp. of the olive oil. Spread in an even layer. Bake 8 minutes or until toasted. Sprinkle with Parmesan and parsley; toss to coat. Transfer to a piece of foil to cool.
2. In a shallow baking pan arrange squash in an even layer; drizzle with 2 Tbsp. of the olive oil. Bake 20 minutes. Add endive, radicchio, and remaining 1 Tbsp. olive oil; toss to coat. Season with salt and pepper. Bake 10 minutes more or until vegetables are tender and browned.
3. Meanwhile, for Brown Butter, in a small saucepan heat butter over low heat until golden brown and nutty-smelling.* Remove from heat. Stir in lemon juice and capers.
4. Arrange vegetable mixture on a platter. Drizzle with brown butter mixture. Sprinkle with croutons and chopped parsley. Makes 6 servings.
*Tip The key to Brown Butter is a watchful eye. Use a light-color saucepan so you can see the butter go from creamy pale yellow to golden brown.
EACH SERVING *194 cal, 16 g fat, 16 mg chol, 358 mg sodium, 11 g carb, 3 g fiber, 4 g pro.*

ROASTED CHICORIES WITH BROWN BUTTER

SPINACH & FETA TART

SPINACH & FETA TART

This savory tart is loaded with spinach in the feta and egg filling and the salad-like topping. Sautéed lemon slices give this tart a beautiful presentation. A quick cook in the skillet mellows flavor and slightly caramelizes them to concentrate their lemony deliciousness.

HANDS-ON TIME 30 min.
TOTAL TIME 1 hr., 15 min.

- 3 Tbsp. extra-virgin olive oil
- 1 bunch green onions (6), thinly sliced
- 1 lb. fresh spinach
- ½ 17.3-oz. pkg. frozen puff pastry sheets (1 sheet), thawed
- 1 small lemon
- 2 eggs
- ½ cup crème fraîche
- 2 Tbsp. snipped fresh dill
- ½ tsp. kosher salt
- ¼ tsp. black pepper
- ⅛ tsp. freshly grated nutmeg
- 4 oz. feta cheese, crumbled
- ½ cup fresh mint leaves, torn if large
- ¼ cup fresh dill sprigs
- 1 recipe Sautéed Lemons

1. In an extra-large skillet heat 1 Tbsp. of the olive oil over medium-high heat. Add green onions; cook and stir until tender and fragrant, about 2 minutes.
2. Gradually add about 12 cups of the spinach, tossing with tongs until wilted, about 2 minutes. Remove and cool slightly. Coarsely chop spinach mixture. Set aside.
3. Preheat oven to 400°F. Line a baking sheet with parchment; set aside. On a lightly floured surface, roll out puff pastry sheet to a 13×11-inch rectangle. Carefully transfer pastry to prepared baking sheet. Moisten edges of pastry with water. Fold over a ½-inch border on all sides; press border lightly. Using the back of a paring knife, make evenly spaced indentations around the outer edge of the pastry to ensure even rising). Chill 15 minutes or up to 1 hour.
4. Meanwhile, zest and juice lemon. In a medium bowl whisk together 1 tsp. of the lemon zest, eggs, crème fraîche, snipped dill, salt, pepper, and nutmeg. Stir in chopped spinach and feta cheese. Spread filling on pastry. Bake 30 minutes or until pastry is puffed and browned on the bottom and filling is set. Transfer to a wire rack; cool.

5. Just before serving, toss remaining spinach, mint leaves, and dill sprigs with 1 Tbsp. lemon juice and remaining 2 Tbsp. oil. Season with salt and pepper. Cut pastry into six pieces. Top with Sautéed Lemons. Serve with tossed spinach and additional feta. Makes 6 servings.
Sautéed Lemons Thinly slice 1 lemon; season with salt and pepper. In a large skillet heat 1 Tbsp. olive oil over medium heat. Cook slices 3 to 5 minutes or until browned, turning once. Remove from heat; let cool.
EACH SERVING *704 cal, 54 g fat, 146 mg chol, 866 mg sodium, 36 g carb, 5 g fiber, 15 g pro.*

TOASTED COUSCOUS & CHARD SALAD

Chard's sturdy-yet-tender texture and mild flavor—between spinach and kale—make it the green to reach for often. Here, it wilts into a warm bowl of toasted couscous, soaking up flavors of pomegranate dressing.

TOTAL TIME 20 min.

- 1 cup reduced-sodium chicken broth
- 2 Tbsp. butter
- 1 tsp. Aleppo pepper
- ½ tsp. kosher salt
- ¼ tsp. black pepper
- 1 bunch green onions (6), trimmed and finely chopped
- 1 cup Israeli couscous (large pearl)
- 1 cup grated uncooked golden beets
- 1 cup lightly packed fresh Italian parsley
- ½ cup pomegranate seeds
- ⅓ cup chopped, toasted walnuts
- ¼ cup mint leaves
- 2 Tbsp. red wine vinegar
- 1 Tbsp. pomegranate molasses
- 8 oz. rainbow chard, stemmed and thinly sliced

1. In a small saucepan bring chicken broth to a boil. Reduce heat to low. Cover; keep warm.
2. Meanwhile, in an extra-large nonstick skillet melt butter with Aleppo pepper, salt, and black pepper over medium-high heat. Add green onions; cook 1 minute or until fragrant. Add couscous; cook 5 minutes or until toasted. Slowly stir in chicken broth. Cook until all liquid is absorbed. Stir in beets; heat through.
3. Remove skillet from heat. Add parsley, pomegranate seeds, walnuts, mint, vinegar, and molasses; toss to combine. Toss with chard and drizzle with olive oil before serving. Makes 8 servings.
EACH SERVING *198 cal, 8 g fat, 8 mg chol, 293 mg sodium, 25 g carb, 2 g fiber, 5 g pro.*

TOASTED COUSCOUS & CHARD SALAD

DRINK UP!

Need a little restart? Pick your potion and sip your way to feeling healthy with deliciously simple juices and smoothies.

CUCUMBER-MINT REFRESHER

Start the day with a hydrating mix of cooling mint, cucumber, and honeydew melon. "Honeydew adds liquid volume to juices, and you can throw it in the juicer peel and all," Candice Kumai says. Just be sure to wash it first.

TOTAL TIME 10 min.

3	cups baby spinach
1	large cucumber
¾	cup honeydew melon
½	cup fresh mint
¼	cup fresh basil

In a high-powered juicer carefully place all ingredients; juice into a clean pitcher. Whisk well and serve immediately. Makes 2 servings.
Blender option Peel, seed, and chop cucumber and honeydew. Place all ingredients in a high-powered blender. Blend until nearly smooth. Pour juice through a fine-mesh sieve into glasses to serve.
EACH SERVING *76 cal, 0 g fat, 0 mg chol, 87 mg sodium, 16 g carb, 5 g fiber, 4 g pro.*

CINNAMON & GINGER CARROT JUICE

Ginger and cinnamon give sweet carrot juice a zippy edge and calm indigestion. "Fresh ginger is one of my favorites to juice," Candice says. "It's anti-inflammatory, full of antioxidants, and good for digestion."

TOTAL TIME 10 min.

10	carrots (1 lb.), scrubbed
½	medium cucumber
1	Tbsp. peeled, chopped fresh ginger*
1	tsp. ground cinnamon

In a high-powered juicer carefully place carrots, cucumber, and ginger; juice into a clean pitcher. Whisk in cinnamon. Serve immediately. Makes 2 servings.
Blender option Peel and chop carrots; peel, seed, and chop cucumber. Place all ingredients in a high-powered blender. Blend until nearly smooth. Pour juice through a fine-mesh sieve into glasses to serve.
* For fresh ginger whenever you need it, peel and chop ginger root into 1-inch pieces. Transfer to a resealable bag and freeze up to 3 months.
EACH SERVING *102 cal, 1 g fat, 0 mg chol, 158 mg sodium, 24 g carb, 7 g fiber, 2 g pro.*

VITAMIN C BERRY SHAKE

Need a winter immuno-boost? Vitamin C-rich berries, OJ, and bee pollen will do the trick. "Probiotics aid digestion and boost immunity, and the powder goes undetected in smoothies," Candice says. "Bee pollen is chock-full of amino acids and gives the shake a little sweetness."

TOTAL TIME 10 min.

½	cup water
1	cup fresh-squeezed orange juice (3 to 4 oranges)
1	cup frozen blackberries
½	cup frozen raspberries
1	cup plain 2-percent Greek yogurt
1	Tbsp. bee pollen powder
1	tsp. probiotic powder

In a blender combine all ingredients; blend until smooth. Serve immediately. Makes 3 servings.
EACH SERVING *153 cal, 2 g fat, 4 mg chol, 32 mg sodium, 25 g carb, 5 g fiber, 10 g pro.*

Candice Kumai, a celebrity chef and clean-food eating expert, has written five books, including Clean Green Drinks. Her latest, *Clean Green Eats* ($27.99; Harper Wave).

CUCUMBER-MINT
REFRESHER

CINNAMON & GINGER
CARROT JUICE

VITAMIN C BERRY
SHAKE

BEETROOT BLEND

MATCHA SMOOTHIE

JUICES ARE BEST MADE IN A MASTICATING JUICER, WHICH EXTRACTS THE JUICE FROM WHOLE PRODUCE AND REMOVES THE PULP. A SMOOTHIE IS MADE IN A BLENDER AND CONTAINS THE WHOLE PRODUCE, INCLUDING ROUGHAGE.

BEETROOT BLEND

"Beet" the afternoon slump with a sweet and tart wake-me-up of beets, apples, and lemon juice. "Lemon juice gives the drink brightness that lets all the flavors shine," Candice says. "The citric acid in the fruit also slows oxidation so it keeps its beautiful color as you sip."

TOTAL TIME 10 min.

- 3 cups baby spinach
- 2 stalks celery, cut up
- 2 medium beets (8 oz.), scrubbed, trimmed, and quartered
- 1 Fuji or Gala apple, quartered and seeds removed
- 2 Tbsp. lemon juice

In a high-powered juicer carefully place spinach, celery, beets, and apple; juice into a clean pitcher. Add lemon juice. Serve immediately. Makes 2 servings.
Blender option Peel and chop beets; seed and chop apple. Place all ingredients in a high-powered blender. Blend until nearly smooth. Pour mixture through a fine-mesh sieve into glasses to serve.
EACH SERVING *126 cal, 0 g fat, 0 mg chol, 187 mg sodium, 29 g carb, 8 g fiber, 4 g pro.*

MATCHA SMOOTHIE

Matcha (aka powdered green tea) promotes mental clarity and helps you chill out. "Matcha is showing up everywhere, and for good reason," Candice says. "Not only can it boost metabolism, it helps you relax and is a natural detoxifier."

TOTAL TIME 10 min.

- 1½ cups refrigerated unsweetened coconut milk
- 2 cups baby spinach
- 1 banana, cut up and frozen
- 2 tsp. matcha (green tea powder)
- 1 tsp. bee pollen powder (optional)
- 1 cup ice cubes

In a blender combine all ingredients. Blend until smooth. Serve immediately. Makes 3 servings.
EACH SERVING *67 cal, 2 g fat, 0 mg chol, 52 mg sodium, 10 g carb, 2 g fiber, 1 g pro.*

CLEAN GREEN PROTEIN SMOOTHIE

"Frozen bananas are a must," Candice says. "Peel them before you freeze them to avoid a nightmare."

TOTAL TIME 10 min.

- 1½ cups refrigerated unsweetened almond milk
- 2 cups chopped kale
- 1 banana, cut up and frozen
- 2 Tbsp. unsweetened almond butter
- ½ tsp. spirulina powder (optional)
- 1 cup ice cubes

Combine all ingredients in a blender and blend until smooth. Serve immediately. Makes 3 servings.
EACH SERVING *142 cal, 8 g fat, 0 mg chol, 110 mg sodium, 16 g carb, 4 g fiber, 5 g pro.*

IF YOU DON'T OWN A JUICING MACHINE, any of these juices can be made in a blender then strained. Note that the texture might differ slightly. Use a high-powered blender for best results.

TO ENSURE A SMOOTH DRINK, pour in the liquids first, then add the hearty fruits and vegetables followed by leafy greens and herbs. Finish with fleshy/watery fruits and vegetables. Start on the lowest speed and wait a few seconds for the bigger pieces to break down, then turn to high.

wake up your
OATS

If the thought of a bowl of oatmeal has you yawning, rethink the breakfast mainstay with steel-cut oats! These inspiring recipes are worth jumping out of bed.

PEANUT BUTTER, BANANA & BACON OATMEAL

Elvis would swoon over this peanut butter-bacon combo, and you will, too! The oats are cooked on the stove to achieve the perfect texture, then finished in the oven to caramelize the bananas and brown sugar.

HANDS-ON TIME 25 min.
TOTAL TIME 45 min.

4   cups milk
1   cup steel-cut oats
1   tsp. salt
½   cup crunchy peanut butter
2   Tbsp. packed brown sugar
2   bananas, peeled and cut into chunks
4   strips bacon, crisp-cooked and crumbled
2   Tbsp. flaxseed, ground
2   Tbsp. grape jelly
½   cup chopped strawberries

1. In a large saucepan bring milk just to boiling over medium heat (watch carefully so milk doesn't boil over). Add oats and salt. Reduce heat to medium-low. Cook, uncovered, 25 to 30 minutes or until oats are tender and mixture is thickened and creamy, stirring frequently to prevent skin from forming and to prevent sticking. Remove from heat.
2. Preheat oven to 400°F. Stir peanut butter, brown sugar, bananas, bacon, and flaxseed into oats. Spoon into a 9-inch cast-iron skillet or a 1½-quart casserole. Bake 10 to 15 minutes or until heated through. Stir in jelly. Top with strawberries and additional bacon. Drizzle with additional jelly. Makes 6 to 8 servings.
EACH SERVING *417 cal, 19 g fat, 18 mg chol, 371 mg sodium, 51 g carb, 17 g pro.*

STEEL-CUT VS. ROLLED

STEEL-CUT Also known as Irish, Scotch, coarse-cut, or pinhead oats, the steel-cut variety is made from whole oat groats (the inner portion of the kernel) chopped into ricelike pieces. The flavor is nuttier and earthier and the texture is heartier and chewier than rolled oats.

ROLLED Often labeled old-fashioned rolled oats, these are also whole oat groats, but they've been steamed and rolled. This process creates a flat, flaky shape that allows them to cook quickly.

THE RATIO FOR MAKING STEEL-CUT OATMEAL ON THE STOVETOP IS 1 CUP OATS TO 4 CUPS LIQUID, FOR CREAMY TEXTURE. IF YOU PREFER OATS CHEWIER, USE A LITTLE LESS LIQUID.

TROPICAL SLOW COOKER OATMEAL

STOVETOP SAVORY HAM & VEGGIE OATMEAL

Denver omelet-inspired oats are delicious morning, noon, or night. Top with an over-easy egg for additional protein punch.

HANDS-ON TIME 15 min.
TOTAL TIME 35 min.

4   cups reduced-sodium chicken broth
1   cup steel-cut oats
2   cups Broccolini or broccoli (4 oz.)
2   Tbsp. olive oil
    Salt
    Black pepper
2   red and/or yellow sweet peppers, chopped
1   medium onion, chopped
4   oz. cheddar cheese, shredded (1 cup)
4   oz. cooked ham, diced
2   Tbsp. toasted wheat germ
2   Tbsp. snipped fresh Italian parsley

1. In a large saucepan bring broth to boiling. Stir in oats. Reduce heat to medium-low. Cook, uncovered, 25 to 30 minutes or until oats are tender and mixture is thickened and creamy.
2. Meanwhile, preheat oven to 400°F. In a shallow baking pan toss Broccolini with 1 Tbsp. of the oil. Season with salt and pepper. Roast 8 to 10 minutes or until crisp-tender and starting to brown, stirring once.
3. In a large skillet heat remaining oil over medium-high heat. Add sweet peppers and onion. Cook, stirring occasionally, 5 to 6 minutes or until tender and starting to brown.
4. Stir cheese into oat mixture until melted and creamy. Stir in pepper mixture, ham, wheat germ, and parsley. Spoon into a serving dish. Top with Broccolini. If desired, top with an over-easy egg. Makes 4 servings.
EACH SERVING *426 cal, 22 g fat, 45 mg chol, 1,147 mg sodium, 38 g carb, 23 g pro.*

TROPICAL SLOW COOKER OATMEAL

HANDS-ON TIME 20 min.
TOTAL TIME 3 hr., 20 min.

6   cups unsweetened vanilla almond milk
2   cups steel-cut oats
1   tsp. salt
¼   cup chia seeds
2   cups chopped pineapple
3   Cara Cara oranges, peeled and sliced
½   cup plain Greek yogurt
¼   cup toasted coconut chips
⅓   cup honey

In a 4-qt. slow cooker stir together milk, oats, and salt. Cover; cook on low 6 to 8 hours or on high 3 to 4 hours. To serve, stir in chia seeds and top with pineapple, oranges, yogurt, and coconut. Drizzle with honey. Makes 6 servings.
EACH SERVING *390 cal, 12 g fat, 1 mg chol, 516 mg sodium, 68 g carb, 14 g pro.*

STOVETOP SAVORY
HAM & VEGGIE
OATMEAL

NO-KNEAD
HONEY BREAD
Recipe on page 44

february

Take a peek inside America's oldest test kitchen—*Better Homes and Gardens®* Test Kitchen—and learn how to cook like a pro. With step-by-step instructions, you can cook at home confidently.

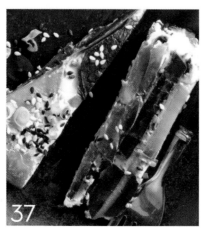

how to cook
BOLOGNESE

This homey sauce is the ultimate winter comfort food.

BOLOGNESE (pronounced boh-luhn-yeyz) is more than just meat sauce. It's one of the most versatile sauces in the kitchen. A lazy Sunday afternoon simmer develops the layered flavors into something more than its humble ingredients. Though there's debate over the traditional version (even in the Northern Italian city of Bologna where it originated), most recipes start with a few basics: meat, vegetables, and wine. Some include tomato, and others use milk or cream for complexity. This version has a spin that will make it worth making again and again.

BOLOGNESE

BUILDING THE SAUCE

MEAT Ground beef (85 percent lean ground chuck) is the primary ingredient, while pork provides a bit of sweetness, and pancetta a smoky flavor. There will be a fair amount of fat. Remember: Fat is flavor! Any excess can be skimmed at the end.

VEGETABLES Traditional recipes call for onion, carrot, and celery. This recipe trades celery for fennel stems, which are similar shaped but deliver a mellow anise flavor. The sauce should have texture, so skip precise chopping—rough will do.

WINE Use any good dry wine that you'd be happy to serve with dinner. White wine melds right into the sauce, but you can also use red, which tends to give a slightly more assertive flavor.

MILK To give the sauce a layer of unexpected richness, add milk before adding the tomatoes.

TOMATOES Some recipes call for tomato paste, but when whole canned San Marzano tomatoes (Italian plum tomatoes that have a sweet flavor and low acidity) are cut into pieces, they fleck the sauce without overpowering it.

BOLOGNESE

*Leftover sauce freezes like a dream.
Divide it into resealable bags, and
you'll have slow-simmered sauce at the
ready any time the craving strikes.*

HANDS-ON TIME 1 hr.
TOTAL TIME 4 hr., 15 min.

2	Tbsp. butter
1	Tbsp. olive oil
4	oz. pancetta, chopped
1	large onion, chopped (1 cup)
2	medium carrots, chopped (1 cup)
	Stems of 1 head fennel, chopped (1 cup)
2	lb. ground beef
1	lb. ground pork
½	tsp. kosher salt
½	tsp. black pepper
2	cups dry white or red wine
1½	cups whole milk
⅛	tsp. ground nutmeg
1	28-oz. can whole tomatoes, cut up (undrained)
1	Parmesan cheese rind (1 to 2 inches)

1. In a 4-qt. Dutch oven heat butter and olive oil over medium-high heat. Add pancetta. Cook and stir 8 minutes or just until starting to brown. Reduce heat to medium. Add onion. Cook and stir until translucent, about 5 minutes. Add carrots and fennel. Cook 2 minutes more.
2. Add beef and pork to Dutch oven. Season with the salt and black pepper. Using a fork, break up meat (retain some larger pieces for texture). Cook until browned. Add wine. Using a wooden spoon, scrape up browned bits from bottom of pan. Simmer, uncovered, until wine has evaporated.
3. Add milk and nutmeg to Dutch oven. Simmer, uncovered, until milk has evaporated, stirring frequently. Add tomatoes; stir to combine. When tomatoes just start to bubble, reduce heat to low; add Parmesan rind. Simmer, uncovered, 2½ to 3 hours, stirring occasionally. As the sauce cooks, liquid will evaporate and the sauce will start to look dry. Add ½ cup water at a time (2 to 3 cups total), continuing to simmer as liquid evaporates. Makes 12 servings.
EACH SERVING *408 cal, 28 g fat, 94 mg chol, 444 mg sodium, 8 g carb, 5 g fiber, 23 g pro.*

1 BROWNING This is the first step to creating the layers of flavor that make this sauce so hard to resist. Take your time. Deep caramelizing on the veggies and meat adds to the richness.

2 DEGLAZING When you add the wine, the liquid helps release all those flavorful browned bits at the bottom of the pan. A wooden spoon is the best tool for scraping them up.

3 REDUCING It might seem like an odd stage to add milk, but cooking away the liquid before adding the tomatoes makes the meat even richer and sweeter without making the sauce overtly creamy.

4 SIMMERING For ultra-tender meat, keep the heat as low as possible, for the slightest bubbling. Add a little water to keep the sauce from sticking—each addition concentrates the flavor.

Bolognese is delicious over pasta, in casseroles, and sandwiches, and as a dip.

ON PASTA Chunky shapes such as rigatoni, penne, tagliatelle, or egg noodles are best. Rigid tubes or wide noodles allow the sauce to cling.

IN LASAGNA Alternate layers of lasagna noodles, ricotta cheese, and Bolognese then top with mozzarella and grated Parmesan.

IN A SANDWICH Spoon meat into buns or serve like Italian sloppy joes.

AS A PARTY DIP Keep Bolognese warm in a slow cooker with crostini nearby for dunking. Make it even more indulgent: Top the warm dip with pieces of fresh mozzarella.

new ways with
BEETS

Roasted, pickled, or eaten fresh—this versatile root intrigues with a splash of color and a hit of sweet, earthy flavor.

The best beets are firm and round with smooth skin and can be deep red, golden yellow, or bright pink. If greens are attached, look for crisp, bright leaves. Leaves pull moisture from the root, so cut and store separately in the refrigerator (add leaves to salads and stir-fries).

We find beets are easiest to peel after roasting. Cool slightly, then rub the beets with paper towels to pull off the skin. For raw beets, use a small sharp knife to slice away the peel along the contour of the root.

CHILLED BEET TART

BEET "NOODLE" SALAD

PICKLED BEET SANDWICHES

GRAB SOME GLOVES. THE STUNNING RUBY COLOR OF SOME BEETS WILL STAIN YOUR HANDS. IF YOU COME AWAY RED-HANDED, WASH WITH LEMON JUICE.

CHILLED BEET TART

HANDS-ON TIME 45 min.
TOTAL TIME 1 hr., 45 min.

- 2   lb. beets
       Olive oil
       Salt
       Black pepper
- 2   8-oz. pkg. cream cheese, softened
- 1   Tbsp. tahini (sesame seed paste)
- 1   to 2 fresh jalapeño peppers*, halved, seeded, if desired, and finely chopped
- ¼   tsp. salt
- ⅓   cup sliced green onions
- ¼   cup black and/or white sesame seeds, toasted **

1. Preheat oven to 350°F. Scrub beets and place in a 3-qt. rectangular baking dish. Drizzle with olive oil and sprinkle with some salt and pepper. Add 2 to 3 Tbsp. water to the dish. Cover and roast 1 hour or until tender. Cool, peel, and slice beets.
2. In a medium bowl stir together the cream cheese, tahini, jalapeño pepper, and salt.
3. Line a 9-inch springform pan with plastic wrap. Set aside 1 Tbsp. green onion and 1 tsp. sesame seeds. Place about one-third of the sliced beets in the prepared pan. Spread about one-third of the cream cheese mixture in the center of the pan and gently spread over the beets toward the edges. Top with one-third of the remaining green onions and sesame seeds. Repeat layers. Cover with foil and chill at least 1 hour or up to 24 hours. Remove sides of pan. Invert tart onto a serving platter and remove bottom of pan and plastic wrap. Top with reserved green onions and sesame seeds. Makes 16 servings.

*Tip Hot chile peppers, such as jalapeños, contain oils that can irritate your skin and eyes. Wear plastic or rubber gloves when working with them. If your bare hands do touch the chile peppers, wash hands and nails well with soap and water.
**Tip To toast nuts, seeds, or coconut, place in a single layer in a shallow baking pan. Bake in a 350°F oven for 5 to 10 minutes or until pieces are golden brown, stirring once or twice. Watch closely to prevent burning them.
EACH SERVING *139 cal, 11 g fat, 31 mg chol, 186 mg sodium, 8 g carb, 2 g fiber, 3 g pro.*

BEET "NOODLE" SALAD

HANDS-ON TIME 20 min.
TOTAL TIME 4 hr., 20 min.

- ⅓   cup balsamic vinegar
- ⅓   cup extra-virgin olive oil
- ½   tsp. salt
- ½   tsp. ground black pepper
- 2   lb. beets, scrubbed and peeled
- 1½   cups green seedless grapes, halved
- 4   oz. ricotta salata cheese, crumbled
- ½   cup chopped toasted almonds

In a large bowl whisk together the vinegar, oil, salt, and pepper. Use a spiral vegetable slicer to cut beets into spirals. Using kitchen shears, snip beet spirals a few times. Add spirals to bowl with dressing; toss to coat. Cover and chill 4 to 24 hours. Just before serving, top beets with grapes, cheese, and almonds. Makes 8 servings.
EACH SERVING *221 cal, 16 g fat, 13 mg chol, 448 mg sodium, 17 g carb, 3 g fiber, 5 g pro.*

PICKLED BEET SANDWICHES

TOTAL TIME 20 min.

- 3   oz. thinly sliced prosciutto
- ¼   cup mayonnaise
- 8   slices hearty wheat bread, toasted
- 1   16-oz. jar pickled beets, drained and sliced*
- 2   cups watercress
- 1½   cups potato chips, coarsely crushed (½ cup)

In an extra-large skillet crisp prosciutto over medium heat, turning occasionally; drain. Spread mayonnaise over 4 four slices of the toasted bread. Top mayonnaise-coated bread with remaining ingredients, topping each sandwich with bread. Makes 4 servings.
EACH SERVING *371 cal, 19 g fat, 21 mg chol, 877 mg sodium, 40 g carb, 4 g fiber, 12 g pro.*

*For Fresh Pickled Beets Omit the jar of pickled beets. Preheat oven to 350°F. Scrub 8 to 12 ounces of small beets and place in a 2-qt. rectangular baking dish. Drizzle with a little olive oil, then sprinkle lightly with salt and pepper. Add 1 to 2 Tbsp. water to the dish. Cover; bake 1 hour or until tender. Cool, peel, and slice. Place in a nonreactive bowl. In a small saucepan heat together ½ cup cider vinegar, ¼ cup water, 1 Tbsp. sugar, 2 whole cloves, 1 whole allspice, and 1½ tsp. salt. Heat and stir over medium heat until sugar and salt dissolve. Pour over beets; cover and chill overnight or up to 1 week.

FAST & FRESH

Easy, healthy recipes for a better dinner tonight.

ROOT VEGETABLE & POMEGRANATE COUSCOUS

Seed the pomegranate without a mess: Cut into quarters, hold each segment in a bowl of water, and pry out seeds with your fingers. When you've worked your way through the pomegranate, strain out the seeds.

HANDS-ON TIME 30 min.
TOTAL TIME 1 hr.

- ½ tsp. ground cumin
- ¼ tsp. ground ginger
- ½ tsp. ground cinnamon
- 1½ tsp. kosher salt
- ¼ tsp. black pepper
- 2 lb. root vegetables, such as carrots, parsnips, turnips, and winter squash, peeled and chopped or sliced ½ inch thick
- 1 red onion, cut into wedges (1 cup)
- 2 Tbsp. extra-virgin olive oil
- 1 cup boiling water
- 1 cup uncooked couscous
- ½ cup almonds, toasted and chopped (tip, page 37)
- ½ cup pomegranate seeds
  Fresh mint or cilantro sprigs
  Orange wedges

1. Preheat oven to 425°F. In a large heatproof bowl combine cumin, ginger, cinnamon, 1 tsp. of the salt, and the black pepper. Add vegetables and oil; toss to coat. Spread in two shallow baking pans. Roast, uncovered, 25 to 30 minutes or until tender, stirring once.
2. In the same large bowl combine boiling water, couscous, and remaining ½ tsp. salt; stir. Cover tightly; let stand 5 minutes. Fluff with a fork. Serve vegetables on couscous. Sprinkle with almonds, pomegranate seeds, and herbs. Squeeze orange wedges over top. Makes 4 servings.
EACH SERVING *492 cal, 17 g fat, 0 mg chol, 514 mg sodium, 77 g carb, 13 g fiber, 13 g pro.*

CHICKEN & WINTER GREENS SALAD

ARCTIC CHAR WITH WARM OLIVE & LEMON DRESSING

A close cousin to salmon and trout, Arctic char has a pinkish-orange flesh but is slightly milder and more delicate. It's available year-round, but if you can't find it, salmon makes a great substitute.

TOTAL TIME 35 min.

1	lemon
½	cup green olives with pits (3 to 4 oz.), rinsed, pitted, and coarsely chopped
1	Tbsp. capers, drained and rinsed
4	Tbsp. extra-virgin olive oil
4	Arctic char or salmon fillets, skin on, ½ to ¾ inch thick (5 oz. each)
	Kosher salt
	Black pepper
½	cup loosely packed fresh Italian parsley, coarsely chopped

1. For Warm Olive and Lemon Dressing, zest and juice lemon. In a small saucepan combine olives, capers, lemon zest, and juice. Slowly stir in 3 Tbsp. of the olive oil until combined. Warm over low heat 5 to 10 minutes, stirring occasionally (do not simmer). Remove from heat.
2. Preheat broiler. Season fish with kosher salt and black pepper. Rub both sides lightly with remaining 1 Tbsp. olive oil. Place skin sides down in a baking pan. Broil 7 minutes or until fish flakes easily with a fork. Just before serving, stir parsley into dressing; spoon over fish. Makes 4 servings.
EACH SERVING *303 cal, 21 g fat, 0 mg chol, 613 mg sodium, 2 g carb, 1 g fiber, 28 g pro.*

CHICKEN & WINTER GREENS SALAD

It's easy to make chicken cutlets. Buy large boneless, skinless chicken breasts and cut them in half horizontally, placing one hand on top to steady. If the cutlets aren't as thin as you'd like, place them in a single layer between two pieces of plastic wrap then pound evenly to about ½ inch thickness.

TOTAL TIME 30 min.

½	large head radicchio, halved, cored, and sliced (3 cups)
2	heads Belgian endive, sliced crosswise (3 cups)
3	cups baby kale or other hearty greens
1	large clove garlic, minced
1	Tbsp. balsamic vinegar
½	tsp. Dijon-style mustard
½	tsp. kosher salt
¼	tsp. black pepper
5	Tbsp. extra-virgin olive oil
4	chicken breast cutlets (4 oz. each)
1	lemon, quartered
1	2-oz. wedge Parmesan, shaved

1. In an extra-large serving bowl combine radicchio, endive, and kale. For dressing, in a small bowl stir together garlic, vinegar, mustard, salt, and black pepper. Drizzle in ¼ cup of the oil slowly, whisking constantly.
2. Season chicken with additional kosher salt and black pepper. In a large skillet heat remaining 1 Tbsp. oil over medium-high heat. Add chicken; cook 2 to 3 minutes per side until done (165°F). Place chicken on top of greens. Squeeze lemon over. Drizzle with dressing. Sprinkle with Parmesan. Makes 4 servings.
EACH SERVING *429 cal, 25 g fat, 114 mg chol, 557 mg sodium, 11 g carb, 4 g fiber, 41 g pro.*

ARCTIC CHAR WITH
WARM OLIVE & LEMON
DRESSING

test kitchen
CONFIDENTIAL

Ever wonder how to make cookies that are crunchy on the outside and chewy inside, or roasted vegetables that are seared just right? *Better Homes and Gardens*® Test Kitchen has these answers—and a lot more. Meet the talented team—and learn techniques from these pros.

THE ROAD TO RECIPE PERFECTION

One of the goals of the early Testing-Tasting Kitchen was to nudge the American public into a new, more scientific era of cooking, which included an overhaul of how recipes were written. Until then, writers of recipes had assumed that all cooks knew how to make a piecrust or even how long something needed to cook. Early cooks in the Test Kitchen knew that wasn't the case—there were too many questions. Then and now, the BHG Test Kitchen champions a style of recipe writing that leaves nothing to chance. Today, all the cooks are trained food professionals with degrees in food science, food and nutrition, culinary arts, or dietetics. All understand the science behind the art of cooking and love to get to the bottom of how recipes work. Each kitchen professional tests an average of five recipes daily. Then all tested recipes are edited by a team of food editors and eventually appear in a wide array of *Better Homes and Gardens*® publications.

GARLIC ROASTED VEGETABLES

Tip #1: Sear Perfection. Toss veggies with seasonings and a bit of oil. Spread on a hot pan and then top with another hot pan, and weight with a heavy skillet. "No need to turn them," Colleen Weeden, culinary specialist, says. "By weighting the hot pans with a heavy skillet, the veggies sear evenly on both sides."

HANDS-ON TIME 15 min.
TOTAL TIME 40 min.

2   to 3 Tbsp. extra-virgin olive oil
1   to 1½ lb. vegetables, such as cauliflower, broccoli, leeks, sweet potatoes, and/or delicata squash, sliced ¾ inch thick
    Onion wedges (optional)
8   to 10 cloves garlic, peeled
1   Tbsp. chopped fresh thyme and/or sage leaves
½   tsp. kosher salt
½   tsp. black pepper

Preheat oven to 450°F, placing two shallow baking pans in the oven as it preheats. Drizzle one of the pans with 1 Tbsp. of the oil. Carefully arrange

vegetables and garlic in one layer in the oiled pan (do not crowd the pan). Drizzle with remaining olive oil. Sprinkle with thyme, salt, and black pepper. Carefully place remaining hot pan over vegetables, bottom side down. Place a heavy skillet or foil-wrapped brick on top of stack. Roast 25 to 30 minutes or until vegetables are browned and tender. Makes 6 servings.
EACH SERVING *101 cal, 5 g fat, 0 mg chol, 209 mg sodium, 14 g carb, 3 g fiber, 3 g pro.*

THE BETTER HOMES AND GARDENS® TEST KITCHEN IS THE OLDEST TEST KITCHEN LINKED TO A PUBLICATION IN THE UNITED STATES. IN 2016, THE KITCHEN CELEBRATED ITS 88TH BIRTHDAY.

"ALMOST ANY HERB WILL WORK FOR TOPPING THE BREAD," LYNN SAYS. "JUST REMOVE ANY HARD OR WOODY STEMS BEFORE PLACING THEM ON."

NO-KNEAD HONEY BREAD

Tip #2: Take the Temp. The color of baked bread can be deceiving—gorgeous and golden doesn't always mean perfectly baked. The best way to check doneness is temperature. "Fully baked bread is about 200°F in the center. To get the most accurate reading, make sure you take the temperature from the thickest part of the bread," says Lynn Blanchard, Test Kitchen director.

HANDS-ON TIME 25 min.
TOTAL TIME 6 hr., 30 min.

¾ cup warm water (105°F to 115°F)
1 package active dry yeast
⅓ cup milk
2 Tbsp. honey
2 Tbsp. butter or olive oil
1½ tsp. salt
2¾ cups all-purpose flour
  Cornmeal
1 egg white
2 tsp. water
  Fresh thyme, sage, oregano, and/or Italian parsley sprigs

1. In a large mixing bowl stir together the ¾ cup water and yeast. Let stand 5 minutes. Meanwhile, in a small saucepan heat and stir milk, honey, butter, and salt just until warm (120°F to 130°F) and butter almost melts. Stir milk mixture into yeast mixture. Stir in flour (dough will be sticky). Lightly coat a medium bowl with nonstick cooking spray; transfer dough to bowl. Lightly coat a sheet of plastic wrap with cooking spray; cover bowl with greased plastic wrap, coated side down. Chill at least 4 hours or up to 24 hours.
2. Using a dough scraper or spatula, carefully loosen dough; turn out onto a floured surface. Cover with greased plastic wrap. Let stand 30 minutes.
3. Grease a baking sheet; sprinkle with cornmeal. Shape dough into an 8- to 9-inch oval loaf, lightly flouring dough. Transfer loaf to prepared sheet, using dough scraper if necessary. Cover with a clean kitchen towel; place on the middle rack of an unheated oven. Place a bowl of warm water on lower rack. Let rise until nearly double in size (about 1 hour).
4. Remove loaf from oven. Uncover; set aside. Preheat oven to 400°F. In a small

bowl whisk together egg white and the 2 tsp. water; brush over loaf. Arrange herbs on loaf. Brush herbs with egg mixture. Bake 23 to 25 minutes or until an instant-read thermometer inserted in center registers about 200°F. Most breads are done throughout between 195°F and 200°F. Remove from baking sheet; cool on a wire rack. Makes 12 to 16 servings.
No time to chill? Prepare the dough as directed in Step 1, except skip chilling it. Let dough stand in the bowl, covered, at room temperature 30 minutes, then continue as directed in Step 2. The bread will have the same taste, but will spread a little more and won't rise as high.
EACH SERVING *142 cal, 2 g fat, 6 mg chol, 315 mg sodium, 26 g carb, 1 g fiber, 4 g pro.*

RASPBERRY-WALNUT DRESSING

Tip #3: Creamy Dressing; No Dairy. "We love walnuts, but other high-fat nuts will help to emulsify the dressing, too," says Carla Christian, nutrition specialist. "Pecans or cashews also lend a creamy texture."

TOTAL TIME 10 min.

½ cup fresh raspberries
⅓ cup toasted walnut pieces
¼ cup raspberry or red wine vinegar
2 Tbsp. honey
1 Tbsp. Dijon-style mustard
¼ tsp. kosher salt
¼ tsp. black pepper
⅓ cup extra-virgin olive oil

In a blender combine raspberries, walnuts, vinegar, honey, mustard, salt, and black pepper. Cover. Blend until nearly smooth. With blender running, drizzle in oil until well combined. Serve with tossed or fruit salads. Makes 1 cup.
EACH 1-TBSP. SERVING *66 cal, 6 g fat, 0 mg chol, 95 mg sodium, 3 g carb, 0 g fiber, 0 g pro.*

NO-KNEAD
HONEY BREAD

CRANBERRY-
CHOCOLATE CHIP
COOKIES

RASPBERRY-
WALNUT DRESSING

Lynn Blanchard
sets eggs that
were poached
ahead of time in
a steamer basket
to reheat them
before serving.

FRESH PINEAPPLE
CAKE WITH
CANDIED CARROT
RIBBONS

CRANBERRY-CHOCOLATE CHIP COOKIES

Tip #4: Cookie Tricks. "Use an ice cream scoop for shaping. Freeze scoops until firm, then bake. Leave them on the cookie sheet for a few minutes after baking to make cookies both crispy and chewy," culinary specialist Sammy Mila says. "And don't skip the corn syrup. Even that small amount makes these cookies stay fresh longer."

HANDS-ON TIME 25 min.
TOTAL TIME 45 min.

¼ cup butter, softened
¼ cup shortening
½ cup packed brown sugar
¼ cup granulated sugar
½ tsp. baking soda
½ tsp. salt
1 egg
1 Tbsp. light-color corn syrup
1½ tsp. vanilla
1½ cups all-purpose flour
1 cup semisweet chocolate chunks or pieces
½ cup dried cranberries

1. Preheat oven to 375°F. In a large mixing bowl beat butter and shortening with an electric mixer on medium to high speed 30 seconds. Add brown sugar, granulated sugar, baking soda, and salt. Beat on medium speed 2 minutes, scraping sides of bowl occasionally. Beat in egg, corn syrup, and vanilla until combined. Beat in as much of the flour as you can with the mixer. Stir in any remaining flour. Stir in chocolate and dried cranberries.
2. Using a small ice cream scoop, drop dough 2 inches apart onto ungreased cookie sheets. Freeze uncooked scoops of dough on the cookie sheet 20 minutes or just until firm. Bake 6 to 8 minutes or just until edges are lightly browned (centers of cookies might not appear set). Cool on cookie sheet 2 minutes. Transfer to wire racks. Cool completely. Makes 30 cookies.
EACH COOKIE *121 cal, 6 g fat, 10 mg chol, 79 mg sodium, 17 g carb, 1 g fiber, 1 g pro.*

FRESH PINEAPPLE CAKE WITH CANDIED CARROT RIBBONS

Tip #5: Cakes Sing! "Listening to the sizzle takes practice," Sarah Brekke, culinary specialist, says. "If you hear it, the cake is still cooking and needs a few minutes. You can always back it up with the toothpick test. Stick a toothpick into the center of the cake. If it comes out clean, the cake is done."

HANDS-ON TIME 30 min.
TOTAL TIME 3 hr., 30 min.

2 cups all-purpose flour
1½ cups sugar
1 tsp. baking powder
½ tsp. baking soda
½ tsp. salt
1 cup chopped fresh pineapple
3 eggs
1 cup plain Greek yogurt
½ cup vegetable oil
1 tsp. vanilla
½ cup toasted, chopped pecans (optional)
1 recipe Cooked White Frosting
1 recipe Candied Carrot Ribbons

1. Preheat oven to 350°F. Grease and lightly flour two 8-inch round cake pans.
2. In a large mixing bowl combine flour, sugar, baking powder, baking soda, and salt. Add pineapple, eggs, yogurt, oil, and vanilla. Stir until combined. Stir in pecans, if using. Divide batter between prepared pans, spreading evenly.
3. Bake 30 to 35 minutes or until you no longer hear a sizzling sound and the top springs back when lightly touched. Cool in pans on wire racks 10 minutes. Remove from pans; cool completely on wire racks.
4. Frost cooled cake with Cooked White Frosting. Top with Candied Carrot Ribbons. Makes 16 servings.
Cooked White Frosting In a medium saucepan whisk together 1½ cups sugar, ⅓ cup all-purpose flour, and ¼ tsp. salt. Whisk in 1½ cups milk. Cook and stir over medium heat 12 minutes or until thickened and bubbly. Cook and stir 1 minute more. Remove from heat; stir in 2 tsp. vanilla. Transfer to a large mixing bowl. Cover. Cool completely at room temperature (2½ to 3 hours). Gradually beat in 1½ cups unsalted butter, cut up and softened, with an electric mixer on medium speed, scraping sides of bowl occasionally. Frosting will look curdled even after all the butter is incorporated. Continue beating 1 minute more or until smooth and fluffy.
Candied Carrot Ribbons Using a vegetable peeler, cut 3 carrots lengthwise into ribbons (1 cup). In a large skillet heat 2 Tbsp. butter over medium heat until melted. Stir in 2 Tbsp. sugar. Add carrots and 1 Tbsp. water; cook 2 to 4 minutes or until carrots are softened and glazed, stirring occasionally. Transfer to a waxed paper-lined tray; cool completely.
EACH SERVING *490 cal, 27 g fat, 87 mg chol, 227 mg sodium, 57 g carb, 1 g fiber, 6 g pro.*

game day
UPGRADE

Score big with make-it-your-way homemade hummus. It's quick to whip up, and the variations offer tasty choices.

HUMMUS

TOTAL TIME 15 min.

- 1 15-oz. can garbanzo beans (chickpeas), rinsed and drained
- ¼ cup tahini (sesame seed paste)
- ¼ cup lemon juice
- ¼ cup olive oil
- 1 clove garlic, minced
- ½ tsp. salt
- ¼ tsp. paprika
  Stir-ins (optional): ¼ cup sliced green onions, ¼ cup crumbled feta cheese, ⅓ cup chopped pitted ripe olives or Kalamata olives, ⅓ cup chopped roasted red sweet pepper, 2 to 3 chopped chipotle peppers in adobo sauce, 1 Tbsp. snipped fresh dill, or ¼ cup basil pesto
- 1 Tbsp. snipped fresh Italian parsley
- 2 to 3 tsp. olive oil (optional)
- 2 Tbsp. toasted pine nuts and/or paprika (optional)
  Pita wedges, tortilla chips, and/or cut-up vegetables

1. In a blender or food processor combine beans, tahini, lemon juice, oil, garlic, salt, and paprika. Cover and blend or process until smooth, stopping to scrape container as needed. If desired, add stir-ins.
2. Spoon hummus onto a serving platter. Sprinkle with parsley. If desired, drizzle with oil and sprinkle with pine nuts and/or paprika. Serve with pita wedges, tortilla chips, and/or cut-up vegetables. Makes 14 servings.
EACH SERVING *84 cal, 7 g fat, 0 mg chol, 156 mg sodium, 5 g carb, 1 g fiber, 2 g pro.*

craving
CHOCOLATE

Sometimes you just want a little something sweet and familiar. Top this pudding with a heart of whisper-pink whipped cream.

DARK CHOCOLATE PUDDING

Splurge on rich, creamy chocolate pudding for Valentine's Day. This recipe makes enough for family and friends.

HAND-ON TIME 20 min.
TOTAL TIME 2 hr., 20 min.

¾	cup sugar
3	Tbsp. cornstarch
2	Tbsp. unsweetened cocoa powder
3	cups half-and-half, light cream, or milk
1	Tbsp. butter
2	tsp. vanilla
¼	tsp. salt
8	oz. bittersweet or semisweet chocolate, chopped

1. In a large saucepan combine sugar, cornstarch, and cocoa powder. Add half-and-half. Cook and slowly stir over medium heat until thickened and bubbly. Cook and stir 2 minutes more.
2. Remove from heat. Stir in butter, vanilla, and salt. Stir in chocolate until melted. Ladle into serving bowls. Cover surface with plastic wrap; chill 2 hours or up to 24 hours. Top with whipped cream and sprinkle with additional cocoa powder. Makes 8 (½-cup) servings.
EACH SERVING *363 cal, 23 g fat, 38 mg chol, 123 mg sodium, 42 g carb, 3 g fiber, 5 g pro.*
Heart How-To Tint whipped cream with one drop of red food coloring. Dollop two spoonfuls onto the pudding. Use the back of a spoon to smooth into a heart.

**SPRING SALAD
WITH GRAPEFRUIT
& FETA**
Recipe on page 72

march

Spring invites lessons in the kitchen on the art of making brioche and recipes for celebrations as well as for everyday meals.

53

60

69

how to cook
BRIOCHE

Good things, like this classic French yeast bread, take time. And the buttery crust and feathery interior are worth every minute.

BRIOCHE gets its irresistibly tender crumb (that's fancy pastry speak for a bread's interior texture) from eggs and copious amounts of butter—gotta love French cooking. Making brioche is less fuss than you'd imagine, but it does require a bit of patience. This dough is brightened with lemon zest to make it just right for spring, and you can shape it any way you wish. Brioche à tête, the cute little fluted rolls with the iconic topknots shown here, are classic. Loaves are simple to make and the stuff of French toast dreams. And if you want to make it extra-special, there's an Easter surprise on page 55.

LEMON BRIOCHE

Each square gets shaped into two balls—one large and one small—to make classic brioche à tête.

HANDS-ON TIME 1 hr.
TOTAL TIME 14 hr. (includes chill time)

2   pkg. active dry yeast
⅓   cup warm water (105° to 115°F)
⅓   cup warm milk (105° to 115°F)
4   cups all-purpose flour
1½ tsp. salt
4   eggs, room temperature
¼   cup sugar
2   Tbsp. lemon zest
1   cup (2 sticks) butter, room temperature

1. In a stand mixer fit with a dough hook, dissolve yeast in the warm water and milk. Let stand 5 to 10 minutes until softened. Add flour and salt. Mix on medium-low speed until flour is moistened, about 2 minutes.

2. Reduce speed to low. Separate 1 egg. Add yolk and remaining 3 eggs (refrigerate egg white for later). Add sugar and lemon zest. Increase speed to medium. Beat 3 minutes. Reduce speed to low. Add butter 2 Tbsp. at a time, beating until each addition is incorporated before adding the next. Once all the butter is added, increase speed to medium-high. Continue to beat until dough pulls away from sides of bowl, about 10 minutes. Transfer to a greased bowl. Cover; let rise in a warm place until double in size, about 1 hour. Using a spatula, release dough from sides of bowl to deflate slightly. Cover with plastic wrap. Chill overnight, 12 to 24 hours.

3. Grease eighteen 3- to 4-inch fluted individual brioche molds or large muffin cups. Pat the cold dough into a 12×6-inch rectangle. Using a dough scraper or sharp knife, cut into 18 equal portions. From each remove a small piece; roll into eighteen 1-inch balls. Roll remaining portions into 18 larger balls; place in prepared pans. Using your fingers, make a deep indentation in the center of each dough ball. Brush with water. Press small balls into indentations. Cover; let rise in a warm place until double in size, about 45 minutes.

1 START WITH YEAST First, check the expiration date on the yeast to ensure freshness. Second, the milk and water should be warm (not hot) to the touch. If you scorch the yeast, the bread won't rise.

2 MOISTEN THE FLOUR At this point the dough will be dry and crumbly. Add eggs and sugar. Now the dough will be wet and sticky; eventually it will start to form around the dough hook.

3 MIX IN THE BUTTER Each addition will take several minutes to incorporate before you can add the next. Be patient. This is how the dough develops its flaky texture.

4 LISTEN TO THE DOUGH "Slap, slap, slap." That's the sound of the dough hitting the sides of the bowl and saying "I'm ready to go!" It will look silky smooth and be wrapped around the dough hook.

4. Preheat oven to 375°F. In a small bowl combine reserved egg white and 1 Tbsp. water; brush over dough. Bake 13 to 15 minutes or until golden brown. Let cool 5 minutes. Remove from pans. Cool on wire racks. Makes 18 rolls.
EACH ROLL *223 cal, 12 g fat, 69 mg chol, 294 mg sodium, 25 g carb, 1 g fiber, 5 g pro.*

Make it sweeter with a simple glaze after removing from the oven: 1 cup powdered sugar, 1 Tbsp. milk, and ¼ tsp. vanilla.
For loaves Divide dough into 18 portions as above. Roll pieces into balls, placing 9 each in two greased 9×5-inch loaf pans. Increase baking time to 18 to 20 minutes.

WHEN YOU ARRANGE BALLS OF DOUGH IN LOAF PANS, YOU MIGHT THINK YOU'RE MAKING PULL-APART BREAD. BUT AS THE DOUGH RISES, THE BOTTOMS OF THE BALLS MELD TOGETHER TO MAKE A SOLID LOAF WITH A TEXTURAL TOP PERFECT FOR SLICING.

HOLIDAY TREAT They're almost too cute to eat! With some simple snipping and shaping, brioche dough transforms into adorable bunnies for an Easter buffet.

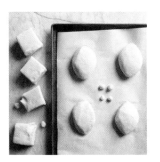
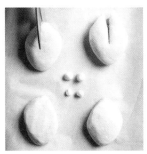
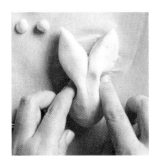

1 Pat dough and cut squares as for brioche à tête. For each bunny, remove a tiny bit from a square and shape into a ¼-inch ball for a nose. Shape remaining piece into an oval, about 3 inches long and 2¼ inches wide.

2 Using kitchen shears or a dough scraper, make a 2-inch cut lengthwise through the center of the oval (about two-thirds from the top to make the bunny's ears).

3 Pinch dough oval where the cut stops to define the head (head might seem small but will become bigger during rising and baking). Gently shape head. Using the side of your pinky, make indentations in the ears.

4 Make a small indentation in the center of the head with your finger, brush with water, and add the small ball for the nose. Let rise, brush with egg white mixture, and bake as directed on page 53.

the power of
PURPLE

Reason No. 422 to add more color to your plate: The hidden component that gives fruits and veggies a violet or indigo blush also makes them extra-good for you.

PURPLE POTATO SOUP

The color wows, but it's the flavor that will win you over. Fresh marjoram and garlic make the potato base mouthwatering and memorable. The purple potatoes turn this soup into a vibrant showstopper. Russets or Yukon golds achieve delicious flavor with softer hues.

HANDS-ON TIME 20 min.
TOTAL TIME 50 min.

- 1 Tbsp. butter
- 1 cup chopped onion
- 2 cloves garlic, minced
- ½ tsp. kosher salt
- 1½ lb. purple potatoes, peeled and cut up
- 4 cups reduced-sodium chicken broth
- 1 tsp. dried marjoram
- ¼ cup pomegranate juice
  Sour cream
  Freshly ground black pepper
  Fresh marjoram

In a 4-qt. Dutch oven melt butter over medium heat. Add onion, garlic, and salt. Cook 5 minutes or until tender, stirring occasionally. Add potatoes, broth, and dried marjoram. Bring to boiling. Reduce heat. Simmer, uncovered, 20 minutes or until tender, stirring occasionally. Using an immersion blender, puree until smooth. Stir in pomegranate juice. Season to taste with additional kosher salt. Top with sour cream, freshly ground black pepper, and fresh marjoram. Makes 4 to 6 servings.
EACH SERVING *224 cal, 6 g fat, 14 mg chol, 736 mg sodium, 37 g carb, 5 g fiber, 8 g pro.*

WHAT'S IN A COLOR? Compounds called anthocyanins make produce purple. They're in kohlrabi, red kale, a variety of potatoes, bell peppers, berries, eggplant, and more. They range from red-orange to violet.

WHY IS IT SO HEALTHFUL? Anthocyanins seem to have an anti-inflammatory effect, which could help lower the risk of heart disease and cancer.

HOW DOES COOKING AFFECT ANTHOCYANINS? Because they're water-soluble, their concentration is highest in produce that's steamed, roasted, or raw.

WHAT'S IN IT FOR THE PLANT? Anthocyanins protect delicate parts against damage from intense sunlight, and the color attracts pollinators.

CAULIFLOWER GRATIN
Recipe on page 60

SPICED KOHLRABI
OVEN CHIPS
Recipe on page 60

ALMOST ALL YOUR FAVORITE PRODUCE HAS A PURPLE SIDEKICK. SOME ARE MERELY TINGED; SOME ARE A FULL-ON RIOT OF COLOR. ALL OF THEM CARRY THE EXTRA NUTRITIONAL BENEFITS THAT COME WITH THE COLOR.

CAULIFLOWER GRATIN

Photo on page 58.

The potato slices should be about ¼ inch thick in this recipe. For a quick and easy way to keep slices uniform, use a mandoline.

HANDS-ON TIME 10 min.
TOTAL TIME 1 hr., 15 min.

1   lb. purple potatoes, peeled and sliced
1¼   cups whipping cream
2   tsp. herbes de Provence
1¼   tsp. kosher salt
1¼   cups Gruyère cheese, shredded (5 oz.)
1   1¾- to 2-lb. head purple cauliflower, sliced ½ inch thick
4   shallots, peeled and halved
⅓   cup panko bread crumbs
3   Tbsp. butter, melted
     Thyme sprigs and lemon zest

1. Preheat oven to 425°F. Arrange potatoes in the bottom of a 2-qt. rectangular gratin dish or baking dish. In a small bowl stir together cream, 1 tsp. of the herbes de Provence, and 1 tsp. of the kosher salt; pour over potatoes. Sprinkle potato layer with ½ cup of the cheese. Top with cauliflower slices and any pieces that break off, shallots, and 1 remaining ¼ tsp. kosher salt. Cover; bake 40 minutes.
2. Meanwhile, stir together the remaining ¾ cup cheese, panko, remaining 1 tsp. herbes de Provence, and butter. Uncover cauliflower; sprinkle with panko mixture. Bake, uncovered, 15 minutes more or until golden. Remove; let stand 10 to 15 minutes. Sprinkle with thyme and lemon zest. Makes 8 servings.
EACH SERVING *310 cal, 24 g fat, 82 mg chol, 374 mg sodium, 16 g carb, 2 g fiber, 8 g pro.*

SPICED KOHLRABI OVEN CHIPS

Photo on page 59.

Like beet greens, kohlrabi greens are edible. Eat them raw in a salad or sauté them for a quick side dish.

HANDS-ON TIME 20 min.
TOTAL TIME 1 hr., 30 min.

1¼   lb. kohlrabi (3), trimmed (don't peel)
1   Tbsp. extra-virgin olive oil
½   tsp. ground cumin
¼   tsp. ground coriander
½   tsp. kosher salt
⅓   cup sour cream
¼   cup mayonnaise
⅛   tsp. black pepper
     Chopped fresh rosemary
     Finely chopped purple-color green onions or shallots

1. Preheat oven to 275°F. Using a mandoline, slice kohlrabi ¹⁄₁₆ inch thick. In a large bowl whisk together olive oil, cumin, coriander, and ¼ tsp. of the kosher salt. Add kohlrabi slices; toss to coat. Arrange slices in a single layer on two extra-large baking sheets. Place baking sheets on two separate oven racks near the center of the oven.
2. Bake 40 to 75 minutes or until chips are golden brown and crisp, rotating the pan, switching rack placement, and turning chips once after 30 minutes. Chips will begin browning quickly after 30 minutes. Check every 5 minutes after this, removing chips from baking sheets as they are done. Cool on a wire rack.
3. For dip, in a small bowl stir together sour cream, mayonnaise, remaining ¼ tsp. kosher salt, and black pepper. Sprinkle chips and dip with rosemary and onions before serving. Makes 2 to 3 servings.
EACH SERVING (WITHOUT DIP) *142 cal, 7 g fat, 0 mg chol, 199 mg sodium, 19 g carb, 11 g fiber, 5 g pro.*

BARELY ROASTED PURPLE VEGETABLES

Quick roasting leaves veggies delightfully crisp-tender. If you prefer them softer, roast a few minutes more.

HANDS-ON TIME 15 min.
TOTAL TIME 30 min.

12   oz. purple baby carrots with tops trimmed and halved lengthwise
8   oz. fresh purple-color green beans, trimmed
3   to 4 purple-color green onions, trimmed and halved
1   bulb purple garlic, halved horizontally
2   Tbsp. extra-virgin olive oil
½   tsp. kosher salt
2   Tbsp. honey
2   Tbsp. butter, melted
1   Tbsp. snipped fresh thyme
½   tsp. fresh cracked black pepper
1   to 2 oz. goat cheese, crumbled

1. Preheat oven to 425°F. In a shallow roasting pan combine the carrots, beans, onions, and garlic. Drizzle with oil and sprinkle with ½ tsp. kosher salt; toss to coat, placing garlic halves cut sides down.
2. Roast, uncovered, 12 to 15 minutes or just until tender, stirring once. Meanwhile, stir together the honey, butter, fresh thyme, and black pepper.
3. To serve, transfer the roasted vegetables to a platter. Drizzle with honey mixture. Sprinkle with goat cheese and additional fresh snipped thyme. Makes 8 servings.
EACH SERVING *110 cal, 7 g fat, 10 mg chol, 201 mg sodium, 10 g carb, 2 g fiber, 2 g pro.*

BARELY ROASTED
PURPLE
VEGETABLES

CORNMEAL
CAKES WITH
BERRY-FIG
CHUTNEY

CORNMEAL CAKES WITH BERRY-FIG CHUTNEY

We love a smear of goat cheese, but any spreadable cheese will work. Try Boursin or a triple-cream Brie.

TOTAL TIME 30 min.

- ¼ cup all-purpose flour
- 1½ tsp. baking powder
- 1 tsp. sugar
- ¼ tsp. salt
- 1 cup boiling water
- 1 cup yellow cornmeal
- 1 Tbsp. butter, melted
- 1 slightly beaten egg
  Milk (optional)
  Goat cheese or Quark (European-style fresh cheese)
- 1 recipe Berry-Fig Chutney
  Fresh blueberries, blackberries, and/or mint leaves

1. In a small bowl combine flour, baking powder, sugar, and salt. In a medium bowl whisk boiling water into cornmeal. Whisk in melted butter until smooth; whisk in egg. Add flour mixture and whisk just until combined. If necessary, whisk in milk (up to 4 Tbsp.) to thin batter.

2. Heat a greased griddle or skillet over medium heat. Drop rounded tablespoons of batter onto griddle. Cook 2 to 3 minutes or until golden brown, turning once. Transfer to a platter. Cover; keep warm. Repeat with remaining batter. Top with cheese, Berry-Fig Chutney, berries, and mint. Makes 16 cakes.

Berry-Fig Chutney In a medium saucepan combine 2 cups blueberries and/or blackberries, 3 Tbsp. balsamic vinegar, ½ cup finely chopped dried figs, ½ cup finely chopped red onion, 1 Tbsp. honey, and 3 sprigs fresh thyme. Bring to boiling; reduce heat. Simmer, uncovered, 8 to 10 minutes or until thickened, stirring occasionally. Remove from heat; stir in ½ cup fresh blackberries and/or blueberries. Cool. Remove and discard thyme stems. Makes 2 cups.

EACH CAKE PLUS 2 TBSP. CHUTNEY *175 cal, 3 g fat, 31 mg chol, 205 mg sodium, 32 g carb, 4 g fiber, 4 g pro.*

BEET HUMMUS

BEET HUMMUS

Sweet potato chips, pita wedges, or crisp cucumber slices are delicious with this dip.

TOTAL TIME 20 min.

- 1 15-oz. can cannellini beans, rinsed and drained
- 1 lb. beets, cooked and peeled*
- ¼ cup tahini (sesame seed paste)
- 2 Tbsp. lemon juice
- 1 Tbsp. prepared horseradish
- 2 cloves garlic, peeled and halved
- ½ tsp. kosher salt
- ¼ cup olive oil
  Kimchi and chopped fresh Italian parsley (optional)

In a food processor combine cannellini beans, beets, tahini, lemon juice, horseradish, garlic, and salt. Cover; process until nearly smooth. With the motor running, add oil in a thin, steady stream through the feed tube, processing until smooth. Transfer to a serving bowl. Cover; chill until serving time. Drizzle with additional olive oil. Top with kimchi and parsley, if desired. Makes 3 cups.

*To cook beets: Trim and scrub beets; cut each in half. In a medium saucepan bring water to boiling; add beets. Reduce heat; cook, covered, 40 minutes or until fork-tender. Drain and cool. Scrape peel from beets.

EACH ¼-CUP SERVING *115 cal, 7 g fat, 0 mg chol, 193 mg sodium, 10 g carb, 3 g fiber, 3 g pro.*

PARTY
like it's 1965

Old is new at this throwback party starring thrift store scores and vintage touches. Welcome spring with classic cocktails and easy day-of prep.

MANHATTAN

FROZEN GRASSHOPPERS

SIDECAR

VODKA GIMLET

MANHATTAN

TOTAL TIME 5 min.

- 2 oz. bourbon
- ½ oz. sweet vermouth
  Dash aromatic bitters
- ½ cup ice cubes
  Maraschino cherry

In a cocktail shaker combine bourbon, vermouth, and bitters. Add ice cubes; cover and shake until very cold. Strain into an ice-filled glass. Serve with a cherry. Makes 1 serving.

EACH SERVING *163 cal, 0 g fat, 0 mg chol, 5 mg sodium, 5 g carb, 0 g fiber, 0 g pro.*

FROZEN GRASSHOPPERS

TOTAL TIME 5 min.

- ½ cup green crème de menthe
- ½ cup white crème de cacao
- 2 cups vanilla ice cream
- 1½ cups ice cubes
  Layered chocolate-mint candies, chopped (optional)

In a blender combine crème de menthe, crème de cacao, and ice cream. Add ice; cover and blend until smooth. Top with chopped candies. Makes 8 servings.

EACH SERVING *177 cal, 4 g fat, 16 mg chol, 30 mg sodium, 22 g carb, 0 g fiber, 6 g pro.*

SIDECAR

TOTAL TIME 5 min.

- 2 oz. brandy
- 1 oz. lemon juice
- 1 oz. orange liqueur
- ½ cup ice cubes
  Thinly sliced lemon peel

In a cocktail shaker, combine brandy, lemon juice, and orange liqueur. Add ice cubes; cover and shake until very cold. Strain into an ice-filled glass. Serve with a lemon peel. Makes 1 serving.

EACH SERVING *234 cal, 0 g fat, 0 mg chol, 1 mg sodium, 12 g carb, 0 g fiber 0 g pro.*

VODKA GIMLET

TOTAL TIME 5 min.

- 1½ oz. vodka
- ½ oz. sweetened lime juice
- ½ cup ice cubes
  Lime wedge

In a cocktail shaker combine vodka and lime juice. Add ice cubes; cover and shake until very cold. Strain into an ice-filled glass. Serve with a lime wedge. Makes 1 serving.

EACH SERVING *98 cal, 0 g fat, 0 mg chol, 0 mg sodium, 1 g carb, 0 g fiber, 0 g pro.*

CHIPOTLE CHEESE FONDUE

Give classic cheese fondue a Southwest spin with Monterey Jack cheese and chipotle peppers.

HANDS-ON TIME 30 min.
TOTAL TIME 4 hr., 30 min.

- 3 cups reduced-sodium chicken broth
- 3 cups whipping cream
- 1 cup dry white wine
- 3 cloves garlic, minced
- ½ cup butter, softened
- ½ cup all-purpose flour
- 1 to 2 Tbsp. finely chopped chipotle peppers in adobo sauce
- 16 oz. shredded Monterey Jack cheese
- 8 oz. shredded Colby cheese
  Rustic bread cubes, mini sweet peppers, steamed broccoli, and/or boiled potatoes

1. In a 4- to 5-qt. slow cooker combine broth, cream, wine, and garlic. Cover and cook on low-heat setting 4 to 5 hours.
2. Meanwhile, in a medium bowl stir together butter and flour until a paste forms. Stir into broth mixture until combined. Cover and cook 30 minutes more or until slightly thickened.
3. Whisk chipotle peppers into broth mixture. Gradually whisk in cheeses until smooth. Serve with bread and vegetables for dipping. Makes 36 servings.
EACH SERVING *177 cal, 16 g fat, 51 mg chol, 184 mg sodium, 2 g carb, 0 g fiber, 5 g pro.*

CHIPOTLE CHEESE FONDUE

new ways with
LOX

Even favorite combos deserve a little reinvention now and then.

Traditional lox is salt-cured or brined salmon from the belly of the fish. Purists will say lox is only cured, not smoked, but it is available both ways.

COLD LOX
NOODLE
BOWL

BAGEL & LOX
SKILLET STRATA

NIÇOISE-STYLE
LOX SALAD

COLD LOX NOODLE BOWL

TOTAL TIME 25 min.

- 8 oz. dried spaghetti
- ¼ cup extra-virgin olive oil
- ¼ cup lime juice
- 1 Tbsp. grated fresh ginger
- ¼ tsp. salt
- 1 romaine heart, thinly sliced (4 cups)
- 6 oz. radishes, very thinly sliced (1 cup)
- 1 fresh jalapeño pepper, thinly sliced (tip, page 37)
- 2 green onions, thinly sliced
- 8 oz. thinly sliced smoked lox-style salmon, cut into strips
  Crushed red pepper (optional)

1. Cook pasta according to package directions. Drain and rinse under cold water. Drain well.

2. Meanwhile, for dressing, in a small bowl whisk together olive oil, lime juice, ginger, and salt. To each serving bowl add cooled spaghetti, romaine, radishes, jalapeño, and green onions. Top with lox. Drizzle with dressing and sprinkle with crushed red pepper, if desired. Makes 4 servings.

EACH SERVING *413 cal, 16 g fat, 25 mg chol, 731 mg sodium, 48 g carb, 4 g fiber, 21 g pro.*

NIÇOISE-STYLE LOX SALAD

TOTAL TIME 30 min.

- 1 lb. small red potatoes, quartered
- 1¼ tsp. salt
- 10 oz. haricot verts or thin green beans, trimmed
- ½ cup olive oil
- ¼ cup champagne vinegar
- 2 tsp. Dijon-style mustard
- 6 oz. thinly sliced smoked lox-style salmon
- 1 small head Bibb lettuce, quartered
- 4 hard-cooked eggs, sliced
- ½ cup niçoise olives, pitted
- ¼ cup chopped fresh Italian parsley

1. Place potatoes in a large saucepan. Cover with cold water; add 1 tsp. of the salt. Bring to a simmer over medium-high heat. Cook 10 minutes or until fork-tender, adding green beans the last 2 minutes. Drain; transfer to a bowl of ice water. Drain well.

2. In a screw-top jar combine the oil, vinegar, mustard, and remaining ¼ tsp. salt. Arrange potatoes, green beans, lox, lettuce, eggs, olives, and parsley on plates. Drizzle each with dressing. Makes 4 servings.

EACH SERVING *564 cal, 41 g fat, 205 mg chol, 965 mg sodium, 31 g carb, 6 g fiber, 19 g pro.*

BAGEL & LOX SKILLET STRATA

HANDS-ON TIME 20 min.
TOTAL TIME 50 min.

- 1 4-oz. plain bagel, cut into pieces
- 1 Tbsp. unsalted butter
- 1 leek, thinly sliced
- 5 oz. asparagus, trimmed and cut into pieces (1½ cups)
- 5 eggs
- 1 cup whole milk
- 3 oz. feta cheese, crumbled
- 1 Tbsp. chopped fresh dill
- ¼ tsp. black pepper
- 8 oz. thinly sliced smoked salmon (lox-style), chopped
  Crème fraîche, capers, and/or fresh dill

1. Preheat oven to 450°F. Spread bagel pieces on a baking sheet. Bake 7 minutes or until toasted. Remove and set aside.

2. Meanwhile, in a 10-inch oven-going skillet, melt butter over medium-high heat. Add leek. Cook 3 minutes or until tender, stirring occasionally. Add asparagus. Cook 5 minutes more.

3. In a medium bowl whisk together eggs, milk, feta cheese, dill, and pepper. Add the lox and dried bagel pieces; stir to combine. Pour mixture over leek and asparagus in skillet, stirring gently to combine. Cover with foil. Transfer to oven. Bake, covered, 10 minutes. Uncover. Bake 12 to 14 minutes more or until a knife inserted in the center comes out clean. Let cool 5 minutes. Serve with crème fraîche, additional feta cheese, capers, and dill. Makes 6 servings.

EACH SERVING *279 cal, 15 g fat, 204 mg chol, 774 mg sodium, 15 g carb, 1 g fiber, 20 g pro.*

KNOW YOUR CURED AND SMOKED FISH

GRAVLAX A Scandinavian favorite. Cured much like lox, except sugar, lots of fresh dill, and, in some instances, spices are added to the salt.

NOVA LOX Cured or brined like lox, then rinsed and cold-smoked. Traditionally "Nova" referred to salmon from Nova Scotia, but now it more broadly reflects the smoking method.

COLD-SMOKED A low and slow method. Fish is smoked around 80°F for many hours to impart the smoky flavor without changing the texture of the fillet.

HOT-SMOKED Fully cooked with hot smoke, just like barbecued meats. You get the smoky flavor and a texture that flakes easily with a fork.

FAST & FRESH

Easy, healthy recipes for a better dinner tonight.

VIETNAMESE PORK MEATBALLS

VIETNAMESE PORK MEATBALLS

A big dose of ginger and lemongrass makes these meatballs bright and zesty. Serve with handfuls of crunchy raw veggies and a big squeeze of lime.

TOTAL TIME 35 min.

1¼ lb. ground pork
1 stalk lemongrass, smashed and minced (1 Tbsp.)
4 tsp. grated fresh ginger
1 clove garlic, minced
2 tsp. Asian fish sauce
1½ tsp. lime zest
1 Tbsp. canola oil
　Finely shredded green cabbage
　Shredded carrots
　Thinly sliced radishes
　Cilantro sprigs
　Lime wedges

1. In a large bowl combine pork, lemongrass, ginger, garlic, fish sauce, and lime zest. Using damp hands, form into twenty 1½-inch meatballs.
2. In a large skillet heat oil over medium-high. Add meatballs. Cook 12 to 15 minutes or until done (165°F), turning occasionally.
3. Serve meatballs with cabbage, carrots, radishes, cilantro, and lime wedges. Drizzle with lime juice. Makes 4 servings.

EACH SERVING *344 cal, 26 g fat, 96 mg chol, 322 mg sodium, 2 g carb, 0 g fiber, 26 g pro.*

Tip Double the recipe and freeze extras for nights you don't have time to cook. Store individual portions in freezer bags up to 3 months. To reheat, thaw in the refrigerator, then place in a skillet with a little broth. Simmer, covered, until heated through.

CRISPY CORNMEAL SHRIMP SANDWICH

CRISPY CORNMEAL SHRIMP SANDWICH

Crispy shrimp without the deep fryer hassle: You need only ¼ inch of oil for pan-frying. Keep your eye on the oil, and if it starts to bubble, turn down the heat slightly to avoid splattering.

TOTAL TIME 30 min.

20 large shrimp (1 lb.), peeled and deveined
½ cup milk
½ cup cornmeal
¼ cup all-purpose flour
½ tsp. smoked paprika
½ tsp. kosher salt
　Vegetable oil for frying
4 5-inch portions French-style baguette, split
¼ cup mayonnaise
⅔ cup sliced pickled hot cherry peppers
4 green onions, thinly sliced
4 butter lettuce leaves

1. Place shrimp in a shallow bowl. Pour milk over, turning to coat. In a medium dish toss together cornmeal, flour, paprika, and salt. Place half the shrimp at a time in flour mixture; toss to coat. Remove to a tray.
2. In a 10-inch skillet heat ¼ inch oil over medium-high heat (about 2 cups). Carefully place shrimp, half at a time, in pan. Cook 2 minutes or until golden brown on one side. Turn and cook 1 minute more or until shrimp turn opaque. Transfer to a paper towel-lined tray.
3. Spread bread tops with mayonnaise. Layer shrimp in baguettes. Top with peppers, onions, and lettuce. Makes 4 servings.

EACH SERVING *553 cal, 25 g fat, 167 mg chol, 896 mg sodium, 51 g carb, 1 g fiber, 27 g pro.*

**LENTIL SOUP WITH
LEMON & DILL**

SPRING SALAD WITH GRAPEFRUIT & FETA

For an interesting salad, use different textures, such as tender butterhead lettuce (Bibb or Boston) and sturdier mustard greens. Cucumbers, fennel, and pine nuts add crunch, tart grapefruit some juiciness, and feta the crumbly cheese factor.

TOTAL TIME 30 min.

½	cup extra-virgin olive oil
½	cup pine nuts
	Kosher salt
2	shallots, finely chopped
2	Tbsp. white wine vinegar
½	tsp. kosher salt
¼	tsp. black pepper
¼	cup sour cream
2	Tbsp. finely chopped fresh tarragon
8	cups butter lettuce, mustard greens, and/or spinach
1	small fennel bulb, trimmed, halved, cored, and sliced into thin wedges
½	medium cucumber, thinly sliced
2	medium pink grapefruit, peeled and cut into ¼-inch slices
4	oz. crumbled feta cheese
	Smoked turkey breast (optional)

1. In a medium skillet heat 1 Tbsp. of the oil over medium heat. Add pine nuts and heat 3 to 5 minutes or until toasted, stirring occasionally. Season with kosher salt.

2. For dressing, in a small bowl whisk together shallots, vinegar, salt, and black pepper. Whisk in remaining olive oil, sour cream, and tarragon.

3. In a large bowl toss together lettuce, fennel, and cucumber. Add dressing; toss to combine. Add grapefruit and cheese; toss gently to combine. Top with pine nuts and, if desired, turkey. Makes 4 servings.

EACH SERVING *557 cal, 48 g fat, 31 mg chol, 631 mg sodium, 27 g carb, 7 g fiber, 11 g pro.*

LENTIL SOUP WITH LEMON & DILL

Top this cozy soup with fresh dill, tangy lemon, and tart yogurt to balance the lentils' warm, earthy flavor. Why use whole cumin seeds instead of ground? When toasted, the seeds release their oils, making them nutty and aromatic. Ground cumin lacks that depth of flavor.

HANDS-ON TIME 20 min.
TOTAL TIME 45 min.

1	Tbsp. extra-virgin olive oil
1	tsp. cumin seeds
1	32-oz. carton vegetable stock
2	cups water
1½	cups French green lentils, rinsed and drained
3	carrots, chopped (1½ cups)
2	cloves garlic, minced
1	bay leaf
½	tsp. kosher salt
3	Tbsp. lemon juice
	Freshly ground black pepper
	Plain yogurt
½	cup lightly packed fresh dill sprigs, coarsely chopped
2	green onions, finely chopped

1. In a large saucepan heat oil over medium-high heat. Add cumin seeds and heat 30 seconds or until toasted and fragrant. Stir in stock, the water, lentils, carrots, garlic, bay leaf, and salt. Bring to boiling; reduce heat. Simmer, covered, 25 minutes or until lentils are tender. Remove bay leaf.

2. Add lemon juice to soup. Season with freshly ground black pepper. Serve with yogurt, dill, and green onions. Makes 4 servings.

EACH SERVING *346 cal, 5 g fat, 2 mg chol, 858 mg sodium, 56 g carb, 9 g fiber, 20 g pro.*

SPRING SALAD WITH
GRAPEFRUIT & FETA

MELTY TINY TOMATOES
Recipe on page 89

Keep it simple. Find recipes and techniques to show off garden-fresh produce this spring. The finale? A dreamy carrot cake.

77

92

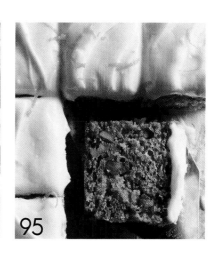

95

how to cook PESTO

Greens, nuts, cheese—so many possibilities. Learn the tricks to this versatile sauce, then choose your own pesto adventure.

PESTO is quick to make, easy to customize, and has a punchy, bright flavor you'll crave. Classic pesto is made with basil, garlic, pine nuts, Parmesan, and olive oil—but that's merely a blueprint. Sure, you can go old-school and use a mortar and pestle (pesto means "pounded" in Italian), but the food processor combines everything in a snap while maintaining some texture. Try basic basil or one of our changeups. Or—now that you have the formula—design your own!

BASIL PESTO

Some people like to squeeze lemon juice in pesto to get a little more zip and to balance the fat of olive oil and cheese. A tablespoon or two is all you need. Try it with and without to see which you prefer.

TOTAL TIME 20 min.

- ⅓ cup olive oil
- 2 cups firmly packed fresh basil leaves
- ½ cup pine nuts, toasted (tip, page 37)
- 2 to 4 cloves garlic, peeled and coarsely chopped
- ¼ tsp. kosher salt
- 2 oz. Parmesan cheese, grated (¾ cup)

In a food processor combine olive oil, basil, nuts, garlic, and salt. Process until nearly smooth, scraping sides as necessary. Stir in Parmesan. Add enough additional olive oil to reach desired consistency. Makes 1 cup.

To store Cover the surface of the pesto with plastic wrap (to prevent from turning brown) and refrigerate up to 1 week.

EACH TABLESPOON *85 cal, 8 g fat, 3 mg chol, 101 mg sodium, 1 g carb, 0 g fiber, 2 g pro.*

1 TOAST THE NUTS When toasted, nuts release oils that make them even more flavorful. Cool them completely before using to prevent the pesto from becoming gummy.

2 EMBRACE TEXTURE Process, don't pulverize! Overprocessing results in bruised greens and a dull, lifeless sauce. Stop before the pesto is completely smooth—a few big flecks give it character.

3 GRATE FRESH Get significantly more flavor by grating the cheese by hand. Because texture is key, stir it in after you've processed the other ingredients to avoid a thick, homogenous paste.

4 ADD EXTRA OIL Everyone has a style of pesto they prefer (thick for smearing on sandwiches, thin for pasta and veggies). Add olive oil as you wish for the consistency you like best.

IT'S ALL ABOUT THE TRIFECTA: FRESH GREENS AND/OR HERBS, AGED SALTY CHEESE, AND TOASTY NUTS. TRY BASIC BASIL OR ONE OF THE VARIATIONS.

PESTO REIMAGINED It's your turn to play! Keep it simple and pair strong assertive herbs with mild greens for the tastiest balance.

PROVENÇAL

MAKE IT Baby greens (2 cups) + Thyme (2 Tbsp.) + Lavender buds (1 Tbsp.) + Almonds (½ cup) + Pecorino (2 oz.)

USE IT Give potluck fare a facelift. Stir into a bowl of boiled new potatoes or pasta salad with shredded chicken.

ARUGULA-MINT

MAKE IT Arugula (1 cup) + Mint (1 cup) + Hazelnuts (½ cup) + Manchego (2 oz.)

USE IT This stuff was made for veggies. Go green with blanched green beans and snap peas or grilled zucchini. It also partners well with lamb or pork.

SPINACH-OREGANO

MAKE IT Spinach (1½ cups) + Oregano (½ cup) + Walnuts (½ cup) + Asiago (2 oz.)

USE IT Next time you make pizza, swap out the tomato sauce for this tasty blend, or whirl it into scrambled eggs with a sprinkle of crushed red pepper.

new ways with PEAS

Snap to it—when fresh peas are in season! Try the everyday veggie at its absolute tastiest in soup, sauce, and pasta.

Garden (also called English) peas have a short shelf life. Look for firm, bright green pods—the smaller, the sweeter—and shell just before using.

Delicate pea shoots (the emerging plants' young tops) are tender with subtle pea flavor. Enjoy raw in a salad or toss into a stir-fry at the last minute.

DIJON & DILL CREAMED PEA SAUCE

DOUBLE-PEA SOUP

LEMONY MAC & PEAS

REMOVE THE STEM END AND PEEL THE STRING FROM THE SEAM. GENTLY PRY OPEN THE POD AND RUN YOUR THUMB ALONG THE INTERIOR TO RELEASE THE PEAS.

DIJON & DILL CREAMED PEA SAUCE

This sauce pairs deliciously with grilled salmon or roast chicken.

TOTAL TIME 30 min.

- 2   Tbsp. butter
- 2   Tbsp. all-purpose flour
- ½   tsp. salt
- ⅛   tsp. ground turmeric
- 1   cup chicken stock or reduced-sodium chicken broth
- 1   Tbsp. Dijon-style mustard
- 1   cup whipping cream
- 2   cups shelled fresh peas*
- 3   Tbsp. snipped fresh dill
       Pea shoots (optional)

In a medium saucepan heat butter over medium heat until melted. Whisk in flour, salt, and turmeric; cook and stir 2 minutes. Add stock all at once; cook, stirring frequently, until thickened and bubbly. Whisk in mustard and cream; bring to boiling. Stir in peas. Reduce heat and simmer, uncovered, 9 minutes or just until peas are tender and sauce reduces to gravy-like consistency, stirring frequently. Remove from heat and stir in dill. Makes 6 servings.

*Tip If using frozen peas, stir in with dill and heat through.

EACH SERVING *223 cal, 19 g fat, 65 mg chol, 380 mg sodium, 10 g carb, 3 g fiber, 4 g pro.*

LEMONY MAC & PEAS

HANDS-ON TIME 25 min.
TOTAL TIME 45 min.

- 2   cups shelled fresh sweet peas
- 8   oz. dried rigatoni pasta
- ¾   cup ricotta cheese
- 1   cup milk
- ¼   cup purchased basil pesto
- 2   tsp. lemon zest
- 1   cup cubed ham
- 4   oz. part-skim mozzarella cheese, shredded (1 cup)

1. Preheat oven to 425°F. Grease a 2-quart square baking dish; set aside. In a medium saucepan cook 1 cup of the peas in enough boiling salted water to cover 6 minutes or until peas are bright green and tender. Drain and run under cold water to cool. Drain well.
2. Cook pasta according to package directions, adding remaining peas the last 4 minutes; drain, return to saucepan and set aside.
3. Meanwhile, in a food processor combine the cooked peas, ricotta, milk, pesto, and lemon zest. Cover and process until smooth.
4. Add ricotta mixture to the cooked pasta mixture along with ham. Transfer to prepared baking dish. Top with cheese. Bake, uncovered, 20 minutes or until golden brown and bubbly. Makes 6 servings.

EACH SERVING *388 cal, 15 g fat, 47 mg chol, 514 mg sodium, 41 g carb, 4 g fiber, 22 g pro.*

DOUBLE-PEA SOUP

TOTAL TIME 30 min.

- 2   Tbsp. butter
- 1   cup shelled fresh sweet peas*
- 2   carrots, peeled and chopped (1 cup)
- ¾   cup thinly sliced green onions and/or shallots
- 1   Tbsp. grated fresh ginger
- 1   tsp. ground coriander
- 4   cups vegetable stock
- 2   cups fresh snap pea pods, trimmed and halved, if desired
- 2   cups 1-inch cubes country-style bread
- 2   oz. Gruyère cheese, shredded (½ cup)
       Pea shoots (optional)

1. Preheat broiler. In a large saucepan melt butter over medium heat. Add shelled peas, carrots, onions, ginger, and coriander. Cook 5 minutes, stirring frequently. Stir in vegetable stock; bring to boiling. Reduce heat; simmer, uncovered, 5 minutes. Add pea pods; simmer 2 minutes more.
2. Meanwhile, line a shallow baking pan with foil and place bread cubes in pan. Broil 3 to 4 inches from the heat 1 minute or until toasted. Sprinkle bread with cheese. Broil 1 minute more or until cheese melts and starts to brown. Serve soup topped with cheesy croutons and, if desired, pea shoots. Makes 4 servings.

*Tip If using frozen peas, add to broth mixture with the pea pods.

EACH SERVING *244 cal, 12 g fat, 36 mg chol, 818 mg sodium, 24 g carb, 5 g fiber, 9 g pro.*

TINY
TOMATO
PIE

TINY TOMATOES

As small as a dime to slightly bigger than a quarter, tiny tomatoes are a gardener's proof that good things come in small packages.

TINY TOMATO PIE

Cups of whole tiny tomatoes pile onto a feta and Parmesan layer, then bake and melt into a tender, flaky crust. Go freeform with the top crust of this rustic pie. Use an assortment of round cutters—or any shape—and layer as you please.

HANDS-ON TIME 20 min.
TOTAL TIME 3 hr., 40 min.

- 1   14.1-oz. pkg. rolled refrigerated unbaked piecrust (2 crusts)
- 4   oz. feta cheese, crumbled
- ⅔   cup finely shredded Parmesan cheese
- ¼   cup mayonnaise
- 1   egg, separated
- 1   Tbsp. chopped fresh oregano
- ¼   tsp. black pepper
- 4   cups assorted tiny tomatoes
- 1   to 2 Tbsp. drained capers
- ½   tsp. kosher salt

1. Let piecrusts stand at room temperature 15 minutes. Meanwhile, preheat oven to 375°F. In a medium bowl stir together feta, 2 Tbsp. of the Parmesan, mayonnaise, egg yolk, oregano, and black pepper. Unroll one pastry into a 9-inch pie plate. Ease into plate, pressing lightly into bottom and sides; crimp edge as desired. Sprinkle crust with remaining Parmesan cheese.
2. Spoon feta mixture into pie plate, spreading over Parmesan. Top with tomatoes and capers. Sprinkle with salt. Using round cutters, cut rounds from remaining pastry; place on filling. In a small bowl whisk together the egg white and 2 tsp. water; brush over top pastry.
3. To prevent overbrowning, cover edge of pie with foil. Place a foil-lined baking sheet on the rack below the pie in oven. Bake 35 minutes. Remove foil. Bake 45 minutes more or until crust is golden brown. Cool 2 hours on a wire rack. Store any leftovers in the refrigerator. Makes 8 servings.
EACH SERVING *339 cal, 23 g fat, 49 mg chol, 656 mg sodium, 29 g carb, 1 g fiber, 7 g pro.*

WHERE TO FIND Cherry and grape varieties represent the larger end of the spectrum. As growing season unfolds, availability of smaller varieties increases. Come summer, you'll find tomatoes as small as currants in gardens, farmers markets, and some grocery stores.

HOW TO STORE Store just as you would any other tomato, which means the fridge is off limits. Don't be fooled by their small size—they come with a sturdy, firm skin that gives them lasting power on the kitchen counter.

CHERRY VS. GRAPE These two varieties are roughly the same size, although the oblong shape of grape tomatoes gives them visual distinction. Cherry tomatoes are juicier and sweeter than grape tomatoes, whose dense flesh makes them excellent for longer cooking.

USE THEM ALL THE WAYS YOU WOULD A LARGE TOMATO—THESE TINY TOMATOES DELIVER BIG FLAVOR.

**ROASTED TOMATO
KETCHUP**
Recipe on page 86

TINY TOMATO SALAD WITH CHAMPAGNE VINAIGRETTE
Recipe on page 86

FROM WHOLE VINE ROASTING TO A MUDDLED COCKTAIL WITH A DELICIOUSLY WICKED HEAT, THESE LITTLE TOMATOES DELIVER BIG FLAVOR.

ROASTED TOMATO KETCHUP

Tiny tomatoes show off their savory side in this chunky salsa-inspired ketchup. Hits of jalapeño and lime make it the condiment to serve with grilled meats and smoky favorites.

HANDS-ON TIME 15 min.
TOTAL TIME 45 min.

3   cups assorted tiny tomatoes
½   medium onion, finely chopped (¼ cup)
1   fresh jalapeño chile pepper, stemmed, seeded, and finely chopped (tip, page 37)
1   Tbsp. lime juice
1   Tbsp. honey
¼   tsp. kosher salt

Preheat oven to 400°F. Line a 15×10×1-inch baking pan with foil. Place all ingredients in prepared pan. Sprinkle with salt. Toss to combine. Roast, uncovered, 20 to 25 minutes or until skins have burst and most of the liquid has evaporated, stirring once or twice. Remove; cool slightly. Place in a food processor or blender; process until smooth. Refrigerate, covered, up to 1 week or freeze up to 3 months. Makes 1¼ cups.
EACH 1-TBSP. SERVING *10 cal, 0 g fat, 0 mg. chol., 31 mg sodium, 2 g carb. 0 g fiber, 1 g pro.*

TINY TOMATO SALAD WITH CHAMPAGNE VINAIGRETTE

This twist on tomato salad tosses the sweet jewels with peppery arugula and paper-thin fennel slices. Double the punchy shallot vinaigrette, and keep it in a jar in the fridge for dressing salads throughout the week.

TOTAL TIME 20 min.

4   cups assorted tiny tomatoes
2   cups arugula or watercress
1   small fennel bulb, quartered, cored, and very thinly sliced (1 cup)
⅓   cup chopped fresh Italian parsley
2   shallots, finely chopped (¼ cup)
¼   cup olive oil
3   Tbsp. champagne vinegar
1   tsp. lemon zest
¼   tsp. kosher salt
⅛   tsp. black pepper

In a salad bowl toss together tomatoes, arugula, fennel, and parsley. For Champagne Vinaigrette, in a screw-top jar combine shallots, oil, vinegar, lemon zest, salt, and black pepper. Cover; shake well. Pour over salad. Makes 12 servings.
EACH SERVING *58 cal, 5 g fat, 0 mg chol, 58 mg sodium, 4 g carb, 1 g fiber, 1 g pro.*

SPICY TOMATO GIN & TONIC

Part gin and tonic, part bloody mary, this spicy cocktail starts with tiny tomatoes and dill muddled in the glass. Add more garden flavor with whole serrano peppers and thin slices of Persian cucumbers.

TOTAL TIME 10 min.

½   cup assorted tiny tomatoes, coarsely chopped
    Steak seasoning
    Fresh dill
1   Tbsp. lime juice
    Splash Worcestershire sauce
    Splash bottled hot pepper sauce
    Kosher salt
    Black pepper
1   oz. gin (2 Tbsp.)
2   oz. tonic water (¼ cup)
    Ice cubes
    Serrano chile peppers (tip, page 37), fresh dill, thinly sliced Persian cucumber, and/or lime wedges.

Rub the rim of a 12-oz. glass with the cut side of a tomato. Dip rim in steak seasoning to coat. Using a wooden spoon, mash tomatoes and dill in bottom of glass. Stir in lime juice, Worcestershire, and hot pepper sauce. Season with kosher salt and black pepper. Add gin, then tonic water and ice. Serve with serrano pepper, dill, cucumber slices, and/or lime wedges. Makes 1 serving.
EACH SERVING *106 cal, 0 g fat, 0 mg chol, 476 mg sodium, 10 g carb, 0 g fiber, 1 g pro.*

SPICY TOMATO
GIN & TONIC

MELTY TINY
TOMATOES

MELTY TINY TOMATOES

With a little sweet and a little spice, whole tomatoes melt into a delicious puddle. Roast the tomatoes on the vine for a dramatic presentation and smush over crusty bread.

HANDS-ON TIME 10 min.
TOTAL TIME 25 min.

- 4 cups assorted tiny tomatoes
- 2 Tbsp. olive oil
- 2 tsp. chili powder
- ½ tsp. sugar
- ½ tsp. kosher salt

Preheat oven to 400°F. Place tomatoes in a shallow baking dish. Drizzle with oil. Stir to coat. Sprinkle with chili powder, sugar, and salt. Roast, uncovered, 12 to 15 minutes, or just until skins start to burst, gently stirring once halfway through roasting time. Serve warm with crusty bread. Makes 3⅓ cups.

EACH ⅓-CUP SERVING *39 cal, 3 g fat, 0 mg chol, 75 mg sodium, 3 g carb, 1 g fiber, 1 g pro.*

TINY TOMATO SAUCE

Serve this garden-fresh sauce over polenta or with blanched green beans or zucchini noodles. It also makes a tasty accompaniment to chicken Parmesan or grilled steak.

HANDS-ON TIME 15 min.
TOTAL TIME 1 hr.

- 8 cups assorted tiny tomatoes
- 1 medium sweet yellow onion, peeled and quartered
- 5 Tbsp. butter
- 1¼ tsp. kosher salt
  Cooked polenta (optional)
  Fresh oregano (optional)

In a 4-qt. saucepan combine 6½ cups of the tomatoes, onion, butter, and salt over medium heat. Once tomatoes begin to bubble, reduce heat to a simmer. Cook 30 minutes, stirring every 10 to 15 minutes. Stir in remaining tomatoes; cook 15 minutes more or until butter has separated from the tomatoes and most of the liquid has evaporated. If desired, serve over cooked polenta and top with fresh oregano. Makes 4 cups.

EACH ⅔-CUP SERVING *124 cal, 10 g fat, 25 mg chol, 571 mg sodium, 9 g carb, 2 g fiber, 2 g pro.*

TINY
TOMATO
SAUCE

FAST & FRESH

Easy, healthful recipes for a better dinner tonight.

ROSEMARY
CHICKEN WITH
SWEET PEPPERS

ROSEMARY CHICKEN WITH SWEET PEPPERS

Weighting the chicken and peppers with a heavy skillet while cooking gives a deep sear that almost caramelizes the meat and veggies for big-time flavor. Serve with a simple arugula and Parmesan salad drizzled with balsamic vinegar and olive oil.

TOTAL TIME 35 min.

8   skinless, boneless chicken thighs
1   tsp. kosher salt
¼   tsp. black pepper
2   Tbsp. extra-virgin olive oil
2   large red sweet peppers,
    stemmed, cored, and each cut
    into eighths
1   Tbsp. chopped fresh rosemary

1. Preheat oven to 200°F. Season chicken with salt and black pepper. Heat a 12-inch skillet over medium-high heat; add 1 Tbsp. of the oil. Place 4 chicken thighs and 8 pepper pieces in a single layer in skillet. Cover with a smaller heavy pan or heatproof dish weighted down with cans. Cook 5 to 7 minutes or until browned.
2. Remove weight; turn chicken and peppers. Sprinkle with half the rosemary. Reduce heat to medium. Return pan and weights. Continue cooking 4 minutes or until done (170°F). Transfer chicken and peppers to a baking sheet; cover and keep warm in oven. Repeat with remaining oil, chicken, peppers, and rosemary. Makes 4 servings.

EACH SERVING *356 cal, 16 g fat, 213 mg chol, 456 mg sodium, 5 g carb, 2 g fiber, 45 g pro.*

CHICKPEA, LEEK & SPINACH SOUP

CHICKPEA, LEEK & SPINACH SOUP

Other tender greens could take the place of the spinach. Try baby kale, watercress, or even dandelion greens.

TOTAL TIME 25 min.

2   Tbsp. extra-virgin olive oil
2   medium leeks, white and light green
    parts only, thinly sliced
2   15- to 16-oz. cans chickpeas,
    drained and rinsed
2   cloves garlic, thinly sliced
4   cups reduced-sodium chicken or
    vegetable stock or broth
3   Tbsp. fresh lemon juice
2   5-oz. pkg. baby spinach
1   Tbsp. fresh thyme, chopped
    Kosher salt and black pepper

1. In a 4-qt. pot heat oil over medium heat. Add leeks. Cook, stirring occasionally, 5 to 7 minutes or until very tender but not browned (reduce heat if leeks begin to brown). Stir in chickpeas and garlic. Cook about 2 minutes, stirring occasionally.
2. Add stock and 1 cup water. Bring to boiling. Reduce heat. Add lemon juice. Simmer, uncovered, 5 minutes. Gradually stir in the spinach and thyme. Cook until the spinach is wilted, about 1 minute. Season to taste with kosher salt and black pepper. Serve immediately. Makes 4 servings.

EACH SERVING *265 cal, 10 g fat, 0 mg chol, 856 mg sodium, 33 g carb, 9 g fiber, 13 g pro.*

HOISIN-GLAZED TOFU & GREEN BEANS

LAMB & CUCUMBER SALAD PITAS

Cooking these thin lamb burgers diner-style (scooping the ground meat right into the skillet as opposed to forming the patty first) ensures a tender patty with a dark brown, crusty exterior. Store the raw lamb in the refrigerator until just before cooking to keep the patties from falling apart.

TOTAL TIME 30 min.

1   large cucumber, peeled and
    coarsely chopped (2 cups)
1   cup thinly sliced red onion
½   cup pitted Kalamata olives,
    halved
½   cup packed fresh mint leaves
1   jalapeño chile pepper, seeded,
    and thinly sliced (tip, page 37)
1½ tsp. dried oregano, crushed
¼   cup lemon juice
3   Tbsp. olive oil
½   cup plain yogurt
2   cloves garlic, minced
½   tsp. kosher salt
¼   tsp. black pepper
1   lb. ground lamb
4   soft flatbreads

1. For Cucumber Salad, in a medium bowl combine cucumber, onion, olives, half the mint leaves, jalapeño, and oregano. Add lemon juice and 2 Tbsp. of the oil; toss to coat.
2. In a small bowl combine yogurt and 1 clove garlic. Chop remaining mint and stir into yogurt mixture. Season to taste with kosher salt and black pepper.
3. In a large bowl combine lamb, remaining clove of garlic, salt, and black pepper. Heat remaining oil in a 12-inch skillet over medium-high heat. Using a slightly rounded ½-cup measure, spoon meat into four mounds in skillet, leaving space between mounds. Cook 2 minutes. Press mounds into thin patties using the back of a wide spatula. Cook 2 to 3 minutes more or until browned. Turn; cook 2 minutes more or until done (160°F).
4. Serve lamb patties in flatbread topped with yogurt sauce and Cucumber Salad. Makes 4 servings.
EACH SERVING *658 cal, 38 g fat, 79 mg chol, 968 mg sodium, 48 g carb, 6 g fiber, 30 g pro.*

HOISIN-GLAZED TOFU & GREEN BEANS

Soy sauce and tamari sauce can be used interchangeably in this dish. Japanese tamari tends to be thicker and less salty than Chinese soy sauce and contains less (or no) wheat so it can work as a gluten-free option.

TOTAL TIME 40 min.

16 oz. extra-firm tofu
2   Tbsp. hoisin sauce
1   Tbsp. soy sauce or tamari sauce
1   Tbsp. grated fresh ginger
¼   tsp. crushed red pepper (optional)
2   Tbsp. vegetable oil
3   cloves garlic, thinly sliced
8   oz. fresh green beans, trimmed and
    halved lengthwise
    Hot cooked rice noodles or rice
    Lime wedges

1. Cut tofu lengthwise into four 1-inch-thick slices. Lay tofu slices on a double layer of paper towels. Top with another double layer of paper towels. Weight with a plate topped with cans to remove excess water from tofu. Let stand 10 minutes. Cut tofu into 1-inch cubes.
2. Meanwhile, stir together 3 Tbsp. water, hoisin, soy sauce, ginger, and crushed red pepper, if using.
3. In an extra-large skillet heat 1 Tbsp. of the oil over medium-high heat. Add tofu. Cook, without stirring, until tofu begins to brown, 4 to 5 minutes. Turn; cook 4 to 5 minutes more, stirring occasionally until tofu is golden brown on all sides.
4. Transfer tofu to a plate. Add remaining 1 Tbsp. oil to skillet. Add garlic; cook 30 seconds. Add beans; cook 4 minutes or until barely tender. Return tofu to skillet. Add hoisin mixture; bring to boiling, stirring to coat. Serve with rice noodles and lime wedges. Makes 4 servings.
EACH SERVING *236 cal, 14 g fat, 0 mg chol, 402 mg sodium, 17 g carb, 2 g fiber, 14 g pro.*

LAMB & CUCUMBER
SALAD PITAS

craving
CARROT CAKE

This is one of those gloriously everyday cakes. It's unpretentious, not too sweet, and full of carrots (so it's healthy ... ish).

CARROT SNACK CAKE

Swapping half the all-purpose flour for whole wheat is undetectable and the texture remains tender.

HANDS-ON TIME 25 min.
TOTAL TIME 2 hr.

4	eggs
1	cup olive oil
¾	cup packed brown sugar
1	Tbsp. orange zest
½	cup orange juice
1	tsp. vanilla
1	cup all-purpose flour
1	cup whole wheat flour
2	tsp. baking powder
2	tsp. ground cinnamon
1	tsp. baking soda
½	tsp. salt
½	tsp. ground nutmeg
2½	cups shredded carrots
1	cup chopped toasted walnuts
1	recipe Cream Cheese Frosting
	Orange zest (optional)

1. Preheat oven to 350°F. Grease a 13×9×2-inch baking pan; set aside.
2. In a large bowl whisk together eggs, oil, brown sugar, orange zest, orange juice, and vanilla until combined. Whisk in flours, baking powder, cinnamon, soda, salt, and nutmeg until combined. Stir in carrots and walnuts. Pour into prepared pan.
3. Bake 35 minutes or until a wooden toothpick inserted in center comes out clean. Cool in pan on a wire rack. Spread with Cream Cheese Frosting. Sprinkle with orange zest, if desired. Makes 20 servings.
Cream Cheese Frosting In a bowl beat together 8 oz. cream cheese and 3 Tbsp. softened butter with a mixer on medium speed until combined and smooth. Add 2 cups powdered sugar; beat on low until combined. Stir in 1 tsp. orange zest.
EACH SERVING *316 cal, 21 g fat, 54 mg chol, 252 mg sodium, 28 g carb, 2 g fiber, 4 g pro.*

THERE ARE CAKES THAT YOU LAYER AND FROST IN SWIRLS AND PUT ON A PEDESTAL. THEN THERE ARE CAKES THAT ARE EASY AND RELAXED, WHICH NEED NO SPECIAL OCCASION OTHER THAN "HEY, IT'S TUESDAY!"

PAVLOVA
Recipe on page 110

may

Find reinvented classics and discover new ingredients—as well as global flavors—in the BHG Dinner Report. Plus, school is in session for pavlova, carnitas, and Vermont-style breakfast.

102

117

123

SALMON POT PIE
CASSEROLE

The DINNER REPORT

Better Homes and Gardens magazine has been a key part of the evolution of the American dinner for nearly 100 years.

SALMON POT PIE CASSEROLE

A classic casserole gets a healthy makeover. Five vegetables pack this lighter, fresher meal-in-a-dish that is crowned with cornmeal biscuits.

HANDS-ON TIME 45 min.
TOTAL TIME 1 hr., 15 min.

- 1   recipe Cornmeal Biscuits
- 1   egg, lightly beaten
-     Kosher salt
- 3   Tbsp. butter
- 1   Tbsp. olive oil
- 2   medium leeks, washed, white and light green parts chopped (1 cup)
- 8   oz. shiitake or cremini mushrooms, stemmed and halved or quartered if large (3 cups)
- 3   cloves garlic, minced
- ½   tsp. black pepper
- ¼   cup all-purpose flour
- 2   cups chicken broth
- ¼   cup whipping cream
- 1½   cups fresh or frozen peas
- 2   large carrots, thinly sliced
- 1   cup broccoli florets
- 1   lb. salmon fillet, skinned and cut into 1-inch cubes
- 3   Tbsp. chopped fresh dill

1. Preheat oven to 400°F. Prepare Cornmeal Biscuits. Place on baking sheet; brush with egg and sprinkle lightly with salt. Partially bake 12 minutes or until lightly golden. Remove from oven. Heat butter and oil in a large skillet over medium heat. Add leeks; cook and stir 4 minutes. Stir in mushrooms, garlic, black pepper, and ¼ tsp. kosher salt. Cook and stir 4 to 6 minutes or just until liquid evaporates and mushrooms are browned.
2. Stir flour into leek mixture; stir 1 minute. Add broth and cream. Cook and stir until bubbly. Add remaining ingredients; bring to boiling. Transfer to a 2-qt. baking dish.
3. Arrange partially baked biscuits on top. Bake 15 to 20 minutes or until biscuits are golden brown. Makes 8 servings.
Cornmeal Biscuits In bowl combine 2 cups all-purpose flour, ½ cup cornmeal, 2 tsp. baking powder, and ½ tsp. salt. Cut in ¼ cup shortening until pea size. Stir in 1 cup buttermilk. Turn out onto floured surface. Knead gently 10 to 15 strokes or until dough comes together. Pat to ¾ inch thickness. Cut into eight 2½-inch rounds, repatting as needed. Partially bake as directed in Step 1. Makes 8 biscuits.
EACH SERVING *454 cal, 21 g fat, 77 mg chol, 644 mg sodium, 47 g carb, 5 g fiber, 21 g pro.*

THE NEW HOME COOKING

People are heading back to the kitchen to prepare dinner in record numbers—and dinner has a lot to live up to these days: When we talk about weeknights, dinner needs to be on the table in less than an hour; comfort foods require a side of healthy; visits to farmers markets reflect renewed interest in where our food comes from; and there are myriad ways to sample the tastes of the world.

DINNER IS CLASSIC Chicken is still the protein of choice, and thighs are now king for economy, flavor, and ability to stay moist and tender.

DINNER IS HEALTHY Eating healthfully means fresh ingredients, and it's a whole lot more veggies—whatever the "it" veg might be.

DINNER IS EXPRESSIVE For most, cooking is a creative outlet, and leads to experimenting and cooking new dishes at home.

DINNER IS PLANNED AHEAD. Let's face it, we haven't found any secret pockets of time, so we cook smarter. Case in point: Sunday roast chicken is also Monday's tacos or Tuesday's salad.

WHATEVER DISH WE COOK, WE'RE DOING IT SMARTER AND FASTER. THESE RECIPES WILL HELP YOU MAKE DINNER MEANINGFUL EVERY NIGHT.

CAULIFLOWER-
POTATO MASH

GREEN BEANS
WITH
TOASTED
PANKO

APRICOT-GLAZED
CHICKEN THIGHS

APRICOT-GLAZED CHICKEN THIGHS

HANDS-ON TIME 15 min.
TOTAL TIME 1 hr.

¼ cup apricot spreadable fruit, large pieces snipped
¼ cup honey
2 Tbsp. soy sauce
2 Tbsp. minced fresh ginger
6 cloves garlic, minced (1 Tbsp.)
½ tsp. cayenne pepper
¼ cup cider vinegar
8 bone-in chicken thighs (3½ to 4 lb. total)

1. Place oven rack in bottom third of oven. Preheat oven to 400°F. For glaze, in a small saucepan combine spreadable fruit, honey, soy sauce, ginger, garlic, and cayenne. Heat over medium-low heat until spreadable fruit is melted. Remove and stir in vinegar; cool.
2. Line a 13×9-inch baking pan with foil. Arrange chicken in a single layer. Pour apricot glaze over chicken, turning pieces to coat. Arrange pieces skin sides up. Bake, uncovered, 40 to 45 minutes or until done (175°F in thickest part) and tops are browned, brushing with glaze twice during baking. Skim fat from pan juices; serve juices over chicken. Makes 8 servings.
EACH SERVING 483 cal, 31 g fat, 193 mg chol, 377 mg sodium, 15 g carb, 0 g fiber, 33 g pro.

CAULIFLOWER-POTATO MASH

HANDS-ON TIME 20 min.
TOTAL TIME 1 hr.

Nonstick cooking spray
1 medium head cauliflower (2 lb.), cut into florets (about 4½ cups)
1 Tbsp. olive oil
1½ lb. Yukon Gold potatoes, scrubbed or peeled, cut into 2-inch pieces
1¼ cups milk
3 Tbsp. coconut oil, melted
1 tsp. salt
¼ tsp. freshly ground black pepper
Green onions, chopped (optional)

1. Preheat oven to 400°F. Lightly coat shallow baking pan with nonstick cooking spray. Place cauliflower in pan; drizzle with oil. Toss to coat. Roast 30 to 40 minutes or just until browned, stirring occasionally.
2. Place potatoes in a large saucepan with salted water to cover. Bring to boiling; reduce heat. Simmer, covered, 15 to 20 minutes or until tender. Drain; return potatoes to saucepan. Mash with potato masher; set aside.
3. Place cauliflower in a food processor; cover and process until finely chopped, adding 2 Tbsp. of the milk. Add cauliflower to potatoes in saucepan. Add remaining milk, the coconut oil, salt, and black pepper. Heat through over medium heat, stirring frequently. Top with green onions, if desired. Makes 8 to 10 servings.
EACH SERVING 123 cal, 6 g fat, 2 mg chol, 151 mg sodium, 14 g carb, 3 g fiber, 3 g pro.

GREEN BEANS WITH TOASTED PANKO

HANDS-ON TIME 15 min.
TOTAL TIME 35 min.

Nonstick cooking spray
1½ lb. green beans, trimmed
1 lemon, sliced
2 Tbsp. olive oil
½ tsp. kosher salt
2 cloves garlic, minced
½ cup panko bread crumbs
2 tsp. lemon zest
2 tsp. chopped fresh tarragon
¼ tsp. freshly ground black pepper

1. Preheat oven to 400°F. Lightly coat a shallow baking pan with nonstick cooking spray. Rinse beans in colander; shake, allowing some water to remain on beans. Place beans and lemon slices on prepared pan; drizzle with 1 Tbsp. of the oil. Toss to coat; spread in an even layer. Sprinkle with salt. Roast, uncovered, 20 minutes or until tender and slightly charred, stirring once.
2. Meanwhile, heat remaining 1 Tbsp. oil in large skillet over medium-high heat. Add garlic; stir 30 seconds. Add panko; stir about 2 minutes or until just golden. Add zest, tarragon, salt, and black pepper; stir to combine. Sprinkle on roasted green beans. Makes 8 servings.
EACH SERVING 68 cal, 4 g fat, 0 mg chol, 156 mg sodium, 8 g carb, 2 g fiber, 2 g pro.

SESAME DAN DAN NOODLE BOWL

Noodles find their way onto about every culture's dinner table. This rendition of dan dan noodles is a takeoff on the traditional dish from China's Szechuan province. It matches spicy-hot sauce with preserved vegetables and pork over noodles.

TOTAL TIME 35 min.

8 oz. dried round Chinese egg noodles or spaghetti
2 Tbsp. soy sauce
2 Tbsp. tahini (sesame seed paste)
1 Tbsp. seasoned rice vinegar
1 Tbsp. toasted sesame oil
1 tsp. sriracha sauce
2 cups reduced-sodium chicken broth
1 Tbsp. peanut or canola oil
8 oz. uncooked lean ground pork
⅓ cup finely chopped dill pickles
2 cloves garlic, minced
Sliced green onions, fresh cilantro leaves, coarsely chopped peanuts, and/or crushed Szechuan or whole black peppercorns

1. Cook noodles according to package directions; drain. Meanwhile, in a small saucepan whisk together soy sauce, tahini, vinegar, sesame oil, and sriracha. Stir in broth; heat over low heat.
2. In a wok or large skillet heat peanut oil over high heat. Add pork and cook until browned, breaking up meat. Drain off any fat. Add pickles and garlic; cook about 2 minutes more or until pork is crispy.
3. Divide noodles among serving bowls. Spoon broth over noodles and top with pork. Top with onions, cilantro, peanuts, and/or crushed peppercorns. Makes 6 servings.
EACH SERVING 311 cal, 16 g fat, 26 mg chol, 686 mg sodium, 27 g carb, 2 g fiber, 15 g pro.

SHRIMP CURRY NOODLE BOWL

TOTAL TIME 35 min.

2   Tbsp. peanut or canola oil
2   shallots, sliced
1   lime
3   cloves garlic, minced
2   tsp. grated fresh ginger
1   to 2 Tbsp. red curry paste
4   cups reduced-sodium chicken broth
     or vegetable broth
2   Tbsp. fish sauce
1   lb. fresh or frozen medium shrimp in
     shells, peeled and deveined
8   oz. rice vermicelli noodles
1   13.5- to 14-oz. can unsweetened
     coconut milk
     Fresh basil leaves and lime wedges

1. Heat oil in Dutch oven over medium heat. Add shallots; cook and stir about 5 minutes or until crisp and browned. Remove shallots; set aside. Using a vegetable peeler, remove zest from lime in strips; cut lime in half. Add garlic, ginger, and curry paste to Dutch oven; cook and stir 1 minute. Add broth, fish sauce, and 2 cups water. Squeeze juice from lime into broth; add strips of zest. Bring to boiling.
2. Stir in shrimp and noodles. Return to boiling; reduce heat. Cook 3 to 4 minutes or just until shrimp turn opaque. Stir in coconut milk; heat through. Remove lime zest. Top bowls with shallots and basil; serve with lime wedges. Makes 6 servings.
EACH SERVING *365 cal, 16 g fat, 106 mg chol, 1,028 mg sodium, 36 g carb, 1 g fiber, 18 g pro.*

ASPARAGUS NOODLE BOWL

TOTAL TIME 45 min.

3   slices bacon
1   8-oz. skinless, boneless chicken
     breast
1   large onion, finely chopped (1 cup)
½   cup dry white wine
4   cloves garlic, minced
1   lb. (3 to 4) ripe tomatoes, finely
     chopped (2 cups)
3   cups reduced-sodium chicken broth
1   tsp. smoked paprika
6   oz. dried angel hair pasta, broken
     in half
8   oz. fresh asparagus, trimmed and
     cut into 1-inch pieces

1. In a large deep skillet cook bacon over medium heat until crisp. Remove and drain on paper towels, reserving drippings. Crumble bacon; set aside.
2. Add chicken to skillet. Cook over medium heat 10 to 12 minutes or until done (165°F). Remove; cover to keep warm.
3. Add onion to skillet. Cook and stir 3 minutes. Remove skillet from heat; add wine and garlic. Return to heat. Bring to boiling; reduce heat. Simmer, uncovered, 5 minutes or until wine evaporates, stirring to scrape up browned bits. Add tomatoes. Bring to boiling; reduce heat. Simmer, uncovered, 5 to 10 minutes or until tomatoes break down, stirring occasionally. Stir in broth and paprika; bring to boiling. Gradually stir in pasta. Return to boiling; reduce heat. Simmer, uncovered, 10 minutes or until pasta is tender, stirring occasionally and adding asparagus the last 2 minutes.
4. Thinly slice chicken. Serve noodle bowls topped with chicken and bacon. Makes 6 servings.
EACH SERVING *285 cal, 9 g fat, 40 mg chol, 428 mg sodium, 29 g carb, 3 g fiber, 18 g pro.*

SOBA NOODLE BOWL
Look for miso in the Asian food section of supermarkets.

TOTAL TIME 40 min.

6   oz. dried soba noodles or dried
     multigrain spaghetti
8   oz. baby bok choy, quartered
     lengthwise
4   cups reduced-sodium chicken broth
     or vegetable broth
¼   cup white miso paste
2   Tbsp. reduced-sodium soy sauce
2   carrots, julienned (1 cup)
4   oz. cremini or shiitake mushrooms,
     stemmed and sliced (1½ cups)
6   soft- or hard-cooked eggs, peeled
     and halved
     Cracked black pepper

1. In a large saucepan cook noodles in lightly salted boiling water according to package directions. Drain; rinse under cold water. Divide among bowls. Top with bok choy.
2. In same saucepan heat broth and 2 cups water over medium-high heat until simmering; whisk in miso and soy sauce.

Add carrots and mushrooms; return to simmering. Reduce heat. Cook 1 to 3 minutes or until carrots are crisp-tender.
3. Ladle broth and vegetables over noodles and bok choy. Top with eggs and cracked black pepper. Makes 6 servings.
EACH SERVING *206 cal, 4 g fat, 124 mg chol, 1,175 mg sodium, 31 g carb, 3 g fiber, 13 g pro.*

PEPPER HAKKA NOODLE BOWL

TOTAL TIME 25 min.

6   oz. flat Chinese egg noodles or
     dried linguine pasta
¼   cup ketchup
¼   cup soy sauce
1   Tbsp. cider vinegar
2   to 3 tsp. chili paste (sambal oelek)
2   Tbsp. peanut or canola oil
2   red sweet peppers, cut into
     bite-size strips
3   cloves garlic, minced
2   tsp. grated fresh ginger
4   oz. fresh snap or snow pea pods,
     trimmed and halved crosswise
     Lime zest and lime wedges

1. In a large saucepan cook noodles in lightly salted water 3 minutes for Chinese noodles or 7 minutes for linguine; drain. Meanwhile, in a small bowl combine ketchup, soy sauce, vinegar, and chili paste; set aside.
2. In a wok or extra-large skillet heat oil over medium-high heat. Add pepper strips, garlic, and ginger. Cook and stir 3 to 4 minutes or until pepper strips are crisp-tender. Add pea pods; cook and stir 1 minute. Add noodles and sauce mixture. Toss to combine; heat through. Top servings with lime zest and additional sliced pea pods. Serve with lime wedges. Makes 6 servings.
EACH SERVING *166 cal, 5 g fat, 0 mg chol, 832 mg sodium, 27 g carb, 3 g fiber, 6 g pro.*

SESAME DAN DAN NOODLE BOWL
Recipe on page 101

ASPARAGUS NOODLE BOWL

SHRIMP CURRY NOODLE BOWL

SOBA NOODLE BOWL

PEPPER HAKKA NOODLE BOWL

ANYTIME
SOCCA

SWEET-SPICY
CHERRIES

OLIVE
RELISH

GARLIC-LENTIL
SALAD
Recipe on page 106

SMOKY
CARROT
SPREAD

CHILE
ZUCCHINI

RADISH
SALAD

ANYTIME SOCCA

Socca—gluten-free chickpea flatbread—is super easy to make and delicious when piled high with bold-flavor toppings.

HANDS-ON TIME 10 min.
TOTAL TIME 35 min.

- 1 cup chickpea (garbanzo bean) flour
- 1 Tbsp. finely chopped Italian parsley
- 1 clove garlic, minced
- ½ tsp. kosher salt
- ½ tsp. chili powder
- 2 Tbsp. plus 2 tsp. olive oil

1. In a medium bowl whisk together chickpea flour, parsley, garlic, salt, and chili powder. Add 1 cup water and the 2 Tbsp. olive oil. Whisk until smooth. Let batter stand 15 minutes.
2. Meanwhile, preheat broiler. Add 1 tsp. of the oil to a 10-inch cast-iron or heavy oven-going skillet. Place the skillet in upper one-third of oven to preheat 5 minutes (bottom of pan should be 5 inches from heat). Holding handle of skillet with hot pads, pour half the batter (about ¾ cup) into skillet; carefully spread batter evenly using an offset spatula.

3. Return skillet to oven and broil about 4 minutes or until golden brown and slightly dark brown in some areas. Loosen from skillet with wide spatula and transfer to paper towels. Repeat with remaining batter, preheating skillet with the remaining 1 tsp. oil 1 minute before adding remaining batter. Serve at room temperature or reheat socca in 350°F oven on baking sheet 5 minutes. Cut rounds in half. Makes 4 servings.
EACH SERVING *192 cal, 11 g fat, 0 mg chol, 157 mg sodium, 18 g carb, 5 g fiber, 6 g pro.*

CHILE ZUCCHINI

TOTAL TIME 30 min.

¼ cup chopped fresh mint
3 Tbsp. olive oil
2 Tbsp. red wine vinegar
1 fresh Fresno chile pepper, stemmed and minced (tip, page 37)
1 clove garlic, minced
  Kosher salt
2 medium zucchini, sliced into ¼-inch rounds (about 32 slices)

1. For vinaigrette, in a small bowl whisk together mint, 2 Tbsp. of the oil, vinegar, chile, and garlic. Season with salt.
2. Brush zucchini slices with remaining 1 Tbsp. oil and sprinkle lightly with salt. Arrange zucchini on rack of covered grill directly over medium-low heat. (Use a grill pan, if desired.) Grill 1 to 2 minutes per side or until charred and softened. Spoon vinaigrette over zucchini. Serve with socca. Makes 4 servings.
EACH SERVING *112 cal, 10 g fat, 0 mg chol, 151 mg sodium, 4 g carb, 1 g fiber, 1 g pro.*

RADISH SALAD

TOTAL TIME 25 min.

1½ cups finely chopped radishes
¼ cup chopped fresh Italian parsley
¼ cup chopped fresh mint
2 Tbsp. finely chopped red onion
1 Tbsp. red wine vinegar
1 Tbsp. olive oil
¼ cup pomegranate seeds
  Kosher salt

In a medium bowl combine radishes, herbs, onion, vinegar, and oil. Toss to combine. Fold in pomegranate seeds. Season with salt. Cover and chill up to 6 hours. Serve with socca. Makes 8 servings.
EACH SERVING *27 cal, 2 g fat, 0 mg chol, 46 mg sodium, 2 g carb, 1 g fiber, 0 g pro.*

SMOKY CARROT SPREAD

TOTAL TIME 20 min.

3 Tbsp. olive oil
1 lb. carrots, peeled and cut into bite-size pieces
2 cloves garlic, peeled
1 roasted red sweet pepper, peeled, stemmed, and seeded*
1 to 2 Tbsp. red harissa paste
2 tsp. smoked paprika
2 Tbsp. red wine vinegar
  Kosher salt
  Pomegranate seeds

1. In a large skillet heat 2 Tbsp. of the oil over medium-low heat. Add carrots and garlic; cook and stir 12 minutes or until carrots are caramelized and tender.
2. Transfer carrots, garlic, and any oil to blender. Add roasted pepper, harissa paste, paprika, vinegar, and the remaining 1 Tbsp. oil. Cover; blend until smooth, scraping sides as necessary. Season to taste with salt. Transfer to a serving bowl; drizzle with additional olive oil; top with pomegranate seeds. Serve with socca. Makes 16 servings.
*To roast sweet pepper, preheat broiler. Place a medium pepper on a foil-lined baking sheet. Broil 4 to 5 inches from heat 5 minutes or until pepper skin is charred. Turn; broil 5 minutes more or until skin is charred. Remove and wrap pepper in foil. Let stand 5 minutes; remove peel, stem, and seeds. Store in refrigerator up to 3 days.
EACH SERVING *44 cal, 3 g fat, 0 mg chol, 62 mg sodium, 4 g carb, 1 g fiber, 0 g pro.*

OLIVE RELISH

TOTAL TIME 10 min.

1 cup green olives, such as Castelvetrano, pitted and chopped
½ cup black olives, such as Kalamata, pitted and chopped
2 Tbsp. red sweet pepper, finely chopped
1 Tbsp. olive oil
2 tsp. orange zest
1 tsp. fresh thyme leaves
1 clove garlic, minced
½ tsp. crushed red pepper

In a small bowl combine all ingredients until well mixed. Serve at room temperature, or cover and chill up to 1 week. Serve with socca. Makes 6 servings.
EACH SERVING *86 cal, 9 g fat, 0 mg chol, 648 mg sodium, 1 g carb, 1 g fiber, 0 g pro.*

SWEET-SPICY CHERRIES

HANDS-ON TIME 15 min.
TOTAL TIME 30 min.

½ cup red wine vinegar
¼ cup sugar
¼ tsp. kosher salt
1½ cups fresh dark sweet cherries, pitted and halved
1 to 2 Fresno chile peppers, stemmed and thinly sliced (tip, page 37)
½ red onion, thinly sliced (½ cup)

1. In a small saucepan combine vinegar, sugar, and salt. Bring just to boiling over medium heat, stirring to dissolve sugar; reduce heat. Simmer, uncovered, 2 minutes. Remove from heat.
2. Meanwhile, in a medium bowl combine cherries, chile peppers, and onion. Pour hot vinegar mixture over cherry mixture; stir to combine. Cover; let stand at least 15 minutes. Serve at room temperature, or cover and chill up to 1 week. Serve with socca. Makes 6 servings.
EACH SERVING *67 cal, 0 g fat, 0 mg chol, 49 mg sodium, 16 g carb, 1 g fiber, 1 g pro.*

MAKE A PARTY OUT OF CHOOSING AND TOPPING PORTIONS OF SOCCA.

WITH 59 PERCENT OF WOMEN DECLARING THEY EAT MORE HEALTHFULLY THAN JUST A FEW YEARS AGO, IT COMES AS NO SURPRISE THAT WE PAY CLOSER ATTENTION TO HOW FOOD MAKES US FEEL.

GARLIC LENTIL SALAD

Photo on page 104.

HANDS-ON TIME 15 min.
TOTAL TIME 35 min.

⅔ cup halved cherry tomatoes
3 cloves garlic, peeled
3 Tbsp. olive oil
Kosher salt
2 Tbsp. red wine vinegar
2 cups vegetable broth
1 cup dried brown lentils
2 carrots, peeled and chopped
½ cup halved cherry tomatoes
1 large shallot, minced
2 Tbsp. snipped fresh chives
⅓ cup microgreens

1. For dressing, preheat oven to 375°F. Line a shallow baking pan with foil. Add the ⅔ cup tomatoes, garlic, and 1 Tbsp. of the oil to pan; toss to coat. Lightly sprinkle with salt. Roast 20 minutes, stirring once. Remove from oven and place tomato mixture in blender. Add the remaining 2 Tbsp. oil and vinegar; cover and blend until smooth. Set aside.

2. Meanwhile, in a medium saucepan combine broth and lentils. Bring to boiling; reduce heat. Simmer, uncovered, 20 to 25 minutes or until tender and all the broth is absorbed, stirring occasionally.

3. In a large bowl combine lentils, carrots, the ½ cup tomatoes, shallot, and chives. Drizzle with dressing; toss to coat. Serve with Anytime Socca (recipe, page 104), and top with microgreens. Makes 16 servings.

EACH SERVING *75 cal, 3 g fat, 0 mg chol, 125 mg sodium, 10 g carb, 2 g fiber, 3 g pro.*

VERDE RISOTTO

This dish offers the creamy richness of traditional comfort food—thanks to silky spinach and basil pesto and plenty of stirring. It's heavy on vegetables, completely vegan, and gluten-free.

TOTAL TIME 1 hr.

6 cups vegetable stock
2 cups packed fresh basil leaves
2 cups packed baby spinach
2 cloves garlic
½ cup olive oil
¼ cup rice vinegar
½ tsp. kosher salt
8 oz. fresh asparagus, trimmed and cut into 1-inch pieces (1 cup)
1 cup frozen quartered artichoke hearts
1 cup fresh English peas
1 medium yellow onion, finely chopped
1½ cups Arborio rice
1 medium zucchini, shredded (2 cups)
Spinach leaves
Halved cherry tomatoes

1. In a large saucepan bring vegetable stock just to boiling; reduce heat to a simmer. Fill a large bowl half full with ice water. Plunge fresh basil into simmering stock. Using tongs, immediately transfer basil to ice bath to cool. Remove basil from ice bath, shaking off excess water.

2. For pesto, in a blender or food processor combine basil, the 2 cups spinach, garlic, ¼ cup of the oil, vinegar, and ¼ tsp. of the salt. Cover and blend until pesto is smooth.

3. Add asparagus to simmering stock; cook about 1 minute or until bright green and barely tender. Using a slotted spoon, transfer asparagus to ice bath. Remove from ice bath; set aside. Add artichokes to stock; cook 2 minutes. Using slotted spoon, transfer artichokes to ice bath. Remove and set aside. Add peas to stock; cook 30 seconds. Transfer to ice bath with slotted spoon; drain.

4. In a 4- to 5-qt. Dutch oven or large pot heat the remaining ¼ cup olive oil over medium heat. Add chopped onion and remaining ¼ tsp. salt; cook and stir about 5 minutes or until onion is tender. Add rice; cook and stir 2 to 3 minutes or until rice is translucent. Add stock to the rice, 1 cup at a time, while continuously stirring with a wooden spoon. As stock is absorbed, add another cup. Continue cooking and adding stock until all the stock is absorbed and the rice is creamy and tender. (This should take about 20 minutes.) Add zucchini, pesto, and cooked vegetables to the rice the last 2 minutes. Serve topped with fresh spinach leaves and halved cherry tomatoes. Makes 8 servings.

EACH SERVING *259 cal, 14 g fat, 0 mg chol, 504 mg sodium, 29 g carb, 3 g fiber, 5 g pro.*

how to cook
PAVLOVA

There's no shortage of oohs and aahs when you set out this showstopping meringue dessert—and it's easier than you might think!

STRAWBERRY, MANGO & ROSE PAVLOVA
Recipe on page 110

PAVLOVA (pav-LOH-vuh) is a thick cloudlike meringue with a soft, slightly chewy marshmallow interior and delightfully crunchy exterior that is topped with whipped cream and fresh fruit. There's debate about where it originated (Australia and New Zealand both lay claim), but what we know for sure is that it's named after Russian ballerina Anna Pavlova, who's said to have danced as if lighter than air. Making meringue might sound intimidating—but a few secrets will help you get the sometimes tricky texture just right. Plus, one of the fabulous things about pavlova is its built-in forgiveness.

A SWEET-TART SPIN:
SUBSTITUTE LEMON
CURD FOR
TRADITIONAL
WHIPPED CREAM

STRAWBERRY, MANGO & ROSE PAVLOVA

Cream of tartar and lemon juice stabilize the egg whites and contribute to volume. Cornstarch is a stabilizer, too; but it also aids in creating the soft inner texture.

HANDS-ON TIME 1 hr.
TOTAL TIME 4 hr., 30 min.

6	egg whites
⅛	tsp. cream of tartar
	Salt
1½	cups sugar
1	tsp. lemon juice
¼	tsp. rose water or ½ tsp. vanilla
2½	tsp. cornstarch
4	cups sliced mango and strawberries
2	Tbsp. sugar
1½	cups whipping cream
½	cup mascarpone cheese

1. Allow egg whites to stand at room temperature 30 minutes (to create more volume). Meanwhile, line a baking sheet with parchment. Draw a 9-inch circle on the paper. Invert paper so circle is on reverse side.

2. Preheat oven to 250°F. For meringue, in the bowl of a stand mixer fitted with the whisk attachment* beat egg whites, cream of tartar, and a pinch of salt on medium speed until soft peaks form. Add the 1½ cups sugar, 1 Tbsp. at a time, beating on high speed until stiff peaks form and meringue is no longer gritty (18 to 20 minutes), scraping down bowl as needed. Beat in lemon juice and rose water. Using a rubber spatula, gently fold in cornstarch.

3. Spread meringue over circle on parchment, building up edges slightly to form a shell. Bake 1½ hours (do not open door). Turn off oven; let dry in oven with door closed 1 hour. Remove; cool completely on sheet on wire rack.

4. In a large bowl toss mango and berries with the 2 Tbsp. sugar. Let stand 20 minutes.

5. Meanwhile, in a large mixing bowl beat cream and mascarpone with an electric mixer on medium speed until soft peaks form. Place meringue shell on a large platter. Spread cream mixture into meringue shell. Spoon fruit mixture on top. Serve immediately.

*You can also use a hand mixer. Total beating time might be a little longer and the total volume a little less than with a stand mixer.

For individuals Prepare meringue as directed. Spoon eight mounds (¾ cup each) 3 inches apart on a parchment-lined baking sheet. Using the back of a spoon, create an indent in each. Bake 1 hour. Dry in oven; cool as above.

EACH SERVING *284 cal, 15 g fat, 54 mg chol, 55 mg sodium, 34 g carb, 2 g fiber, 3 g pro.*

1 **PAN PREP** Part of the trick to the meringue is getting the right size and thickness so baking time will hit the mark. Trace a 9-inch plate to ensure success.

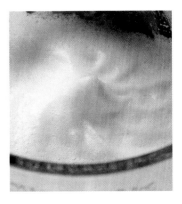

2 **SOFT PEAKS** It's time to add the sugar when the egg whites look foamy and just begin to hold their shape, forming soft, droopy peaks when you lift the beater.

3 **STIFF PEAKS** The meringue is ready when the mixture forms stiff, glossy peaks (tips will stand straight) and all the sugar has dissolved.

4 **GRIT TEST** Rub a little meringue between your fingers. You should feel just a granule or two of sugar. If it feels gritty, beat just another minute.

5 **GENTLY FOLD** Be careful not to deflate the volume created by beating air into the meringue. Use a spatula to lightly fold in cornstarch.

6 **EASY SHAPE** Use the back of a spoon to push meringue toward edges to create a shallow bowl to give cream and fruit a place to sit.

A SWEET-TART SPIN: SUBSTITUTE LEMON CURD FOR TRADITIONAL WHIPPED CREAM.

BAKING POINTERS

CLOSE THE DOOR Keep the oven door closed while the Pavlova bakes. A sudden change in temperature can cause the meringue to crack or collapse.

BAKE LOW AND SLOW If you notice that it's starting to brown, lower the oven temp 15°F. When it's finished baking, the outside will be mostly dry to the touch.

LET IT REST When the Pavlova is baked, turn off the oven and leave the door closed. The Pavlova continues to dry on the outside with a marshmallowy interior.

FAST & FRESH

Easy, healthful recipes for a better dinner tonight.

CREAMY SPRING VEGETABLES & SMOKED TROUT

Hot-smoked trout has an intense salty flavor and flaky texture. You can swap in hot-smoked salmon or high-quality tuna.

TOTAL TIME 20 min.

1   Tbsp. olive oil
1   Tbsp. unsalted butter
8   oz. cremini or other mushrooms, sliced
3   medium carrots, thinly bias-sliced
⅔   cup fresh shelled or frozen peas
½   cup whipping cream
¼   cup water
¼   tsp. kosher salt
¼   tsp. black pepper
8   oz. smoked trout, skin removed
2   Tbsp. chopped fresh chives
1   large bunch watercress, tough stalks removed

1. In a large skillet heat olive oil and butter over medium heat. Add mushrooms; cook 2 minutes or until they release their liquid. Stir in carrots. Cover. Cook 3 minutes. Uncover. Add peas, cream, the water, salt, and black pepper. Bring to boiling; reduce heat. Simmer, uncovered, 4 minutes or until peas are tender, stirring occasionally. **2.** Break trout into large pieces; gently stir into vegetables. Reduce heat to medium. Heat through. Stir in chives. Top with watercress. Makes 4 servings.
EACH SERVING *294 cal, 21 g fat, 84 mg chol, 755 mg sodium, 11 g carb, 3 g fiber, 17 g pro.*

CREAM DOESN'T NEED TO BE CODE FOR HEAVY. PEPPERY WATERCRESS, EARTHY MUSHROOMS, AND A VEGGIE DUO—PEAS AND CARROTS—MAKE THIS SAUCE LIGHT AND SPRINGY.

ASPARAGUS & GREENS WITH FARRO

ASPARAGUS & GREENS WITH FARRO

To significantly cut farro cook time, cover with water and soak in the refrigerator overnight. Then drain and cook as directed; simmer just 10 minutes.

HANDS-ON TIME 20 min.
TOTAL TIME 40 min.

- 1 cup uncooked farro
- 1 bunch thin asparagus, trimmed and cut into 2-inch pieces
  Juice of 1 lemon (3 Tbsp.)
- ½ cup whole almonds, toasted and coarsely chopped (tip, page 37)
- 1 Tbsp. extra-virgin olive oil
- ½ tsp. kosher salt
- ¼ tsp. black pepper
- 3 cups baby spinach, baby kale, and/or baby mustard greens
- ⅓ cup shaved Parmesan cheese (1 oz.)

1. In a medium saucepan bring 3 cups water to boiling; add farro. Reduce heat. Simmer, covered, 30 minutes or just until tender; drain. Meanwhile, place a steamer basket in a large skillet. Add water to just below basket. Bring water to boiling. Add asparagus to basket. Cover; steam 3 minutes or until crisp-tender. Transfer to a large bowl.
2. Add farro to bowl with asparagus. Drizzle with lemon juice while still warm. Stir in almonds, olive oil, salt, and black pepper. Add greens. Toss to combine. Top with Parmesan. Makes 4 servings.
EACH SERVING *360 cal, 15 g fat, 5 mg chol, 447 mg sodium, 43 g carb, 10 g fiber, 15 g pro.*

PROSCIUTTO & ARTICHOKE PANINI

These easy Italian sandwiches are a satisfying dinner on the fly. With prosciutto, artichokes, basil, and lemon zest (let's not forget fresh mozzarella), they're special enough for company. Make them bite-size with mini ciabattas for a spring party buffet. You don't need any special appliance to make panini at home. A second pan weighted with a few cans from the pantry works as a do-it-yourself press.

TOTAL TIME 20 min.

- 4 ciabattas or other crusty rolls, split
- 1 Tbsp. extra-virgin olive oil
- 1 8-oz. ball fresh mozzarella, sliced
- 8 large basil leaves
- 1 6-oz. jar marinated artichoke hearts, drained
- 8 thin slices prosciutto (3 oz.)
- 1 lemon, zested
  Black pepper

1. Drizzle cut sides of rolls with olive oil. For each sandwich, layer mozzarella, basil, and artichokes on bottom bread half. Top with prosciutto. Sprinkle with zest and black pepper. Add roll top.
2. Heat a large heavy skillet over medium heat. Place two sandwiches at a time in pan; top with a pan weighted with canned food. Cook 4 minutes or until golden. Remove weighted pan; turn. Replace weighted pan; cook 3 minutes more or until browned and cheese melts. Makes 4 servings.
EACH SERVING *360 cal, 18 g fat, 55 mg chol, 1,159 mg sodium, 26 g carb, 2 g fiber, 20 g pro.*

PROSCIUTTO &
ARTICHOKE PANINI

The FARMHOUSE LIFE

The food, the dishes, even the table—they're all homemade when this Vermont family sits down to breakfast.

Sometimes life imitates art. And sometimes it's the other way around. For Zoe and James Zilian, their pottery business was a byproduct of their lifestyle. The couple traded city life in Boston for a pastoral one in Vermont, where they fell for a modest-size Colonial ringed with apple trees and blueberry bushes. They took down walls and added plenty of white paint to reinvent it as a sprawling farmhouse—their dream. "We thought we hit the lottery when we moved to Woodstock," James says. "We'd been longing for a slow and simple life, with more inspiring aesthetics, too."

James, then the design director for a glass and pottery company, turned the home's basement into a ceramics workshop—complete with a kiln—where he could create anything he was inspired to. "I wanted our girls to have nice bowls for blueberry picking, so I asked James to make a couple," Zoe says. "I loved them so much, I asked him to make a pitcher." Mixing bowls and crocks followed. The basement soon grew crowded with James' stoneware, and it occurred to the couple that the art he was creating for his family life might appeal to others.

ZOE'S CRÈME FRAÎCHE PANCAKES

TOTAL TIME 30 min.

1½ cups unbleached all-purpose flour
3 Tbsp. sugar
2 tsp. baking powder
1 tsp. kosher salt
1 cup whole milk
½ cup crème fraîche
¼ cup sour cream
2 eggs
1½ tsp. vanilla
3 Tbsp. European-style butter
Pure maple syrup
Fresh blueberries (optional)

1. In a large bowl combine flour, sugar, baking powder, and salt. In a medium bowl whisk together milk, crème fraîche, sour cream, eggs, and vanilla. Add to dry ingredients; whisk to combine.
2. In an extra-large skillet melt 1 Tbsp. of the butter over medium heat. Spoon rounded tablespoons of batter into skillet. Cook 2 to 3 minutes or until undersides are browned; turn. Cook 1 to 2 minutes. Repeat with remaining batter. Serve with syrup and, if desired, berries. Makes 18 to 20 pancakes.
EACH PANCAKE *110 cal, 6 g fat, 34 mg chol, 216 mg sodium, 11 g carb, 0 g fiber, 2 g pro.*

THE FAMILY'S WEEKEND MORNINGS REVOLVE
AROUND HEARTY BREAKFASTS.

ORANGE-HONEY
OVERNIGHT
OATS
Recipe on page 120

"I'M ALWAYS LOOKING FOR A WAY TO HAVE MORE SYRUP IN MY DIET," SAYS JAMES, WHOSE SPECIALTY IS THICK-CUT BACON WITH A MAPLE SYRUP GLAZE AND PECAN COATING.

MASHED POTATO-EGG CASSEROLE

HANDS-ON TIME 25 min.
TOTAL TIME 1 hr., 45 min.

2½ lb. russet potatoes (5 to 6 potatoes)
4 medium leeks, halved and sliced
5 cloves garlic, minced
2 Tbsp. butter
1 8-oz. carton sour cream
4 oz. Asiago cheese, shredded (1 cup)
½ tsp. salt
½ tsp. black pepper
¾ to 1 cup milk
6 eggs
1 Tbsp. olive oil
½ lemon, juiced
2 cups baby spinach and/or arugula

1. Prick potatoes with fork. Microwave on high 12 minutes or until fork-tender, turning once. Remove; cool until easy to handle. Preheat oven to 375°F. Grease a 2-qt. baking dish; set aside. In a large skillet cook leeks and 4 cloves of the garlic in melted butter over medium heat 5 minutes or until tender and browned, stirring occasionally.
2. Peel potatoes; place in a large bowl. Mash with potato masher. Stir in leek mixture, sour cream, half the cheese, and ¼ tsp. each salt and black pepper. Stir in milk to make a creamy consistency. Spread in prepared dish. Bake 40 minutes or until starting to brown. Remove from oven. Make six indents in potato mixture. Place an egg in each indent. Bake 20 minutes more or until whites are set and yolks start to thicken. Sprinkle with remaining cheese. Cool slightly.
3. In a bowl whisk oil, lemon juice, remaining 1 clove garlic, and remaining ¼ tsp. salt and pepper. Add spinach and/or arugula; toss to coat. Serve on casserole. Makes 6 to 8 servings.
EACH SERVING *457 cal, 25 g fat, 238 mg chol, 491 mg sodium, 44 g carb, 3 g fiber, 17 g pro.*

PECAN MAPLE BACON

TOTAL TIME 40 min.

1 lb. thick-sliced bacon
¼ cup pure maple syrup
¼ cup very finely chopped pecans
1 tsp. cracked black pepper

1. Preheat oven to 400°F. Place wire rack in foil-lined 15×10-inch baking pan. Arrange bacon on rack, tucking under any edges that hang over. Bake 10 minutes.
2. Generously brush bacon slices with syrup; sprinkle with pecans and cracked black pepper. Bake 20 minutes or until bacon is browned. Makes 6 servings.
EACH SERVING *196 cal, 14 g fat, 22 mg chol, 478 mg sodium, 10 g carb, 1 g fiber, 9 g pro.*

SPARKLING STRAWBERRY MIMOSA

TOTAL TIME 15 min.

4 cups quartered strawberries
4 oranges, peeled and sectioned
1 750 ml bottle chilled champagne or sparkling apple juice
    Ice
    Maple Syrup (optional)

In a pitcher combine strawberries and orange sections. Muddle with a wooden spoon. Stir in chilled champagne. Serve in glasses over ice. Drizzle with maple syrup, if desired. Makes 6 servings.
EACH SERVING *186 cal, 0 g fat, 0 mg chol, 2 mg sodium, 27 g carb, 4 g fiber, 2 g pro.*

ORANGE-HONEY OVERNIGHT OATS

Photo on page 119.

Oatmeal is a staple in the Zilian house, but these aren't your everyday oats. Topped with coconut, raspberries, and orange zest, this overnight version is a feast.

HANDS-ON TIME 15 min.
TOTAL TIME 12 hr.

2 cups milk or refrigerated coconut milk
2 cups regular rolled oats
1 cup plain Greek yogurt
½ cup flaked coconut
2 oranges, zested (4 tsp.)
2 Tbsp. honey
1 tsp. snipped fresh thyme
    Toppings, such as strawberry preserves, berries, coconut, orange zest, and/or snipped thyme

In a large bowl stir together milk, oats, yogurt, coconut, orange zest, honey, and thyme. Cover; chill overnight. Stir; serve with toppings. Makes 6 to 8 servings.
EACH SERVING *310 cal, 8 g fat, 11 mg chol, 79 mg sodium, 52 g carb, 6 g fiber, 10 g pro.*

SPARKLING
STRAWBERRY
MIMOSA

MASHED POTATO-
EGG CASSEROLE

PECAN MAPLE
BACON

PORK CARNITAS TACOS ON CORN TORTILLAS WITH SALSA VERDE CRUDA

CARNITAS!

Rich, slow-cooked pork—so tender it falls apart at the touch of a fork—is a staple of Mexican kitchens. Cookbook author and TV host Pati Jinich shows how to make the iconic yet versatile dish.

"Carnitas is a loaded word," Pati Jinich, host of the popular PBS television series Pati's Mexican Table, says with a laugh. "When you say you're making carnitas, it means you're going to create irresistible, slow-cooked pork. It also means that dinner's about to turn into an event." Pati's take on the dish, popular in Mexico City, where she was born and raised, begins with an inexpensive cut of pork—most often the shoulder or butt. It gets braised in a slow-simmering mix of garlic, cumin, cloves, orange juice, and Pati's special ingredient: sweetened condensed milk. The milk caramelizes to a sweet coating on the meat. Always a winner, her version is as easy for a weeknight meal as it is for a special gathering.

PORK CARNITAS

HANDS-ON TIME 45 min.
TOTAL TIME 3 hr.

- ½   cup coarsely chopped white onion
- 6   cloves garlic
- 1   tsp. dried marjoram
- 1   tsp. dried thyme
     Pinch ground cumin
- 4   whole cloves, stems removed
- 1   Tbsp. salt
- 1   tsp. black pepper
- 1   Tbsp. lard or canola oil
- 4   to 5 lb. boneless pork shoulder or butt, cut into 2-inch chunks
- ½   tsp. salt
- 2   bay leaves
- 1   cup freshly squeezed orange juice
- 2   Tbsp. sweetened condensed milk
- 1   recipe Corn Tortillas, page 127, or 16 purchased 6-inch tortillas
- 1   recipe Salsa Verde Cruda
     Pickled jalapeños and sliced radishes

1. In a blender add 1½ cups water, the onion, garlic, marjoram, thyme, cumin, cloves, 1 Tbsp. salt, and black pepper. Blend until smooth.
2. In a Dutch oven heat lard over medium-high heat. Add pork; top with ½ tsp. salt. Brown pork 10 minutes; turn occasionally.
3. Pour onion mixture over pork. Bring to a simmer; cook 5 to 6 minutes. Stir in bay leaves, juice, and milk. Cover; simmer 1½ to 2 hours or until meat pulls apart easily, stirring occasionally. Uncover; simmer 5 minutes. Transfer to a bowl.

4. Discard bay leaves. Skim fat from liquid. Shred meat with a fork; toss with cooking liquid to moisten, if desired. For tacos, serve with tortillas, Salsa Verde Cruda, jalapeños, and radishes. Makes 16 tacos.
EACH TACO *298 cal, 10 g fat, 69 mg chol, 275 mg sodium, 15 g carb, 3 g fiber, 23 g pro.*

SALSA VERDE CRUDA

TOTAL TIME 15 min.

- 1   lb. tomatillos, husks removed, rinsed, and halved
- 1   ripe avocado, halved, seeded, and peeled
- ¼   cup cilantro leaves and tops of stems
- 2   Tbsp. coarsely chopped white onion
- 1   fresh jalapeño chile pepper, stemmed and seeded (tip, page 37)
- ½   tsp. kosher salt

In a blender combine tomatillos, avocado, cilantro, onion, chile pepper, and salt. Blend until nearly smooth. Makes 2 cups.
EACH 2-TBSP. SERVING *24 cal, 2 g fat, 0 mg chol, 36 mg sodium, 3 g carb, 0 g pro.*

**PORK CARNITAS
WITH SALSA VERDE
CRUDA**
Recipes on page 123

**MEXICAN
RED RICE**

MEXICAN RED RICE

*"You can't have carnitas without
signature Mexican rice," Pati says.
Cooked in a thin tomato sauce with
onions and garlic, it's the perfect mild
side dish. So is Pati's take on potato
salad with exuberant poblanos.*

HANDS-ON TIME 30 min.
TOTAL TIME 50 min.

2	cups uncooked long-grain rice
1	lb. ripe tomatoes, quartered, or one 14.5-oz. can diced tomatoes
⅓	cup coarsely chopped white onion
4	cloves garlic
1	tsp. salt
3	Tbsp. vegetable oil
3	cups chicken or vegetable broth
1	cup peeled and diced carrots
1	cup fresh or frozen whole kernel corn
1	to 2 fresh jalapeño chile peppers, halved (tip, page 37) (optional)
2	sprigs fresh Italian parsley
½	cup fresh or frozen peas

1. In a bowl soak rice 5 minutes in enough
hot water to cover; drain. Rinse rice
under cold water until water runs clear;
drain well.
2. In a blender puree tomatoes, onion,
garlic, and salt. Pass through strainer;
measure 1 cup liquid (discard solids).
3. In a medium saucepan cook rice in hot
oil over medium-high heat 3 to 4 minutes
or until rice becomes milky white, stirring
often. Stir in tomato puree. Cook,
uncovered, 3 minutes or until puree is
mostly absorbed by the rice.
4. Stir in broth, carrots, corn, chiles (if
using), and parsley. Bring to a rolling
boil. Cover; reduce heat to low. Cook
10 minutes. Add peas; cook 5 minutes
or until most of the liquid has been
absorbed. (Rice should be tender. If it
isn't, add 2 Tbsp. water if needed. Cover;
cook 2 minutes more.) Remove from
heat. Let stand, covered, 5 minutes.
Makes 8 servings.
EACH SERVING *263 cal, 6 g fat, 2 mg chol,
482 mg sodium, 47 g carb, 3 g fiber,
6 g pro.*

**POBLANO
POTATO SALAD**
Recipe on page 127

GRILLED
PINEAPPLE
MARGARITA

HIBISCUS AGUA
FRESCA

CORN TORTILLAS

Pati Jinich cooks her tortillas on a comal, which is a flat round griddle.

TOTAL TIME 1 hr.

2   cups corn tortilla flour (masa harina)
1½ cups water
    Kosher salt

1. Heat a griddle or heavy skillet over medium-high heat 8 minutes or until very hot. Meanwhile, cut two 8-inch circles from plastic produce bags or plastic wrap.
2. In bowl mix flour, the water, and a pinch of salt. Stir to form a smooth dough (if dough feels coarse, add a little more water). Shape into 16 smooth balls. Cover with a damp dish towel or plastic wrap.
3. To make tortillas, place a plastic circle on bottom of tortilla press; top with a dough ball. Place other circle on top of the ball; clamp press down to make a flat disk. (If tortilla edges look cracked and jagged, dough needs a little more water.) To flatten without a press, roll between pieces of plastic wrap with a rolling pin.
4. Open press; remove top plastic piece. Lift tortilla; peel off plastic. Cook tortilla on griddle 30 seconds or until spatula can lift it without sticking. Turn; cook 1 minute. Turn again; cook 10 to 15 seconds or until tortilla puffs in spots; cook 15 to 20 seconds to brown. Transfer to paper towel. Repeat with remaining dough.
5. Store in a resealable plastic bag in refrigerator up to 3 days or freeze up to 3 months. To reheat, place on hot griddle for 30 seconds per side. Makes 16 tortillas.
EACH TORTILLA *55 cal, 1 g fat, 0 mg chol, 9 mg sodium, 12 g carb, 2 g fiber, 2 g pro.*

POBLANO POTATO SALAD

Photo on page 125.

HANDS-ON TIME 15 min.
TOTAL TIME 55 min.

3   fresh poblano chile peppers (tip, page 37)
2   lb. tiny yellow new potatoes, halved
⅓   cup pickled jalapeño pepper brine
¼   cup canola oil
½   tsp. kosher salt
½   tsp. black pepper
½   cup coarsely chopped parsley
    Toasted pepitas (optional)

1. Preheat oven to 450°F. Place peppers on a foil-lined baking sheet. Roast 20 minutes or until skins are blistered and charred. Wrap in foil; let stand 20 minutes or until cool enough to handle. Remove skins, stems, and seeds from peppers; coarsely chop.
2. Cook potatoes in lightly salted boiling water 12 to 15 minutes or until tender. Drain.
3. For dressing, in serving bowl whisk together jalapeño brine, canola oil, salt, and black pepper. Add potatoes, peppers, and parsley; toss to coat. Season to taste. Sprinkle with pepitas, if desired. Makes 8 servings.
EACH SERVING *158 cal, 7 g fat, 0 mg chol, 186 mg sodium, 21 g carb, 3 g fiber, 3 g pro.*

HIBISCUS AGUA FRESCA

Honey balances the tartness of Pati's refreshingly minty nonalcoholic hibiscus agua fresca.

HANDS-ON TIME 15 min.
TOTAL TIME 55 min.

½   cup sugar
3½ cups water
½   cup packed mint leaves
5   hibiscus tea bags (such as Red Zinger)
6   cups cold water
    Ice
    Honey

1. For mint syrup, in a small saucepan stir together sugar and ½ cup of the water. Bring to a simmer, stirring to dissolve sugar. Remove from heat. Stir in mint leaves; let stand 20 minutes.
2. Bring the remaining 3 cups water to boiling. In a heatproof pitcher pour water over tea bags; steep 20 minutes. Remove tea bags. Pour the 6 cups cold water into tea. Discard mint. Stir in syrup. Cover; chill. Serve cold over ice. Drizzle with honey to taste. Makes 8 servings.
EACH SERVING *74 cal, 0 g fat, 0 mg chol, 12 mg sodium, 19 g carb, 0 g fiber, 0 g pro.*

GRILLED PINEAPPLE MARGARITA

Pati's playful spicy-hot tropical margarita features jalapeño and grilled, almost candied, pineapple that lends sweetness.

TOTAL TIME 30 min.

1   pineapple, peeled, cored, and cut into ½-inch rings
1   jalapeño chile pepper, seeded, if desired, and sliced (tip, page 37)
¼   cup chopped fresh cilantro leaves and upper stems
3   Tbsp. grated piloncillo (unrefined cane sugar) or dark brown sugar
3   cups pineapple juice, chilled
1   cup white or silver tequila
¾   cup freshly squeezed lime juice
½   cup agave syrup or simple syrup
1   Tbsp. Mexican chili powder
1   Tbsp. kosher salt

1. Grill pineapple over medium-high heat 4 to 6 minutes, turning once. Cool.
2. In a pitcher combine jalapeño, cilantro, and 2 Tbsp. of the piloncillo. Using a wooden spoon, muddle ingredients. Cut two slices of pineapple into wedges and set aside. Coarsely chop remaining pineapple; muddle with jalapeño mixture. Stir in pineapple juice, tequila, lime juice, and syrup. Let mixture stand 10 minutes or chill up to 4 hours.
3. On a small plate combine remaining piloncillo, chili powder, and salt. Rub glass rims with lime wedges; dip into sugar mixture. Serve margarita in glasses with ice. Add reserved pineapple wedges. Makes 8 servings.
EACH SERVING *240 cal, 0 g fat, 0 mg chol, 261 mg sodium, 46 g carb, 3 g fiber, 1 g pro.*

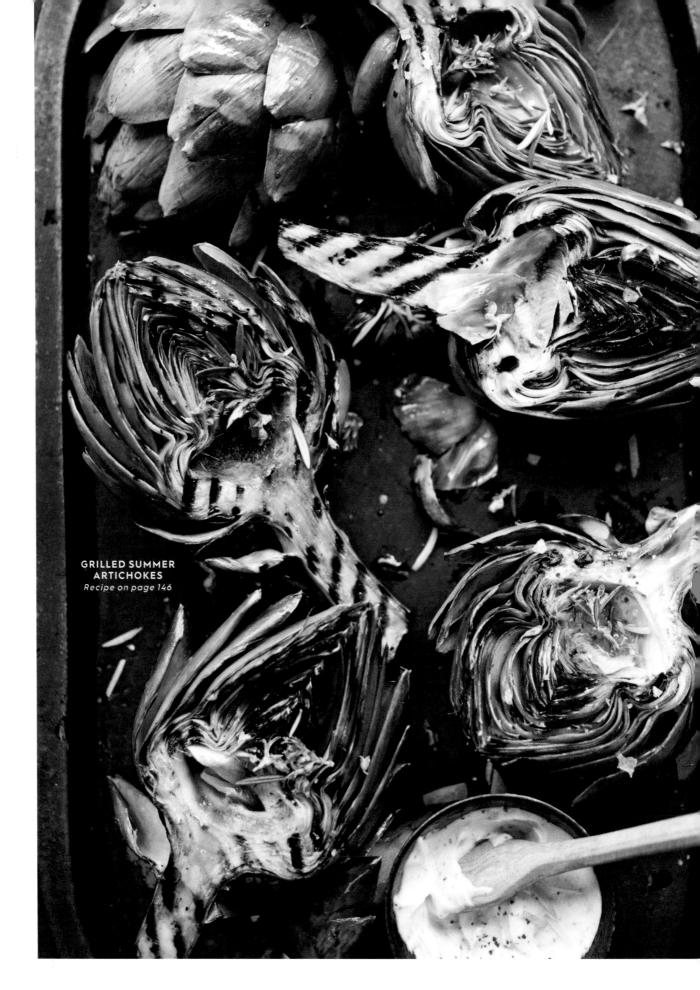

GRILLED SUMMER
ARTICHOKES
Recipe on page 146

june

Welcome summer with a backyard barbecue that features a fabulous fire-roasted menu. Keep the party rolling all month with a trio of make-ahead dumpling appetizers and recipes for new potatoes.

131

135

137

how to cook DUMPLINGS

They're a fave at the Chinese spot around the corner, and with a little know-how you can prepare them at home. Plus, this party food has major make-ahead potential.

STEAMED DUMPLINGS might seem cumbersome to make from scratch, but they're quite simple to master. All you need is a bamboo steamer basket and a bit of practice. Many traditional Chinese versions are packed with a mixture of pork, shrimp, ginger, and garlic, but you can fill dumplings with just about anything. The easier-than-it-looks pleat and twist shaping will win you style points. The best part is they're primed for fuss-free entertaining. Ready a big batch and freeze, and when it's party time, steam them for stunning appetizers.

STEAMED DUMPLINGS

Bamboo steamer baskets absorb excess moisture and condensation while allowing steam to move throughout the circular frame. It's a particularly gentle cooking process that retains flavor and texture.

HANDS-ON TIME 1 hr., 40 min.
TOTAL TIME 2 hr. 55 min.

- 3 cups all-purpose flour
- 1 Tbsp. vegetable oil
- 1 recipe filling (recipes, page 132)
- 1 recipe dipping sauce (recipes, page 132)

1. For dough*, place flour in a large bowl. Make a well in center; pour in 1 cup warm water (about 110°F). Using a fork, stir just until a shaggy dough forms. Cover with plastic wrap. Let stand 15 minutes. Add oil. Mix until combined and dough forms a ball. Transfer to a lightly floured surface. Knead until soft and smooth, about 5 minutes, adding flour as needed to prevent sticking. Sprinkle lightly with flour; cover with plastic wrap. Let stand at room temperature 1 hour.

2. Meanwhile, prepare desired filling; chill. Line the bottom of a bamboo steamer basket with a piece of parchment cut to fit. Using a sharp knife, make several slits in paper; lightly coat with cooking spray.

3. Divide dough into four equal portions. Roll one portion of dough at a time into a 12-inch log (keep remaining dough covered with plastic wrap). Using a ruler as a guide, cut into 1-inch pieces. Press each piece into a circle, then roll to a 4-inch circle. Spoon 1 Tbsp. filling in center. Working your way around the dumpling, pull the dough up over filling, creating pleats to enclose. Pinch dough at the top and twist.**

4. Transfer to prepared steamer basket. Repeat with remaining dough and filling. (Fill and shape remaining batches of dumplings while the first batches steam.)

5. Set basket over a skillet of boiling water (not touching water). Cover; steam 10 minutes or until dumplings reach 165°F when an instant-read thermometer is inserted into filling. Serve with desired dipping sauce. Makes 48 dumplings.

*Tip If you're crunched for time, use purchased wrappers. Look for those labeled dumpling or gyoza. (Avoid wonton wrappers as they tend to be too thin.)

**Make ahead Prepare through Step 3. Place in a single layer on a baking sheet. Cover with plastic wrap. Freeze until firm. Transfer to airtight containers. Freeze up to 3 months. Steam 12 minutes or until done (165°F).

1 **MIX & REST** When you combine the flour and water, the dough will look rough and just barely hold its shape. A 15-minute rest gives the water a chance to permeate the flour.

2 **5-MINUTE KNEAD** The dough comes together quickly and should feel elastic and slightly tacky when finished. Add flour only as needed—too much can make the dough tough.

3 **FOOLPROOF CUT** A ruler makes cutting uniform pieces a cinch. Cover portions you're not working with in plastic wrap to keep the dough from drying out.

4 **ROLL IT RIGHT** Roll from the center out. You want the edges to be slightly thinner so when you shape the dumpling it's not too bulky on top.

5 **STRETCH & FOLD** Lift the dough up and over onto itself, making a pleat that hugs the filling. This eliminates any air between wrapper and filling.

6 **SEAL WITH A TWIST** To finish, pinch dough up in the center and twist. Don't worry about being perfect on the first try—your shaping will improve with each dumpling.

DUMPLING FILLINGS AND DIPPING SAUCES

LEMONGRASS & GINGER PORK

FILLING Combine 1 lb. ground pork; 2 thinly sliced green onions; 1 stalk lemongrass, finely chopped (2 Tbsp.); 1 Tbsp. grated fresh ginger; 2 cloves minced garlic; 1 Tbsp. soy sauce; and 1 tsp. toasted sesame oil.
DIPPING SAUCE Stir together ½ cup rice vinegar, ¼ cup soy sauce, 2 thinly sliced green onions, and 4 slices pickled ginger.
EACH SERVING *55 cal., 2 g fat, 6 mg chol., 100 mg sodium, 6 g carb., 0 g fiber, 3 g pro.*

LEMON-BASIL VEGGIE

FILLING Combine 2 medium zucchini, shredded and squeezed dry; 4 oz. chopped mushrooms; ¼ cup chopped fresh basil; 2 tsp. lemon zest; 2 Tbsp. lemon juice; 2 cloves minced garlic; 1 tsp. olive oil; ½ tsp. dried thyme; ½ tsp. kosher salt; and ¼ tsp. black pepper.
DIPPING SAUCE Blend together ½ cup canola oil, ½ cup fresh basil, ¼ cup lemon juice, and ¼ tsp. kosher salt.
EACH DUMPLING *55 cal., 3 g fat, 0 mg chol., 25 mg sodium, 7 g carb., 0 g fiber, 1 g pro.*

CILANTRO-LIME CHICKEN

FILLING Combine 1 lb. ground chicken; 1 poblano chile pepper, seeded, and finely chopped; ¼ cup chopped cilantro; 2 Tbsp. lime juice; 2 tsp. ground cumin; 1 tsp. crushed red pepper; 1 tsp. olive oil; ½ tsp. kosher salt; and ¼ tsp. black pepper.
DIPPING SAUCE Blend together ½ cup canola oil, ½ cup chopped fresh cilantro, ¼ cup lime juice, and ¼ tsp. kosher salt.
EACH DUMPLING *67 cal., 4 g fat, 8 mg chol., 30 mg sodium, 6 g carb., 0 g fiber, 3 g pro.*

SHRIMP SCAMPI

FILLING Combine 1½ lb. medium shrimp in shells, peeled, deveined, and finely chopped; ⅓ cup capers; 2 finely chopped shallots; 3 Tbsp. chopped fresh parsley; 4 cloves minced garlic; 1 tsp. olive oil; ½ tsp. kosher salt; and ¼ tsp. black pepper.
DIPPING SAUCE Stir together ½ cup melted butter, 2 Tbsp. Worcestershire sauce, and 2 thinly sliced green onions.
EACH DUMPLING *61 cal., 2 g fat, 6 mg chol., 72 mg sodium, 6 g carb., 0 g fiber, 3 g pro.*

new ways with
NEW POTATOES

Potato salad, you're swell, but this thin-skinned gem knows more than one way to make a splash at the summer potluck.

Delicate skins mean new potatoes don't need to be peeled. Be gentle when cleaning them—scrub too hard and the skin will rub off.

ASIAN POTATO
SALAD WITH
SHRIMP

HERB HASH
BROWNS

CHEESY
HASSELBACK
NEW POTATOES

NOT ALL SMALL RED OR WHITE POTATOES ARE NEW. THE DISTINCTION GOES TO FRESHLY HARVESTED IMMATURE POTATOES, WHICH HAVE A CREAMY, WAXY TEXTURE AND LESS STARCH THAN FULL-GROWN POTATOES.

HERB HASH BROWNS

HANDS-ON TIME 15 min.
TOTAL TIME 30 min.

- ¼ cup finely chopped red onion
- ¼ cup cider vinegar
  Salt
- 1 lb. shredded new potatoes
- ⅓ cup chopped fresh Italian parsley
- 2 Tbsp. chopped fresh tarragon
- 1 Tbsp. chopped fresh thyme
- ½ tsp. salt
- ¼ cup butter
- ⅓ cup plain low-fat yogurt
  Chopped fresh Italian parsley (optional)
  Black pepper

1. In a bowl combine red onion, cider vinegar, and a pinch of salt. Set aside.
2. Stir shredded potatoes into a bowl of water; drain. Repeat until water is clear. Place potatoes in a salad spinner; spin until dry. Toss with parsley, tarragon, thyme, and salt.
3. In a nonstick skillet melt butter over medium heat. Add potato mixture. Using a spatula, press into an even layer. Cook 7 to 10 minutes or until browned. Place a baking sheet over top of skillet; invert potatoes. Slide back into skillet, browned side up. Cook 7 to 10 minutes more.
4. Drain onion mixture. Serve on hash browns with plain yogurt and, if desired, parsley. Sprinkle with pepper. Makes 4 servings.
EACH SERVING *210 cal, 12 g fat, 32 mg chol, 408 mg sodium, 23 g carb, 3 g fiber, 4 g pro.*

ASIAN POTATO SALAD WITH SHRIMP

HANDS ON TIME 20 min.
TOTAL TIME 2 hr.

- 2 lb. new potatoes
  Salt
- ¼ cup Asian chili-garlic sauce*
- ¼ cup peanut oil
- 3 Tbsp. rice vinegar
- 2 tsp. fish sauce
- ½ tsp. kosher salt
- 1 lb. cooked, peeled, and deveined shrimp
- ⅓ cup chopped peanuts
- ⅓ cup chopped fresh mint

1. Place potatoes and a dash of salt in a large saucepan. Cover with cold water; bring to boiling. Reduce heat; simmer, uncovered, 25 minutes. Drain. Cool completely.
2. Whisk together chili-garlic sauce, peanut oil, rice vinegar, fish sauce, and salt. Gently smash potatoes; transfer to a bowl. Add shrimp, chopped peanuts, and dressing; toss to coat.
3. Chill 30 minutes or up to 24 hours. Stir in chopped mint before serving. Makes 6 servings.
*Tip Look for Asian chile-garlic sauce where Asian sauces are sold; but don't confuse chili-garlic sauce with Sriracha sauce, which is much hotter.
EACH SERVING *324 cal, 14 g fat, 143 mg chol, 632 mg sodium, 27 g carb, 4 g fiber, 24 g pro.*

CHEESY HASSELBACK NEW POTATOES

HANDS ON TIME 30 min.
TOTAL TIME 1 hr. 30 min.

- 12 new potatoes (about 1¾ lb.)
- 3 Tbsp. butter, melted
- 1 5.2-oz. pkg. semisoft cheese with garlic and herbs
- 2 Tbsp. fine dry bread crumbs
- 2 Tbsp. grated Parmesan cheese
- 1 tsp. chopped fresh rosemary
- 2 tsp. lemon zest

1. Preheat oven to 400°F. Slice into each potato at ⅛-inch intervals, cutting to but not through opposite side. Arrange, cut sides up, on a greased baking pan. Brush with 2 Tbsp. of the butter. Cover with foil; bake 45 minutes.
2. In a small microwaveable bowl heat cheese on 50-percent power 20 seconds. Place in a plastic bag; snip one corner.
3. In a small bowl combine bread crumbs, Parmesan, remaining 1 Tbsp. melted butter, and rosemary. Uncover potatoes; cool slightly. Using a butter knife, pry open layers; pipe cheese between slices. Sprinkle with bread crumb mixture. Bake 10 to 15 minutes more. Sprinkle with lemon zest. Makes 6 servings.
EACH SERVING *271 cal, 17 g fat, 42 mg chol, 255 mg sodium, 26 g carb, 3 g fiber, 5 g pro.*

FAST & FRESH

Easy, healthy recipes for a better dinner tonight.

**ORANGE SALMON
& GREEN ONIONS**

ORANGE SALMON & GREEN ONIONS

A double citrus punch—orange and lime—gives salmon bold, zippy flavor. Serve with a side of rice to soak up delicious juices. When you buy fresh salmon look for bright and metallic skin and firm and vivid flesh. Avoid fillets with visible tears or separation in muscle tissue. Always smell the fish; it should smell clean and briny like the ocean—never fishy!

TOTAL TIME 30 min.

2	navel oranges, halved
2	limes, juiced (¼ cup)
3	Tbsp. tamari or soy sauce
1	Tbsp. grated fresh ginger
4	tsp. vegetable oil
12	green onions, trimmed
1	lb. salmon fillet (skin on)

1. Preheat oven to 425°F. Juice one orange to get ⅓ cup juice. Cut remaining orange into wedges.
2. In a small bowl stir together orange juice, lime juice, tamari, ginger, and 2 tsp. of the oil. Drizzle the bottom of a 3-qt. gratin dish with remaining 2 tsp. oil. Place green onions and orange wedges in dish; toss to coat. Place salmon, skin side down, in center of dish. Drizzle with orange juice mixture.
3. Bake 15 minutes or until salmon is opaque and starting to flake. Remove. Turn oven to broil. Baste salmon with sauce in pan. Broil 4 to 5 inches from heat 5 to 7 minutes or until fish flakes easily with a fork and onions begin to brown, turning onions once or twice. Makes 4 servings.

EACH SERVING *259 cal, 12 g fat, 62 mg chol, 812 mg sodium, 13 g carb, 8 g fiber, 25 g pro.*

TAHINI-GINGER
NOODLES & VEGGIES

TAHINI-GINGER NOODLES & VEGGIES

Tahini, sesame seed paste that's most known for making hummus extra-creamy, has additional roles. Serve it as a dip for apples and carrot sticks, whirl it into salad dressing for more body, or slather a sandwich. Store in the refrigerator to prevent it from going rancid.

TOTAL TIME 20 min.

¼	cup tahini (sesame seed paste)
¼	cup lemon juice
¼	cup water
1	Tbsp. grated fresh ginger
1	Tbsp. agave syrup
¼	tsp. kosher salt
8	oz. dried linguine
3	cups broccoli florets
8	oz. sugar snap pea pods, halved
2	medium carrots, cut in ribbons with a vegetable peeler
¼	cup chopped peanuts or almonds Fresh mint leaves (optional)

1. In a small bowl stir together tahini, lemon juice, the water, ginger, agave syrup, and salt; set aside.
2. In a large pot cook linguine in salted boiling water according to package directions. Drain; rinse under cold water. Return to pot. Add broccoli, peas, carrots, and tahini mixture; toss to combine. Top with nuts and , if desired, mint leaves. Makes 4 servings.

EACH SERVING *429 cal, 15 g fat, 242 mg sodium, 61 g carb, 9 g fiber, 17 g pro.*

**BLACK BEAN &
RAINBOW CHARD
TORTILLAS**

CHICKEN WITH BASIL SAUCE & CUCUMBER-RADISH SALAD

Vegetable sprouts, the plants' first tender stems, are packed with nutrition and crunch. Broccoli sprouts have a mild peppery flavor; radish sprouts, a hint of heat.

TOTAL TIME 30 min.

2   8- to 10-oz. skinless, boneless chicken breast halves, halved horizontally
    Kosher salt
    Black pepper
2   Tbsp. extra-virgin olive oil
½   cup crème fraîche
¼   cup chopped basil leaves
1   Tbsp. Dijon-style mustard
2   Tbsp. lemon juice
1   seedless cucumber, thinly sliced
8   radishes, very thinly sliced
2   oz. radish or broccoli sprouts, washed

1. Place each chicken piece between two pieces of plastic wrap; lightly pound to an even thickness. Season on both sides with kosher salt and black pepper.
2. In a large heavy skillet heat 1 Tbsp. of the oil over medium-high heat. Add chicken; cook 3 minutes or until browned. Turn; cook 2 to 3 minutes more or until done (165°F).
3. Meanwhile, for Basil Sauce, in a bowl stir together crème fraîche, basil, and mustard. For Cucumber-Radish Salad, in a medium bowl whisk together lemon juice, remaining 1 Tbsp. oil, and a pinch of kosher salt. Add cucumber, radishes, and sprouts; toss to coat. Serve chicken with Basil Sauce and Cucumber-Radish Salad. Makes 4 servings.
EACH SERVING *328 cal, 21 g fat, 108 mg chol, 449 mg sodium, 4 g carb, 1 g fiber, 27 g pro.*

BLACK BEAN & RAINBOW CHARD TORTILLAS

Swiss chard stems are too tough to eat raw, but once cooked they become crisp-tender and slightly sweet.

TOTAL TIME 30 min.

1   1-lb. bunch rainbow Swiss chard, stems and leaves separated
½   tsp. cumin seeds
1   Tbsp. vegetable oil
¼   tsp. kosher salt
½   medium red onion, chopped (½ cup)
1   yellow, red, or orange sweet pepper, chopped
1   clove garlic, minced
1   Tbsp. red wine vinegar
1   15- to 16-oz. can black beans, rinsed and drained
4   8-inch flour tortillas
1   cup shredded Monterey Jack cheese
    Sour cream
    Cilantro
    Chili powder (optional)

1. Slice Swiss chard stems into ½-inch pieces. Coarsely shred leaves. Heat a large skillet over medium heat. Add cumin seeds. Heat 2 minutes or until fragrant. Add oil to skillet; increase heat to medium-high. Add chard stems and salt. Cook, stirring occasionally, 3 minutes or until stems are crisp-tender. Add onion, sweet pepper, garlic, and chard leaves. Cook 3 minutes or until vegetables are barely tender and leaves wilted, stirring occasionally. Stir in vinegar and beans; heat through. Remove from heat.
2. Meanwhile, preheat broiler. Arrange tortillas on a baking sheet. Divide cheese among tortillas. Broil 5 to 6 inches from heat 1 minute or until cheese is melted. Spoon chard mixture onto tortillas. Top with sour cream and cilantro. Sprinkle with chili powder, if desired. Makes 4 servings.
EACH SERVING *406 cal, 16 g fat, 25 mg chol, 1,279 mg sodium, 51 g carb, 8 g fiber, 20 g pro.*

CHICKEN WITH
BASIL SAUCE &
CUCUMBER-RADISH
SALAD

FIRE-ROASTED RICOTTA WITH CORN AND PEPPERS
Recipe on page 142

GRILLED SUMMER ARTICHOKES
Recipe on page 146

summer FIRE

The crackle of a big wood fire transforms an ordinary backyard barbecue into summer's hottest party. Portland chefs and grilling experts Greg Denton and Gabrielle Quiñónez Denton share their techniques for cooking over an open flame without getting burned.

Smoke from long-burning oak logs infuses a woodsy depth of flavor into fire-roasted food in ways that are hard to describe. "You will never get that added dimension of smoky flavor with a gas grill," Greg Denton says, as he repositions the meat over the fire.

Greg and his wife, Gabrielle, co-owners of Portland's Ox Restaurant and authors of the book *Around the Fire,* prefer the slow summer time frame that a wood-fired meal demands. "It's a totally different pace—all about cooking slowly and savoring the time together," Gabrielle says. "And the fire remains a focal point of the party even when the meal is over."

The pair light the fire as guests arrive, then cook dishes at varying speeds: some over direct heat and others around the cooler perimeter. They make use of every last ember with unpeeled onion and eggplant nestled into the wood coals to peel and use the next day.

Although it might take longer to nurture the fire and roast the food, the results are amazingly delicious. This is slow food at its finest.

FIRE-ROASTED RICOTTA WITH CORN AND PEPPERS

Photo on page 140.

Serve tangy balsamic butter sauce and toasted bread to cut the richness of grilled ricotta and charred corn spread.

HANDS-ON TIME 10 min.
TOTAL TIME 20 min.

- 1 recipe Homemade Ricotta or one 15-oz. carton whole milk ricotta cheese
- 1 recipe Charred Corn
- 1 recipe Grilled Padrón Peppers
- 1 Tbsp. chopped fresh Italian parsley
- ½ tsp. flaky sea salt
- 1 recipe Balsamic Brown Butter
- 1 recipe Garlic-Rubbed Bread

Heat grill to medium-high. Place ricotta in an 8- or 9-inch cast-iron skillet. Grill about 6 minutes or until bubbly. Cool 10 minutes. Top with Charred Corn and Grilled Padrón Peppers; sprinkle with parsley and salt. Drizzle with Balsamic Brown Butter and serve with Garlic-Rubbed Bread. Makes 8 servings.

Charred Corn Remove husks and silks from 2 ears fresh corn. Brush with 1 Tbsp. extra-virgin olive oil. Grill over medium-high heat 12 minutes, turning often. Remove corn from cobs.

Grilled Padrón Peppers Toss 6 oz. whole Padrón peppers with 2 Tbsp. extra-virgin olive oil and a little kosher salt; transfer to grill basket. Grill over medium-high heat 2 minutes or until peppers begin to blister. Shake basket; cook 1 to 2 minutes more.
EACH SERVING *400 cal, 26 g fat, 62 mg chol, 599 mg sodium, 30 g carb, 2 g fiber, 13 g pro.*

HOMEMADE RICOTTA

HANDS-ON TIME 15 min.
TOTAL TIME 1 hr., 35 min.

- 4 cups whole milk
- 1¼ cups whipping cream
- 2 Tbsp. white vinegar
- 2 tsp. kosher salt

1. In a heavy 4-qt. nonreactive pot heat milk and cream over medium-high heat just until boiling, stirring occasionally. Remove from heat; stir in vinegar and salt. Let stand 20 minutes.

2. Line a colander with a few layers of 100-percent-cotton cheesecloth; set over a large bowl. Pour in milk mixture. Let stand 1 hour. Lift ends of cheesecloth around cheese and squeeze gently; discard whey. Transfer cheese to a storage container. Cover; chill up to 1 week. Makes 8 servings.
EACH SERVING *203 cal, 17 g fat, 55 mg chol, 343 mg sodium, 7 g carb, 0 g fiber, 5 g pro.*

BALSAMIC BROWN BUTTER

TOTAL TIME 15 min.

- ½ cup unsalted butter
- 2 Tbsp. balsamic vinegar
- ½ tsp. kosher salt
- ¼ tsp. black pepper

1. In a saucepan cook butter over low heat about 12 minutes or until browned, stirring occasionally. Remove from heat; cool 2 minutes.
2. Stir in vinegar and season with salt and black pepper. Serve with roasted ricotta. Makes 8 servings.
EACH SERVING *105 cal, 12 g fat, 31 mg chol, 72 mg sodium, 1 g carb, 0 g fiber, 0 g pro.*

GARLIC-RUBBED BREAD

Use the hot grill to quickly toast garlic bread.

TOTAL TIME 10 min.

- 8 ¾-inch slices artisan-style sourdough bread
- 1 large clove garlic, peeled and halved

Heat grill to medium-high. Grill sourdough bread slices 1 to 2 minutes or until toasted, turning once. Rub both sides of warm bread with cut sides of garlic. Serve toasted bread with roasted ricotta. Makes 8 servings.
EACH SERVING *169 cal, 7 g fat, 15 mg chol, 292 mg sodium, 23 g carb, 1 g fiber, 5 g pro.*

GRILLED BONE-IN BEEF RIBEYE STEAK

Photo on pages 143 & 145.

HANDS-ON TIME 10 min.
TOTAL TIME 3 hr., 15 min.

- 2 1¾- to 2¼-lb. bone-in beef ribeye steaks
- 2 Tbsp. extra-virgin olive oil
  Kosher salt
  Black pepper
- ½ cup Black Gold for basting*
  Flaked sea salt

1. Rub steaks with oil and season lightly with kosher salt and black pepper. Cover; chill 2 to 24 hours. Let stand at room temperature 30 minutes before grilling.
2. Heat grill to medium-high, arranging coals on half of grill. Season steaks again with kosher salt and black pepper. Grill on rack of uncovered grill directly over coals about 10 minutes or until well caramelized. (When flare-ups happen, turn and move steaks to a new area of grill to avoid flames.) Move steak to side of grill without coals. Grill, covered, 12 to 18 minutes more for medium doneness (145°F), turning and basting with Black Gold every 5 to 8 minutes.
3. Transfer steak to cutting board; let rest 8 minutes before slicing. Brush with a fresh teaspoonful of Black Gold; sprinkle with sea salt. Makes 8 to 10 servings.
EACH SERVING *460 cal, 40 g fat, 109 mg chol, 196 mg sodium, 0 g carb, 0 g fiber, 25 g pro.*
***Black Gold** Place 1½ cups rendered fat, such as bacon fat, beef fat, good-quality lard, or duck fat; unsalted butter; or extra-virgin olive oil (or any combination of these) in a small pot over low heat. Add 8 to 10 sprigs assorted fresh herbs, such as basil, oregano, thyme, rosemary, and parsley (no more than 3 sprigs of each); 2 green onions; 1 head garlic, halved crosswise; and a lemon half. Cook just until herbs begin to wilt (but not sizzle) and sauce is 140° to 150°F. Remove from heat and let stand 15 minutes so flavors can marry. When using to baste, keep in warm spot on grill. Strain before storing; refrigerate up to 1 week. Add more herbs when rewarmed.

GRILLED BONE-IN
BEEF RIBEYE STEAK

BLISTERED GREEN
BEANS WITH
CHARRED TOMATO
PUTTANESCA
Recipe on page 146

OX BLOOD COCKTAIL
Recipe on page 149

LEAFY SUMMER SALAD
Recipe on page 149

GRILLED RED ONIONS WITH CRUMBLED FETA
Recipe on page 146

GRILLED BONE-IN BEEF RIBEYE STEAK
Recipe on page 142

GRILLED SUMMER ARTICHOKES

Photo on pages 128 & 140.

HANDS-ON TIME 20 min.
TOTAL TIME 55 min.

1   cup mayonnaise
1   Tbsp. ground espelette pepper, or ½ tsp. paprika and ¼ tsp. cayenne pepper
¼   tsp. finely shredded lemon zest
1   Tbsp. fresh lemon juice
¼   tsp. garlic powder
⅛   tsp. kosher salt
4   cloves garlic, peeled
1   lemon, halved
4   large artichokes
¼   tsp. kosher salt
¼   tsp. black pepper
2   Tbsp. extra-virgin olive oil
    Snipped fresh rosemary (optional)

1. For mayo, in a bowl whisk together mayonnaise, espelette pepper, lemon zest, lemon juice, garlic powder, and salt until combined. Cover and refrigerate until ready to use.
2. To cook artichokes, bring a large pot of salted water to boiling. Add garlic cloves and lemon halves, squeezing lemon juice into pot before dropping in halves. Add artichokes; bring water to a simmer and cook about 25 minutes or until tender when pierced with a paring knife. Drain and transfer cooked artichokes to cutting board to cool.
3. Heat grill to high. Cut artichokes in half lengthwise; scoop out choke and some of the soft inner leaves from around each heart. Season remaining parts with salt and black pepper; drizzle with olive oil.
4. Place artichokes on grill, flat sides up; cook about 4 minutes or until golden brown and lightly charred on one side. Turn; cook 4 minutes more or until grill marks appear. Serve with mayo for dipping. Top with additional pepper and/or rosemary, if desired. Makes 8 servings.
Make ahead Prepare artichokes through Step 2. Wrap in plastic wrap; chill up to 2 days. Continue as directed.
EACH SERVING *264 cal, 24 g fat, 12 mg chol, 305 mg sodium, 11 g carb, 5 g fiber, 3 g pro.*

BLISTERED GREEN BEANS WITH CHARRED TOMATO PUTTANESCA

Photo on page 144.

Classic puttanesca—anchovies, olives, and capers—adds zip to grilled beans.

HANDS-ON TIME 20 min.
TOTAL TIME 55 min.

2   large cloves garlic, peeled
½   to 1 tsp. crushed red pepper
2   Tbsp. sherry vinegar
½   cup pitted Kalamata olives, sliced
¼   cup capers
¼   cup extra-virgin olive oil
3   to 4 oil-packed anchovy fillets, drained and chopped
2   tsp. coarsely chopped fresh oregano
1   lb. roma and/or cherry tomatoes
1   tsp. kosher salt
¼   tsp. black pepper
2   lb. haricots verts or other fresh green beans, trimmed
2   Tbsp. extra-virgin olive oil

1. For Charred Tomato Puttanesca, crush garlic with side of a knife; place in a large bowl with red pepper and vinegar. Let stand 20 minutes. Remove garlic; discard. Stir in olives, capers, the ¼ cup olive oil, anchovies, and oregano. Heat grill to medium-high.
2. Cut roma tomatoes in half lengthwise. Place tomatoes (romas cut sides up and cherry tomatoes whole) on hottest part of grill. Cook tomatoes 4 to 5 minutes or until lightly charred. Add tomatoes to olive mixture. Stir in salt and black pepper. Adjust seasoning if necessary.
3. Place green beans in a large bowl with the 2 Tbsp. olive oil; season with additional salt and pepper. Toss to combine. Transfer to grill basket (or place a sturdy metal cooling rack upside-down on grill, grates in opposite direction to form a crosshatch pattern). Cook beans 4 minutes or until lightly charred; gently stir or turn beans. Continue cooking 6 to 7 minutes or until firm-tender (cook 10 to 15 minutes for larger beans). Serve with puttanesca. Makes 6 servings.
EACH SERVING *209 cal, 17 g fat, 2 mg chol, 767 mg sodium, 13 g carb, 5 g fiber, 4 g pro.*

GRILLED RED ONIONS WITH CRUMBLED FETA

Photo on page 145.

"As sharp as an onion can be when it's raw, exposing it to the high level of heat on a grill yields surprisingly quick caramelization, juiciness, and sweetness," Gabrielle says. Soaking the onion helps it steam better and cook more thoroughly.

HANDS-ON TIME 25 min.
TOTAL TIME 35 min.

2   red onions (about 1½ lb. total, each 3 inches in diameter), peeled
1   Tbsp. extra-virgin olive oil
    Kosher salt
    Black pepper
¼   cup honey
¼   tsp. ground chipotle chile pepper
¼   tsp. kosher salt
½   cup crumbled feta cheese
½   cup walnuts, toasted (tip, page 37)
2   Tbsp. snipped fresh chives

1. Heat grill to medium. Quarter onions lengthwise. Place in bowl of cold water; let stand 10 minutes. Drain. Drizzle with olive oil and season with salt and black pepper. Transfer to grill rack. Grill 15 to 18 minutes or until charred and tender inside, turning to brown.
2. Combine honey, chile pepper, and salt. Serve onions topped with feta, walnuts, and chives. Drizzle with honey mixture. Makes 8 servings.
Make ahead Cool onions after grilling. Cover; chill up to 24 hours. To reheat, place in cast-iron skillet; grill 5 minutes or until warm, turning once. Top as directed.
EACH SERVING *147 cal, 8 g fat, 8 mg chol, 125 mg sodium, 18 g carb, 2 g fiber, 3 g pro.*

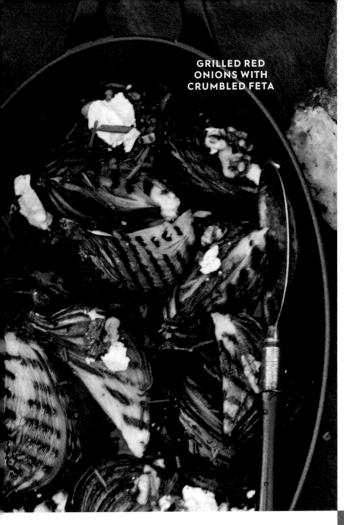

GRILLED RED ONIONS WITH CRUMBLED FETA

OX BLOOD COCKTAIL
Recipe on page 149

GRILLED
PARMESAN
CAKE

A LITTLE PARMESAN IN THE BATTER ADDS UMAMI—A RICH, IRRESISTIBLE SALTY-SWEET CHARACTER—AND PERFECTLY BALANCES THE SWEETNESS IN THIS DESSERT.

LEAFY SUMMER SALAD

Photo on page 145.

Crisp fresh greens, crunchy cucumbers and onion, and cool avocados are a refreshingly delicious contrast to grilled food.

TOTAL TIME 20 min.

- 12 cups loosely packed baby lettuce leaves, red or green leaf, or baby romaine (12 oz. total)
- 1 small English cucumber, halved and thinly sliced (1½ cups)
- ¾ cup very thinly sliced sweet onion
- ⅓ cup extra-virgin olive oil
- 2 Tbsp. red wine vinegar
- 1 tsp. kosher salt
- ¼ tsp. black pepper
- 2 avocados, halved, seeded, peeled, and cut into ¾-inch chunks
- ¾ cup loosely packed fresh dill sprigs

In an extra-large bowl, combine lettuce, cucumber, and onion. In a screw-top jar combine olive oil, vinegar, salt, and black pepper. Cover and shake to combine. Pour over salad; toss gently to coat. Top with avocados and dill. Makes 6 to 8 servings.

EACH SERVING *209 cal, 19 g fat, 0 mg chol, 198 mg sodium, 9 g carb, 5 g fiber, 3 g pro.*

OX BLOOD COCKTAIL

Photo on pages 144 & 147.

The sweet earthiness of beet juice plays brilliantly with the bourbon in one of Ox Restaurant's signature cocktails.

TOTAL TIME 20 min.

- 1 cup red beet juice* (from 1 lb. beets or available in the produce or juice section of supermarkets)
- ⅓ cup sugar
- 1½ cups good quality bourbon
- ¾ cup fresh lemon juice
- ¼ tsp. kosher salt
  Ice
- 1 bunch fresh tarragon
- 8 slices fresh beet

1. For beet syrup, in small nonreactive pot cook red beet juice and sugar over medium heat 4 to 5 minutes or until sugar dissolves, stirring constantly. Cool completely. Store in sterilized, sealed container in refrigerator up to 1 week (syrup is best when used fresh).
2. In a pitcher combine bourbon, beet syrup, lemon juice, and salt. Stir to dissolve salt. Add ice and tarragon, reserving 8 sprigs. Garnish drinks with reserved tarragon sprigs and beet slices. Makes 8 servings.
*Use a vegetable juicer to juice beets, or peel and chop beets and add to a high-powered blender or food processor with ¼ cup water. Cover and process or blend 5 minutes or until as smooth as possible. Press mixture through a fine-mesh sieve.
EACH 3-OZ. SERVING *150 cal, 0 g fat, 0 mg chol, 64 mg sodium, 14 g carb, 1 g fiber, 1 g pro.*

GRILLED PARMESAN CAKE

Bake and chill this buttery cake one to two days before grilling. Freeze for longer storage.

HANDS-ON TIME 35 min.
TOTAL TIME 1 hr., 20 min.

- 2 cups all-purpose flour
- 2 tsp. baking powder
- 1 tsp. kosher salt
- 5 oz. Parmigiano-Reggiano cheese, finely grated (1¼ cups)
- 1 cup unsalted butter, softened
- 2 cups granulated sugar
- 4 eggs, lightly beaten
- ½ 8-oz. pkg. cream cheese, cut into cubes and softened
- 1 8-oz. carton sour cream
- 1 cup whipping cream
- 2 Tbsp. powdered sugar
- ¼ tsp. ground cinnamon
  Fresh blackberries
  Fresh mint sprigs

1. Preheat oven to 350°F. Butter and lightly flour a 13×9-inch baking pan. In a large bowl stir together flour, baking powder, and salt. Stir in grated cheese.
2. In bowl of a stand mixer fitted with a paddle attachment, beat butter and granulated sugar on medium-high speed 5 minutes, stopping to scrape down sides of bowl. Reduce speed to medium; slowly drizzle in beaten eggs and beat thoroughly. Add cream cheese and beat until combined (batter will look slightly curdled). Reduce speed to low; alternately add one-third each of the flour mixture and sour cream until both are nearly incorporated. Stop mixer; use a spatula to finish mixing batter. Evenly spread batter in prepared pan.
3. Bake about 45 minutes or until a toothpick inserted near center comes out clean. Cool in pan on wire rack 10 minutes. Remove cake from pan; cool on wire rack.
4. For sweetened whipped cream, in chilled mixing bowl combine cream, powdered sugar, and cinnamon. Beat with electric mixer on medium speed until soft peaks form. Chill until serving time.
5. Heat grill to medium. Cut cooled cake into 12 pieces. Grill cake slices without moving 1 to 1½ minutes or until lightly toasted. Carefully turn; grill 1 minute more. (Watch carefully; cake toasts quickly.) Using metal spatula, remove from grill. Serve warm slices with sweetened whipped cream, berries, and mint. Makes 12 slices.
EACH SLICE *544 cal, 34 g fat, 153 mg chol, 392 mg sodium, 54 g carb, 1 g fiber, 8 g pro.*

ASIAN BLUEBERRY
COLESLAW
Recipe on page 158

july

With produce at its peak, get ready to celebrate with summer. Blueberries star in chocolaty pie, pork kabobs, and other tasty recipes. Plus farmstand corn on the cob shows off deliciously in unexpected roles.

162

165

167

TRUE BLUE

It's national blueberry month, but who needs an excuse to enjoy this delicious little berry? These recipes feature twists on fresh salads, a classic pie, and even savory kabobs. Grab a pint of the berries at the market while the picking is good.

BLUEBERRY CHOCOLATE PIE

This pie will be the favorite at a Fourth of July potluck, hands down. The cookie dough is easier to shape than regular pie pastry and sweeter.

HANDS-ON TIME 45 min.
TOTAL TIME 3 hr.

- 1 recipe Sour Cream Cookie Dough
- 1 cup semisweet chocolate pieces
- 1 egg
- ½ cup sugar
- 3 Tbsp. all-purpose flour
- 1 lemon, juiced
- 6 cups fresh blueberries

1. Preheat oven to 450°F. Prepare Sour Cream Cookie Dough. On a well-floured surface, roll out half the dough to form a 12-inch circle. Line a 9-inch pie plate with dough. Trim and flute edge. Line with a double thickness of foil. Bake 8 minutes; carefully remove foil. Bake 3 to 4 minutes more or until golden. Remove; sprinkle with chocolate pieces. Set aside.

2. Reduce oven to 375°F. Roll remaining dough to ⅛ inch thickness. Cut into star shapes using assorted-size cutters. In a small bowl whisk together egg and 1 Tbsp. water. Arrange cutouts 2 inches apart on parchment-paper-lined cookie sheets. Brush cutouts with egg mixture. Bake 7 to 9 minutes or until edges are lightly browned. Remove; cool on wire rack.

3. For pie filling, in a large saucepan stir together sugar, flour, and lemon juice. Add 4 cups of the blueberries. Cook and stir over medium heat just until thickened and bubbly. Remove from heat. Stir in remaining berries. Pour into crust.

4. Bake 10 minutes or just until berries are heated through, covering edge of pie with foil if necessary to prevent overbrowning. Remove to wire rack. Top with cookie cutouts; cool completely. Makes 8 servings.

Sour Cream Cookie Dough In a mixing bowl beat ½ cup butter, softened, with mixer 30 seconds. Add ½ cup sugar, ½ tsp. baking powder, ⅛ tsp. baking soda, and a dash of salt; beat until combined. Add 1 egg yolk, ¼ cup sour cream, and 1 tsp. vanilla; beat until combined. Beat in 2 cups all-purpose flour. Divide in half; wrap and chill until easy to handle.

EACH SERVING *520 cal, 21 g fat, 80 mg chol, 182 mg sodium, 82 g carb, 5 g fiber, 7 g pro.*

THE SOUR CREAM COOKIE CRUST AND THE IRRESISTIBLE LAYER OF DARK CHOCOLATE ARE SWEET PROMISES TO WIN RAVE REVIEWS.

PORK KABOBS ARE DOUBLY FLAVORFUL, THANKS TO A GARLIC-CHILI RUB AND EXTRA-RICH BLUEBERRY-JALAPEÑO SAUCE BRUSHED ON HALFWAY THROUGH GRILLING.

GRILLED PORK KABOBS WITH BLUEBERRY BARBECUE SAUCE

Cook a batch of this zippy blueberry, jalapeño, and molasses sauce and prepare to be crowned king of BBQ. Serve the unexpected Blueberry Corn Salad as a stand-alone side or toss it on the grilled kabobs like a relish.

HANDS-ON TIME 30 min.
TOTAL TIME 1 hr.

2	lb. pork tenderloin
2	tsp. chili powder
4	cloves garlic, minced
¾	tsp. kosher salt
½	tsp. black pepper
4	cups fresh blueberries
⅓	cup molasses
⅓	cup cider vinegar
2	fresh jalapeño peppers, seeded and minced (tip, page 37)
¼	cup tomato paste
2	tsp. Worcestershire sauce
1	recipe Blueberry Corn Salad (optional)

1. Trim fat from pork; cut into 1-inch cubes. In a large bowl combine chili powder, garlic, ½ tsp. of the salt, and black pepper. Add pork and toss to coat. Thread pork on sixteen 8-inch skewers.* Cover and chill.
2. For sauce, in a medium saucepan combine blueberries, molasses, vinegar, jalapeños, tomato paste, Worcestershire sauce, and remaining ¼ tsp. kosher salt. Bring to boiling; reduce heat. Simmer, uncovered, 25 to 30 minutes or until thickened, stirring occasionally. Remove from heat; cool. Set aside 1 cup to brush kabobs.
3. Grill pork kabobs on a rack of a covered grill directly over medium heat 6 to 8 minutes or until meat is still slightly pink in the center, turning once and brushing pork with reserved sauce halfway through grilling. Serve with remaining blueberry sauce and, if desired, Blueberry Corn Salad. Makes 8 servings.
*If using wooden skewers, soak in water 30 minutes; drain before using.
EACH SERVING *219 cal, 3 g fat, 74 mg chol, 307 mg sodium, 24 g carb, 2 g fiber, 25 g pro.*

BLUEBERRY CORN SALAD

The combination of grilled veggies, fresh fruit, and garlic-lemon vinaigrette goes well with just about any grilled meat.

HANDS-ON TIME 20 min.
TOTAL TIME 40 min.

½	cup olive oil
½	cup lemon juice
¼	cup chopped fresh mint
4	cloves garlic, minced
½	tsp. kosher salt
½	tsp. black pepper
8	ears fresh corn
2	Tbsp. olive oil
4	cups fresh blueberries

1. In screw-top jar combine ½ cup olive oil, lemon juice, mint, garlic, salt, and black pepper; cover and shake until combined.
2. To grill corn, pull back husks, but leave intact. Remove silks; rinse corn. Brush with olive oil and sprinkle lightly with salt and pepper. Fold husks back around corn. Tie tops of husks closed with 100-percent-cotton kitchen string.
3. Grill corn on a rack of a covered grill directly over medium heat 20 to 25 minutes or until kernels are tender, turning occasionally. Remove and cool. Cut kernels from cobs. In a large bowl combine corn, berries, and dressing. Makes 8 servings.
EACH SERVING *275 cal, 18 g fat, 0 mg chol, 200 mg sodium, 29 g carb, 4 g fiber, 4 g pro.*

BLUEBERRY-
BRAISED BRISKET
SANDWICHES
Recipe on page 158

ASIAN BLUEBERRY
COLESLAW
Recipe on page 158

THIS TINY SUMMER BERRY, PACKED WITH ANTIOXIDANTS AND VITAMIN C, PAIRS WITH SWEET AND SAVORY FOODS ALIKE. DON'T BE SHY—TRY THESE RECIPES AT YOUR NEXT GATHERING—YOU'LL BE HAPPY YOU DID!

BLUEBERRY-BRAISED BRISKET SANDWICHES

Photo on page 156.

The sweet and tangy vinegar-blueberry braising liquid turns out remarkably tender, flavorful brisket with very little hands-on work. Serve it on buns or pile it on a platter with a heap of grilled veggies. Adding berries at the end turns pan juices into a chutney-like sauce.

HANDS-ON TIME 30 min.
TOTAL TIME 3 hr.

1. 3- to 3½-lb. boneless beef brisket flat half
   Salt and black pepper
1. Tbsp. olive oil
2. slices bacon, chopped
1. medium onion, chopped (½ cup)
6. cloves garlic, minced
1. cup cider vinegar
2½ cups fresh blueberries
¼ cup packed brown sugar
½ tsp. salt
   Pretzel buns, split
   Radish sprouts or greens (optional)

1. Preheat oven to 325°F. Season beef with salt and black pepper. In a Dutch oven heat oil over medium-high heat. Brown beef well on both sides. Remove from pan; set aside.
2. In the same pan cook bacon until lightly browned. Add onion and garlic; cook about 5 minutes or until onion is tender. Stir in vinegar, 2 cups of the berries, sugar, and salt. Bring to boiling; stir to dissolve sugar. Reduce heat; boil gently, uncovered, 10 minutes. Return beef to pan. Cover; roast 2½ to 3 hours or until tender.
3. Remove meat from pan, reserving liquid; thinly slice against grain. Skim fat off liquid; stir in remaining berries. Serve meat on buns with reserved liquid. Top with sprouts, if desired. Makes 8 servings.
EACH SERVING *521 cal, 23 g fat, 120 mg chol, 662 mg sodium, 37 g carb, 2 g fiber, 41 g pro.*

ASIAN BLUEBERRY COLESLAW

Photos on pages 150 & 157.

Not too sweet, with just the right amount of creamy, this coleslaw satisfies with extra crunch of slivers of jicama, zings of ginger, and blueberries that burst in your mouth.

TOTAL TIME 25 min.

½ cup mayonnaise
2 Tbsp. sweet Asian chili sauce
1 Tbsp. grated fresh ginger
1 tsp. lime zest
½ medium head red cabbage, shredded (8 cups)
½ jicama, peeled and cut into julienne strips (2 cups)
2 cups fresh blueberries
½ cup fresh basil leaves, cut into slivers
   Freshly ground black pepper

In an extra-large bowl whisk together mayonnaise, chili sauce, ginger, and lime zest. Add cabbage, jicama, and blueberries; toss to coat. Scatter basil over top. Season with freshly ground black pepper. Makes 12 servings.
EACH SERVING *105 cal, 7 g fat, 4 mg chol, 114 mg sodium, 10 g carb, 3 g fiber, 1 g pro.*

SPARKLING ROSÉ BLUEBERRY FLOATS

Crisp bubbly wine cuts the typical sweetness of a float for this grown-up treat. It's pure summer celebration.

HANDS-ON TIME 20 min.
TOTAL TIME 3 hr., 35 min.

3 cups Blueberry Granita
1 pint purchased coconut gelato (2 cups)
2 Tbsp. honey
2 cups fresh blueberries
1 750-ml bottle sparkling rosé, chilled
½ cup very thinly sliced fresh basil leaves

1. Prepare and freeze Blueberry Granita.
2. Scoop granita and gelato into six 10- to 12-oz. glasses. Top each with a drizzle of honey and some blueberries. Pour rosé over each. Garnish with basil and serve immediately. Makes 6 servings.
Blueberry Granita For syrup, in saucepan bring 1 cup water, ¾ cup sugar, and 2 tsp. lemon zest just to boiling over medium heat, stirring to dissolve sugar. Remove from heat; transfer to a large bowl. Freeze 15 minutes. Puree 4 cups fresh blueberries and 2 Tbsp. lemon juice in a food processor until nearly smooth. Strain puree through a fine-mesh sieve; discard solids. Stir blueberry puree and ½ cup sparkling rosé into syrup. Pour into a 3-qt. rectangular baking dish. Cover; freeze 1 hour. Scrape sides with a fork for even freezing. Cover; freeze 2 hours more or until firm, scraping down sides once. Freeze up to 3 months. Makes 5 cups.
EACH SERVING *368 cal, 6 g fat, 20 mg chol, 42 mg sodium, 58 g carb, 3 g fiber, 3 g pro.*

SPARKLING ROSÉ
BLUEBERRY FLOATS

WHAT IS A FINANCIER, ANYWAY? IT'S A SMALL MOIST FRENCH CAKE THAT'S DISTINGUISHED BY THE USE OF ALMOND FLOUR AND LOTS OF BROWNED BUTTER.

BLUEBERRY-OAT FINANCIERS

Fancy name, super easy little cakes that ooze butter and juicy blueberries. With a dollop of whipped cream and a spoon of berries warmed in more butter, they're a simply decadent dessert. Browning butter is key to the subtle nuttiness of financiers. This version includes a hint of rolled oats for texture.

HANDS-ON TIME 15 min.
TOTAL TIME 1 hr., 20 min.

- 1 cup butter
- 1 cup sugar
- 1 cup almond flour
- ⅔ cup all-purpose flour
- ¼ cup plus 1 Tbsp. regular rolled oats
- ½ tsp. kosher salt
- ¾ cup egg whites (6 large), lightly beaten
- 1½ cups fresh blueberries
  Soft whipped cream

1. In a small saucepan melt ¾ cup of the butter over medium heat 15 minutes or until amber color, stirring occasionally and watching carefully the last 3 minutes. Remove from heat. Let stand 30 minutes or until cooled to room temperature.

2. Preheat oven to 350°F. With additional butter, generously butter the bottoms and sides of twelve 2½-inch muffin cups. In a bowl whisk together sugar, almond flour, all-purpose flour, ¼ cup of the oats, and salt.

3. Add egg whites to flour mixture. Stir in browned butter just until blended. Fold in ½ cup of the blueberries. Spoon batter into prepared muffin cups, filling each half-full. Tap pan against counter twice. Sprinkle batter with remaining oats. Bake 20 minutes or until edges are browned and centers are set.

4. Remove from oven and cool in pans 10 minutes. Using a table knife, loosen sides and gently tilt financiers out of pan onto a cooling rack. Wipe out the small saucepan; melt the remaining ¼ cup butter in saucepan over medium-low heat. Add remaining blueberries. Cook about 4 minutes or just until blueberries begin to pop, stirring occasionally. Serve financiers with soft whipped cream and buttered blueberries. Makes 12 financiers.

EACH FINANCIER *331 cal, 22 g fat, 46 mg chol, 250 mg sodium, 30 g carb, 2 g fiber, 6 g pro.*

BLUEBERRY SUMMARY

BLUEBERRY SEASON Although blueberries are available year-round, July is the peak harvest month for fruit grown in the United States. Then is a good time to look for the berry at local farmers markets or to make a trip to a you-pick farm.

CARE AND CHOOSING When shopping for fresh blueberries, look for fruit that's deep blue to blue-black with a silver sheen called bloom. Store berries in the refrigerator and eat within 10 days. Wash just before using.

BERRY NUTRITION This nutritional powerhouse weighs in at 80 calories a cup and ranks among antioxidant super foods. A cup also offers a quarter of the recommended daily dose of vitamin C as well as nearly 4 grams fiber.

PICKLED BLUEBERRIES

BLUEBERRY MUSTARD

BLUEBERRY KETCHUP

BLUEBERRY VINEGAR

BLUEBERRY KETCHUP

Pair with Muenster or smoky cheddar for a sassy burger upgrade.

HANDS-ON TIME 10 min.
TOTAL TIME 30 min.

- 2½ cups fresh blueberries
- ½ cup packed brown sugar
- ⅓ cup red wine vinegar
- 1 Tbsp. lemon juice
- ½ tsp. kosher salt
- ¼ tsp. black pepper
- ½ cup ketchup

1. In a medium saucepan combine 2 cups of the blueberries, brown sugar, vinegar, lemon juice, salt, and black pepper. Bring to boiling, stirring to dissolve sugar. Reduce heat; simmer, uncovered, 20 minutes or until slightly thickened, stirring occasionally. Remove from heat; cool slightly.
2. Use an immersion blender (or transfer to a blender) to puree blueberry mixture until smooth. Let cool (mixture will thicken). Stir in remaining blueberries and ketchup. Chill up to 2 weeks. Makes 2⅓ cups.
EACH 1-TBSP. SERVING *21 cal, 0 g fat, 0 mg chol, 62 mg sodium, 5 g carb, 0 g fiber, 0 g pro.*

BLUEBERRY MUSTARD

Spoon onto grilled brats for a snappy, dressed-up topping.

HANDS-ON TIME 15 min.
TOTAL TIME 30 min.

- 1 Tbsp. butter
- ¼ cup finely chopped red onion
- 1 clove garlic, minced
- 1½ cups fresh blueberries
- ¼ cup dry red wine
- 1 Tbsp. sugar
- 3 Tbsp. Dijon-style mustard

In a small saucepan heat butter over medium heat. Add onion and garlic; cook and stir 4 minutes or until onion is tender. Stir in blueberries, wine, and sugar. Bring to boiling; reduce heat. Simmer, uncovered, 10 minutes. Mash berries lightly with a potato masher. Simmer 2 to 4 minutes more or until thickened. Remove from heat. Stir in mustard; cool. Chill up to 2 weeks. Makes about 1 cup.
EACH 1-TBSP. SERVING *19 cal, 1 g fat, 2 mg chol, 63 mg sodium, 3 g carb, 0 g fiber, 0 g pro.*

BLUEBERRY VINEGAR

HANDS-ON TIME 10 min.
TOTAL TIME 8 hr., 10 min.

- 3 cups fresh blueberries
- 2 cups white wine vinegar
- 2 Tbsp. honey

1. In a stainless-steel or enamel saucepan combine 1½ cups of the blueberries with vinegar. Bring to boiling; reduce heat. Simmer, uncovered, 3 minutes. Stir in honey. Remove from heat; cool. Pour mixture through a fine-mesh strainer and let drain into a bowl. Discard berries.
2. Transfer vinegar to a clean 1-qt. jar or bottle. Add remaining 1½ cups berries to jar or bottle. Cover tightly with nonmetallic lid (or cover with plastic wrap; tightly seal with metal lid). Chill at least 8 hours; strain and discard berries. Store vinegar in cool, dark place up to 2 weeks. Makes 2 cups.
EACH 1-TBSP. SERVING *17 cal, 0 g fat, 0 mg chol, 1 mg sodium, 3 g carb, 0 g fiber, 0 g pro.*

PICKLED BLUEBERRIES

Use as a surprising addition to a salad or include in your favorite martini.

HANDS-ON TIME 15 min.
TOTAL TIME 24 hr.

- 1½ cups white wine vinegar
- ⅓ cup sugar
- ½ tsp. kosher salt
- 3 cups fresh blueberries
- 1 small fennel bulb, trimmed, cored, and quartered

1. In a small nonreactive saucepan heat vinegar, sugar, and salt over medium heat, stirring until sugar and salt are dissolved. Remove and cool mixture.
2. Place berries and fennel in nonreactive bowl or 1-qt. canning jar. Pour vinegar mixture over blueberries. Cover; chill overnight or up to 2 weeks. Makes 3 cups.
EACH ¼-CUP SERVING *57 cal, 0 g fat, 0 mg chol, 255 mg sodium, 12 g carb, 1 g fiber, 0 g pro.*

new ways with
CORN

When midsummer roadside produce stands brim with sweet corn, try these inspiring recipes.

When choosing corn, the husk should be bright green and fit snugly around the cob. Kernels should be plump and packed in tight rows. Strip the husks and silks just before cooking.

Buy and eat corn as soon after picking as possible. Once picked, the sugar in corn immediately starts to convert to starch. The sooner you can enjoy corn, the more you can savor its natural sweetness.

BUCATINI CORN-BONARA

HUSK-WRAPPED CHICKEN & CORN RELISH

GRILLED CORN & HALLOUMI SALAD

A FAVORITE GADGET TO GET RID OF PESKY SILKS—A NEW SOFT-BRISTLE TOOTHBRUSH. IT'S INEXPENSIVE AND MAKES REMOVING THEM A BREEZE.

BUCATINI CORN-BONARA

TOTAL TIME 30 min.

- 6   ears corn on the cob, shucked and silks removed
- 12 oz. dried bucatini pasta
- 1   cup half-and-half
- 2   egg yolks
- 1   to 2 tsp. cracked black pepper
- 8   oz. bacon, chopped
- 1   Tbsp. minced garlic
- ½   cup finely shredded Parmesan cheese

1. In a large pot cook corn in lightly salted boiling water 5 minutes; remove. Add pasta to water and cook according to package. Drain, reserving ¾ cup pasta water.
2. With a sharp knife, cut corn from cobs. In a bowl whisk together half-and-half, egg yolks, and pepper. Set aside.
3. In an extra-large skillet cook bacon over medium heat until crisp; drain, reserving 2 Tbsp. drippings. Add garlic to skillet; cook and stir 30 seconds. Add cream mixture, bucatini, corn, cheese, and bacon. Bring just to boiling, stirring constantly. Add pasta water to reach desired consistency. Makes 6 servings.
EACH SERVING *530 cal, 22 g fat, 104 mg chol, 386 mg sodium, 62 g carb, 4 g fiber, 20 g pro.*

GRILLED CORN & HALLOUMI SALAD

HANDS-ON TIME 20 min.
TOTAL TIME 40 min.

- 4   ears corn on the cob, shucked and silks removed
- 1   12-oz. head radicchio, quartered lengthwise
- 8   oz. Halloumi cheese, cut into ½-inch slices
- 2   Tbsp. olive oil
- ¼   cup chopped pickled hot peppers (such as banana peppers or cherry peppers)
- 2   Tbsp. brine from pickled peppers
- ¼   cup olive oil
- 1   Tbsp. white wine vinegar
     Fresh basil

1. Brush corn, radicchio, and cheese with the 2 Tbsp. oil. Grill corn on rack of a covered grill directly over medium heat 10 minutes; turn. Add radicchio. Grill 5 minutes; turn. Add cheese. Grill 5 minutes, turning once. Remove; cool.
2. In a large bowl whisk together pickled peppers, brine, the ¼ cup oil, and vinegar. With a sharp knife cut corn from cobs and add to bowl. Chop radicchio; add to bowl and toss salad to combine. Top servings with cheese and fresh basil. Makes 4 servings.
EACH SERVING *480 cal, 37 g fat, 218 mg chol, 927 mg sodium, 22 g carb, 3 g fiber, 20 g pro.*

HUSK-WRAPPED CHICKEN & CORN RELISH

HANDS-ON TIME 45 min.
TOTAL TIME 1 hr., 10 min.

- 4   ears corn on the cob, husks intact
- 1   Tbsp. chili powder
- 2   tsp. dried oregano, crushed
- ½   tsp. kosher salt
- 8   boneless, skinless chicken thighs (about 2 lb.)
- 2   Tbsp. olive oil
- 2   Tbsp. red wine vinegar
- 1½ cups chopped fresh pineapple
- ¼   cup chopped red onion
- 1   fresh jalapeño pepper, halved, seeded, and chopped (tip, page 37)

1. Remove husks and silks from corn, reserving husks. Rinse husks. Combine chili powder, oregano, and salt. Sprinkle over chicken. Wrap each thigh in a piece of husk. Tear strips from remaining husks; tie around wrapped chicken to secure.
2. In a large bowl whisk together olive oil and vinegar. With a sharp knife cut corn from cobs; add to bowl. Add pineapple, onion, and jalapeño. Season to taste with additional salt.
3. Grill chicken on rack of a covered grill directly over medium heat 20 to 25 minutes or until done (170°F), turning occasionally. Unwrap chicken; serve with relish. Makes 4 servings.
Make Ahead Tip Prepare corn relish as directed. Chill up to 24 hours. In a large bowl combine corn husks and enough water to cover. Refrigerate until ready to use.
EACH SERVING *455 cal, 18 g fat, 213 mg chol, 497 mg sodium, 27 g carb, 4 g fiber, 48 g pro.*

FAST & FRESH

Easy, healthy recipes for a better dinner tonight.

SHRIMP SALAD WITH LIME DRESSING

SHRIMP SALAD WITH LIME DRESSING

Toss grilled shrimp, juicy tomato, and creamy avocado in a zesty lime dressing with a cayenne kick. Bright, fresh, and ready in a snap, this salad has summer written all over it.

TOTAL TIME 25 min.

1   large lime
¼   tsp. cayenne pepper
½   tsp. kosher salt
2   Tbsp. plus 1 tsp. olive oil
1   lb. uncooked large shrimp in shells, peeled and deveined
2   avocados, halved, seeded, peeled, and sliced
1   large tomato, cut into chunks
½   sweet onion, such as Vidalia or Walla Walla, thinly sliced
½   cup packed fresh cilantro

1. For Lime Dressing, remove 1 tsp. zest and squeeze 3 Tbsp. juice from lime. In a small bowl combine zest, juice, cayenne, and ¼ tsp. of the salt. Slowly whisk in 2 Tbsp. of the olive oil until combined.
2. In a medium bowl toss shrimp with the remaining 1 tsp. oil and remaining ¼ tsp. salt. Grill shrimp on the greased rack of a covered grill directly over medium heat 3 to 4 minutes or until opaque, turning once.
3. On a large platter arrange shrimp, avocados, tomato, and onion. Drizzle with dressing and top with cilantro. Makes 4 servings.
EACH SERVING *291 cal, 19 g fat, 159 mg chol, 373 mg sodium, 12 g carb, 6 g fiber, 22 g pro.*

OPEN-FACE FLOUNDER
SANDWICH

OPEN-FACE FLOUNDER SANDWICH

Flounder has a firm texture and a mild, sweet taste. Tilapia, grouper, or catfish would be equally delicious.

TOTAL TIME 20 min.

1   lemon, halved
⅓   cup mayonnaise
1   shallot, minced
1   Tbsp. pickle relish
1   tsp. Dijon-style mustard
     Black pepper
     Kosher salt
1½   lb. flounder or other firm white fish, cut into 4 portions
2   Tbsp. all-purpose flour
3   Tbsp. vegetable oil
4   slices sourdough bread, toasted
4   cups mixed herbs and greens, such as parsley, chives, basil, cilantro, and/or spinach, coarsely chopped

1. Juice half the lemon. Cut remaining half into wedges. For sauce, in a bowl combine juice, mayonnaise, shallot, relish, and mustard. Season with black pepper.
2. Lightly season flounder with kosher salt. Sprinkle flour onto a large plate. Dip fish into flour, shaking off excess. In a large skillet heat oil over medium-high heat. Carefully add fish to skillet (cook in batches if necessary). Cook 4 to 6 minutes per ½-inch thickness or until fish flakes easily with a fork, turning once.
3. Spread sauce on each bread slice; sprinkle with half the herbs. Top with fish and remaining herbs. Serve with lemon wedges. Makes 4 servings.
EACH SERVING *555 cal, 29 g fat, 89 mg chol, 841 mg sodium, 39 g carb, 4 g fiber, 37 g pro.*

GRILLED BROCCOLI & ORZO

QUICK TANDOORI-STYLE CHICKEN

Madras curry powder, typically a blend of garlic and spices—fenugreek, coriander, cumin, turmeric, and red pepper—tends to be hotter than blends simply labeled curry powder.

TOTAL TIME 40 min.

½   cup plain Greek yogurt
1   Tbsp. cider vinegar
2   tsp. Madras (hot) curry powder
1   clove garlic, minced
½   tsp. kosher salt
1½   lb. skinless, boneless chicken thighs, cut into 1- to 1½-inch pieces
    Cooked basmati rice
    Mango chutney
    Chopped fresh mint leaves

1. In a large bowl whisk together yogurt, vinegar, curry powder, garlic, and salt. Add chicken; toss to coat. Let stand 15 minutes (or cover and chill up to 24 hours).
2. Thread chicken on skewers, leaving ¼ inch between pieces. Grill on the greased rack of a covered grill directly over medium-high heat 8 to 10 minutes or until chicken is done (175°F), turning to brown evenly. Serve over basmati rice and top with mango chutney. Sprinkle with mint. Makes 4 to 6 servings.
EACH SERVING *232 cal, 8 g fat, 162 mg chol, 295 mg sodium, 2 g carb, 1 g fiber, 37 g pro.*

GRILLED BROCCOLI & ORZO

The broccoli stalks stay crisp and tender with flecks of browned goodness on the florets. Rich toasted pine nuts, a sprinkle of Parm, and a big squeeze of orange make this easy vegetarian main irresistible.

TOTAL TIME 35 min.

2   oranges
1   large head broccoli (1½ to 2 lb.), trimmed
2   Tbsp. extra-virgin olive oil
¾   tsp. kosher salt
8   oz. dried orzo pasta
1   clove garlic, minced
⅓   cup pine nuts, toasted (tip, page 37)
¼   cup freshly grated Parmesan cheese
    Small fresh basil leaves
    Black pepper

1. Remove 1 tsp. zest and squeeze to get 3 Tbsp. juice from one orange. Cut remaining orange into wedges.
2. Cut broccoli into eight large spears. In a large serving bowl toss broccoli with 1 Tbsp. of the olive oil and ½ tsp. of the salt. Grill on the rack of a covered grill directly over medium heat 7 to 9 minutes or until lightly charred and crisp-tender.
3. Meanwhile, cook orzo in a large pot of lightly salted boiling water 7 minutes or until al dente; drain. Transfer to a serving bowl.
4. In a small skillet heat remaining 1 Tbsp. oil over low heat. Add garlic; cook 1 minute or until fragrant. Stir in orange juice and remaining ¼ tsp. salt. Stir into orzo. Top with broccoli, pine nuts, Parmesan, and basil. Season with black pepper. Serve with orange wedges. Makes 4 servings.
EACH SERVING *449 cal, 18 g fat, 4 mg chol, 519 mg sodium, 61 g carb, 8 g fiber, 16 g pro.*

QUICK
TANDOORI-STYLE
CHICKEN

ZUCCHINI-OLIVE
OIL CAKE
Recipe on page 194

august

Taste summer at its best with bold flavor veg-centric recipes that family and friends will rave about. Add to the menu a mouthwatering burger recipe with a Kentucky Bourbon Sauce from a master griller.

174

177

180

how to cook
BURGERS

There's the burger you want to eat. And then there's the burger that's so rich, juicy, and bursting with flavor you just want to devour it. Grilling expert Jamie Purviance shares his tips on how to make the best-ever backyard burger.

It's all about the patty: a dark outer crust and juicy interior seasoned to let the flavor of the meat shine. Accessorize with toppings as you please—there's no wrong way!

BURGERS PUFF UP SLIGHTLY WHEN COOKED. JAMIE'S TRICK? MAKE A SHALLOW WELL IN THE CENTER OF EACH RAW PATTY FOR NICE FLAT BURGERS.

Jamie Purviance knows grilling. As a top barbecue expert and Weber's master griller, he's written more than a dozen cookbooks on the subject. "The key to a great burger is quality meat and maintaining juiciness," he says. Here's how to get there:

THE GRIND "Ground chuck (about 18 percent fat) is better for burgers than ground round (about 12 percent). Use 1½ pounds to make four burgers. You want meat that's been ground in the past 24 hours. Avoid packages that have any browning or look smashed. You can ask your butcher to grind some chuck for you to ensure freshness."

EXTRA FLAVOR "Sometimes I also like to throw in a little Worcestershire and grated onion to taste, or even some roasted chiles or bell peppers. Anything that adds moisture to the meat will improve both the taste and the juiciness."

A LIGHT TOUCH "I salt and pepper the meat first along with any flavor additions (this ensures the patty is seasoned throughout), and then use my hands to just incorporate. Avoid overmixing—your burger will have a pasty consistency."

GREAT SHAPE "The ideal patty thickness is ¾ inch. Thinner, and it's likely to dry out before developing a nice crust on the outside; thicker, and the crust might blacken before the center reaches medium doneness."

BACON CHEESEBURGERS WITH KENTUCKY BOURBON SAUCE

This splurge of a burger is what Jamie calls a "full orchestra of flavors."

HANDS-ON TIME 25 min.
TOTAL TIME 55 min.

- 2 large handfuls hickory or mesquite wood chips
- 1 recipe Kentucky Bourbon Sauce
- 1½ lb. ground chuck (80-percent lean)
- 1 tsp. kosher salt
- ½ tsp. black pepper
- 4 oz. smoked cheddar cheese, shredded or sliced
- 4 hamburger buns, split
  Lettuce and sliced tomatoes
- 8 slices cooked bacon

1. Soak wood chips in water at least 30 minutes. Prepare Kentucky Bourbon Sauce.

2. Meanwhile, in a bowl mix ground chuck, salt, and pepper; shape four ¾-inch-thick patties. Make a shallow indentation in the center of patties. Chill until ready to grill.

3. Prepare grill for direct cooking over medium-high heat (400° to 450°F). Drain wood chips; add to charcoal or to smoker box of gas grill, following manufacturer's directions; cover. When smoke appears, grill patties over direct medium-high heat, covered, 8 to 10 minutes for medium doneness (160°F), turning once. During the last minute, top patties with cheese and toast buns, cut sides down, over direct heat.

4. Build burgers on buns with lettuce, tomato, bacon slices, and Kentucky Bourbon Sauce. Makes 4 burgers.

Kentucky Bourbon Sauce In a medium heavy saucepan warm 2 tsp. vegetable oil over medium heat. Add 2 slices bacon, cut into ½-inch pieces; cook 3 to 5 minutes or until crisp. Drain; reserve drippings in pan. Add ⅔ cup finely chopped yellow onion to pan; reduce heat to medium-low. Cook 8 to 10 minutes or until soft and golden brown, stirring occasionally. Stir in 1 clove garlic, minced; cook 1 minute. Add ¼ cup bourbon; increase heat to medium-high. Boil 1 minute. Add 1 cup ketchup, ¼ cup water, 3 Tbsp. cider vinegar, 3 Tbsp. unsulfured molasses (not blackstrap), 2 Tbsp. dark steak sauce, 1 Tbsp. spicy brown mustard, 1 tsp. liquid smoke, and ½ tsp. hot pepper sauce. Bring to boiling over medium-high heat. Reduce heat. Simmer, uncovered, 20 minutes or until reduced to 2 cups, stirring occasionally. Remove from heat; stir in cooked bacon.

EACH BURGER *1,011 cal, 60 g fat, 177 mg chol, 2,152 mg sodium, 57 g carb, 2 g fiber, 349 g pro.*

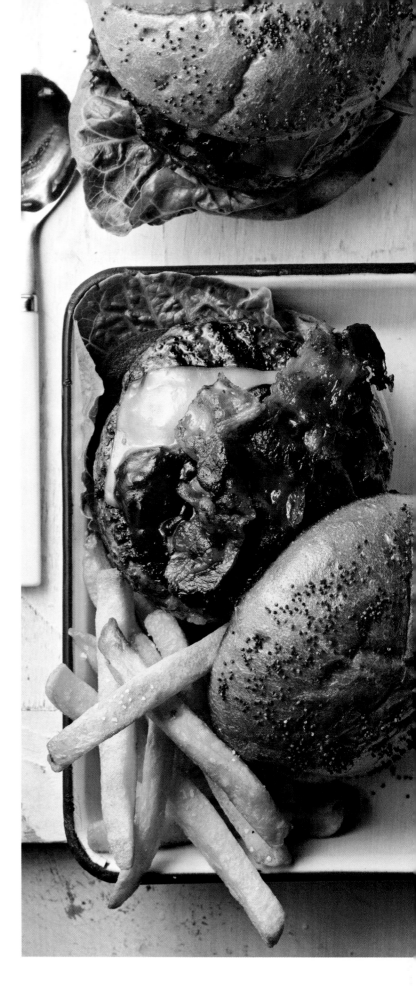

new ways with
GREEN BEANS

Familiar yet seldom extravagant, green beans rise to bold levels in these big-flavor dishes.

Look for slender bright green beans that are crisp and blemish-free. Avoid bulging, leathery-looking beans—they're old! Store beans unwashed in a plastic bag in the fridge up to 1 week.

To trim green beans, stack them on a cutting board with the tough stem ends on one side; press with your palm. Using a chef's knife, make one cut to remove stems. (The tapered tips are tender and fine to eat.)

CHOPPED
GREEN BEAN
SALAD WITH
MANCHEGO

SESAME GREEN
BEAN TART

ITALIAN SAUSAGE &
TWO-BEAN SKILLET

PRESERVE SURPLUS BEANS AT THEIR FRESHEST. TO BLANCH WHOLE OR CUT BEANS, BOIL THEM 3 MINUTES, THEN SUBMERGE IN ICE WATER. DRAIN AND TRANSFER TO FREEZER CONTAINERS, LEAVING ½-INCH HEADSPACE.

SESAME GREEN BEAN TART

This tart gets a kick from gochujang, a spicy, garlicky fermented Korean chili paste. Find it in the Asian section of grocery stores.

HANDS-ON TIME 30 min.
TOTAL TIME 1 hr.

- ½ 14.1-oz. pkg. rolled refrigerated piecrust (1 crust)
- 1 Tbsp. sesame seeds
- 6 slices bacon
- 1 lb. green beans, trimmed and cut into 3- to 4-inch pieces
- ½ tsp. salt
- 1 bunch green onions, sliced (½ cup)
- 2 Tbsp. gochujang (hot pepper paste)
- 2 Tbsp. water
- 5 eggs, lightly beaten
- 1 tsp. toasted sesame oil

1. Preheat oven to 425°F. Let piecrust stand according to package directions. Unroll crust and sprinkle top with sesame seeds. Gently roll over crust with rolling pin to press seeds into dough. Transfer to a 10-inch tart pan with removable bottom, pressing into bottom and up sides; trim even with edge. Line crust with a double thickness of foil. Bake 8 minutes. Remove foil and bake 6 minutes more. Remove to a wire rack; set aside. Reduce heat to 375°F.
2. In an extra-large skillet cook bacon until crisp. Remove and reserve 1 Tbsp. drippings in skillet. Add green beans and salt to skillet. Cook over medium-high heat 5 minutes or until beans are browned and crisp-tender, stirring occasionally. Add green onions; stir to combine. Transfer bean mixture to prepared crust. In a medium bowl combine the gochujang and water; whisk to combine. Add eggs and sesame oil and whisk until combined. Pour egg mixture over beans in crust. Bake 20 minutes or until eggs are set. Crumble bacon and sprinkle over tart. Top with additional sesame seeds. Makes 6 servings.
EACH SERVING *302 cal., 19 g fat, 168 mg chol., 685 mg sodium, 25 g carb., 2 g fiber, 10 g pro.*

CHOPPED GREEN BEAN SALAD WITH MANCHEGO

TOTAL TIME 25 min.

- 1¼ lb. green beans, trimmed and cut into 1-inch pieces
- 6 to 8 oz. Manchego cheese,* divided
- ⅓ cup red wine vinegar
- 1 shallot, peeled and cut up
- ½ tsp. salt
- ¼ tsp. pepper
- ⅓ cup extra-virgin olive oil
- ¾ cup almonds, toasted and chopped (tip, page 37)
- ¾ cup golden raisins
- 2 cups cooked farro**

1. In a large pot cook green beans in lightly salted boiling water 4 minutes or until crisp-tender. Transfer beans with a slotted spoon to a bowl half-filled with ice water to stop cooking; drain and set aside. Meanwhile, finely shred 1 cup of the cheese; cut remaining cheese into bite-size pieces.
2. For dressing, in a blender combine the vinegar, shallot, salt, and pepper. Add the shredded cheese and olive oil; cover and blend until well-combined and creamy. In a large bowl combine the cooked beans, dressing, cheese pieces, almonds, raisins, and farro. Toss to combine. Makes 6 servings.

*Tip Substitute Asiago or Parmesan cheese for the Manchego, if desired.
**Tip For 2 cups cooked farro, in a medium saucepan combine ¾ cup farro and 1½ cups water. Bring to boiling; reduce heat. Cover and simmer 30 minutes or until tender. Drain, if necessary.
EACH SERVING *522 cal., 33 g fat, 28 mg chol., 447 mg sodium, 44 g carb., 8 g fiber, 16 g pro.*

ITALIAN SAUSAGE & TWO-BEAN SKILLET

TOTAL TIME 25 min.

- 1 Tbsp. extra-virgin olive oil
- 4 uncooked Italian sausage links (about 1 lb.)
- 2 shallots, peeled and sliced (½ cup)
- 1 Tbsp. minced garlic (6 cloves)
- 2 cups reduced-sodium chicken broth
- 12 oz. green beans, trimmed
- 1 15- to 16-oz. can cannellini beans, rinsed and drained
- 8 oz. (1¾ cups) cherry tomatoes, halved
- ⅓ cup chopped fresh Italian parsley

In an extra-large skillet heat oil over medium heat. Add sausage; cook 10 minutes, turning occasionally. Add shallots and garlic to skillet with sausages; cook 30 seconds. Add chicken broth and bring to boiling; reduce heat. Simmer, covered, 5 minutes. Add green beans and cannellini beans; return to simmer. Cover; cook 5 minutes or until green beans are crisp-tender and sausage is done (160°F). Stir in tomatoes and parsley. Makes 4 servings.
EACH SERVING *573 cal., 40 g fat, 86 mg chol., 1,345 mg sodium, 28 g carb., 8 g fiber, 26 g pro.*

FAST & FRESH

Easy, healthful recipes for a better dinner tonight.

BLT SALAD WITH CREAMY CHIVE DRESSING

The ultimate summer sandwich turned into a hearty salad, drizzled with a thick and creamy herb dressing that's fresher and tastier than even the best bottle of ranch. Combining the garlic with the vinegar and a pinch of salt mellows its raw flavor in this use-it-on-anything dressing. Make a double batch to keep on hand for veggie dipping throughout the week.

TOTAL TIME 25 min.

12   oz. sliced smoked bacon (14 slices)
2   Tbsp. cider vinegar
1   clove garlic, minced
     Kosher salt
¾   cup sour cream
¼   cup chopped fresh chives
2   Tbsp. extra-virgin olive oil
1   to 2 Tbsp. milk
1   head green leaf or Bibb lettuce, broken into leaves
3   large ripe tomatoes, cut into wedges
2   large croissants or one 8-oz. baguette, sliced and toasted
¼   tsp. black pepper

1. In a large skillet cook bacon until crisp; drain on paper towels. Meanwhile, for dressing, in a small bowl combine vinegar, garlic, and a pinch of kosher salt; let stand 10 minutes. Whisk in sour cream, chives, and olive oil. Thin with milk to desired consistency.
2. On a platter arrange lettuce, tomatoes, croissant slices, and bacon. Season with ¼ tsp. kosher salt and black pepper; drizzle with dressing. Sprinkle with additional chopped fresh chives. Makes 4 servings.
EACH SERVING *428 cal, 24 g fat, 49 mg chol, 890 mg sodium, 35 g carb, 2 g fiber, 16 g pro.*

AMERICA'S FAVORITE SANDWICH IS THE BLT. AND IF EVER A MONTH HAD AN OFFICIAL MEAL, AUGUST WOULD CLAIM THE BLT.

WATERMELON-TOMATO GAZPACHO

CHORIZO & SQUASH QUESADILLAS

Try something unexpected, like this chorizo-squash combo topped with lime-soaked red onions. Chorizo comes in a variety of forms, shapes, and sizes. Dried smoked chorizo is sold in links that can be cut into pepperoni-like slices. Because of its high fat content, cook and drain chorizo before adding it to a dish.

TOTAL TIME 35 min.

1   medium red onion, halved and very thinly sliced (½ cup)
2   Tbsp. fresh lime juice
    Kosher salt
2   dried smoked chorizo sausage links (3¼ oz. total), thinly sliced
8   6-inch corn tortillas
8   oz. Monterey Jack cheese or mild cheddar cheese, shredded
2   small zucchini and/or summer squash, thinly sliced (2 cups)
1   to 2 Tbsp. olive oil
1   cup loosely packed fresh cilantro leaves

1. Preheat oven to 250°F. Place a baking sheet in oven. In a small bowl combine onion, lime juice, and a pinch kosher salt.
2. Meanwhile, heat an extra-large skillet over medium heat. Add chorizo. Cook 5 minutes, stirring occasionally. Transfer to a paper-towel-lined plate. Wipe out skillet.
3. Top four of the tortillas with half the cheese. Arrange zucchini and chorizo on each; top with remaining cheese and remaining tortillas. Add 1 Tbsp. oil to skillet; heat over medium heat. Place two quesadillas in skillet. Cook 2 minutes each side until browned and cheese is melted. Transfer to oven. Repeat with remaining quesadillas, adding more oil, if needed.
4. Stir cilantro into onions. Serve with quesadillas. Makes 4 servings.
EACH SERVING *427 cal, 27 g fat, 63 mg chol, 725 mg sodium, 26 g carb, 4 g fiber, 22 g pro.*

WATERMELON-TOMATO GAZPACHO

In this riff on gazpacho, watermelon replaces traditional cucumber, lime juice offers some zip, and sourdough bread gives the soup body. Top this pretty pink soup with thin slices of watermelon, red onion, and tomato—or serrano chile for a touch of heat. Crumbled feta or a dollop of sour cream would be tangy and delicious, too.

TOTAL TIME 25 min.

2   slices bread, such as sourdough, crusts removed, torn into pieces (1 cup)
3   Tbsp. sherry vinegar or cider vinegar
5   cups cubed watermelon, seeds removed
4   large tomatoes, cored and quartered (about 1½ lb.)
1   medium red sweet pepper, stemmed, seeded, and quartered
1   small red onion, quartered
2   Tbsp. lime juice
1   Tbsp. extra-virgin olive oil
½   tsp. kosher salt

1. In a small bowl combine bread, vinegar, and 1 Tbsp. water. Let stand 10 minutes.
2. Working in batches, in a blender or food processor puree watermelon, bread mixture, tomatoes, sweet pepper, onion, lime juice, olive oil, and salt. Serve immediately or chill up to 2 days. Makes 4 servings.
EACH SERVING *172 cal, 4 g fat, 0 mg chol., 312 mg sodium, 33 g carb, 4 g fiber, 4 g pro.*

CHORIZO & SQUASH
QUESADILLAS

THAI RICE NOODLE
& GRILLED STEAK
SALAD

THAI RICE NOODLE & GRILLED STEAK SALAD

This grilled steak is ultratender, thanks to a lime marinade that's a little bit sweet, a little bit salty, and all kinds of flavorful. Crisp carrot and cucumber plus a handful of mint and basil are a light and bright balance to the juicy meat. Thin slices cut against the grain (across rather than parallel to the muscle fibers) are tender and easy to chew.

HANDS-ON TIME 20 min.
TOTAL TIME 50 min.

3 limes
3 Tbsp. fish sauce
2 Tbsp. sugar
1 Tbsp. vegetable oil
2 cloves garlic, minced
¾ lb. flat iron, flank, or skirt steak
¼ tsp. crushed red pepper
8 oz. flat rice noodles, cooked, drained, and rinsed
2 cups torn green leaf lettuce
1 medium seedless cucumber, thinly sliced
2 carrots, thinly bias-sliced
½ cup basil leaves
⅓ cup mint leaves
½ cup peanuts, coarsely chopped

1. Finely shred zest from two of the limes; juice to get ¼ cup. In a small bowl whisk together 1 Tbsp. of the fish sauce, 1 Tbsp. of the sugar, lime zest, oil, and garlic. Place steak in a resealable plastic bag; pour mixture over steak. Seal bag, turning to coat. Marinate in refrigerator 15 minutes or up to 24 hours. Drain; discard marinade. Grill steak on rack of a covered grill directly over medium heat 15 to 18 minutes or until desired doneness. Cover. Let rest 5 minutes.
2. Meanwhile, for dressing, in a small bowl whisk together lime juice, remaining fish sauce and sugar, 1 Tbsp. water, and red pepper. In a large bowl combine noodles, lettuce, cucumber, carrots, basil, and mint. Thinly slice steak against the grain; arrange on salad. Sprinkle with peanuts. Serve with dressing and remaining lime, cut into wedges. Makes 4 servings.
EACH SERVING *524 cal, 18 g fat, 55 mg chol, 1,138 mg sodium, 65 g carb, 5 g fiber, 28 g pro.*

QUINOA & SUMMER VEGETABLES

QUINOA & SUMMER VEGETABLES

Get ahead by making the quinoa earlier in the week, or save time with prepared quinoa in a microwavable pouch—convenient for hectic nights!

TOTAL TIME 30 min.

1½ cups quinoa, rinsed
¼ cup extra-virgin olive oil
1 medium zucchini, chopped or sliced into ½-inch pieces
 Kosher salt
1 yellow, red, or orange sweet pepper, chopped
½ tsp. smoked paprika
6 green onions, bias-sliced
⅓ cup almonds, toasted and chopped (tip, page 37)
¼ tsp. black pepper
2 cups loosely packed cilantro leaves
 Lemon wedges

1. Cook quinoa according to package directions; transfer to a large bowl.
2. In a large skillet heat oil over medium-high heat. Add zucchini in a single layer. Cook, without stirring, 2 to 3 minutes or until browned on one side. Add a pinch of kosher salt. Stir; reduce heat to medium. Add sweet pepper; cook 2 minutes more or until crisp-tender, stirring occasionally. Stir in paprika; add to quinoa.
3. Stir in green onions, almonds, ¼ tsp. kosher salt, and black pepper. Stir in cilantro just before serving. Serve with lemon wedges. Makes 4 servings.
EACH SERVING *456 cal, 24 g fat, 171 mg sodium, 52 g carb, 9 g fiber, 13 g pro.*

KALAMATA
BAKLAVA

**NASTURTIUM
POPPERS**
Recipe on page 187

FAMILY TREES

When the last olives at Global Gardens are pressed for the season, one item remains on owner Theo Stephan's to-do list: Relax and celebrate the harvest with family and friends over an abundant lunch in her backyard olive grove.

Twenty years into her career as a graphic designer, Dayton, Ohio, native Theo Stephan fell hard for the flowery pastures of California's Santa Ynez Valley.

She purchased a 3-acre plot of land that had a fixer-upper house. Next Theo planted a few olive trees in the backyard, slowly adding guava, pomegranate, persimmon, and Meyer lemon trees. She named her new farm-to-be Global Gardens.

What started with a few trees is now a thriving organic olive oil business and booming weekend farm stand, and a happy life for Theo and her two daughters, Sunita (21) and Anita (20). "They're Nepalese and I'm Greek. Together we've created a global-minded, farm-centric lifestyle that we call 'Caliterranean' and it influences everything—how we live, work, entertain, and even how we make our delicious products."

One of the highlights each year is the rustic luncheon that Theo and her daughters create to celebrate the farm's olive harvest. "We set the table smack-dab in the middle of the olive garden and the menu is our signature low-fuss comfort food," Theo says.

KALAMATA BAKLAVA

"I was in a pinch for an appetizer to take to a party and didn't want to go to the store," Theo says, describing the origin of this recipe. "Being a good Greek girl, I have phyllo in the freezer; the rest I found in the pantry."

HANDS-ON TIME 45 min.
TOTAL TIME 3 hr., 30 min.

- ½ 16-oz. pkg. frozen phyllo dough (14×9-inch rectangles)
- 2 cups finely chopped pitted Kalamata olives
- 1½ cups finely chopped, salted pistachios (6 oz.)
- 4 oz. feta cheese, crumbled (1 cup)
- 1 Tbsp. minced fresh garlic
- 2 tsp. dried oregano, crushed
- ¾ cup extra-virgin olive oil
- 1 orange, zested and juiced
- ¼ cup Sauvignon Blanc or other dry white wine
- 3 Tbsp. honey

1. Thaw phyllo dough according to package directions. Preheat oven to 325°F. For Kalamata filling, in a large bowl combine olives, pistachios, feta, garlic, and oregano. Brush bottom of 13×9-inch baking pan with some of the olive oil. Unroll phyllo. For each layer, place five sheets in prepared pan, brushing each sheet with some of the olive oil. Sprinkle with one-third of the Kalamata filling (about 1⅓ cups). Repeat layers twice.
2. Top with remaining phyllo, brushing each sheet with olive oil. Drizzle with any remaining oil. Using a sharp knife, cut stacked layers into 32 pieces. Bake 40 to 45 minutes or until golden brown. Cool slightly in pan on wire rack.

3. Meanwhile, in a small saucepan combine orange zest and juice, wine, and honey; heat through. Pour over warm baklava; cool 2 hours. Recut into bars. Makes 32 bars.
EACH BAR *139 cal, 11 g fat, 3 mg chol, 293 mg sodium, 8 g carb, 1 g fiber, 2 g pro.*

HALE THE KALE
SALAD

"WE CELEBRATE THE OLIVES WE GROW, THE PRODUCTS WE PRODUCE, AND THE MEALS WE SHARE AT OUR TABLE." THEO STEPHAN

NASTURTIUM POPPERS

Photo on page 184.

In this appetizer, the sharp, spicy flavor of nasturtium blossoms is offset by the lemony herb goat cheese center. Theo uses her lemon-flavor olive oil.

HANDS-ON TIME 15 min.
TOTAL TIME 45 min.

- 2 oz. soft goat cheese (chèvre)
- 2 dried tomatoes (not oil-packed), very finely chopped
- 1 tsp. finely chopped fresh rosemary
- 1 tsp. finely shredded lemon zest
- 2 cloves garlic, minced
- 12 edible fresh nasturtium blossoms or other edible blossoms
- 1 Tbsp. extra-virgin olive oil

1. Let cheese stand at room temperature 30 minutes. In a small bowl stir together tomatoes, rosemary, lemon zest, and garlic. Shape cheese into twelve ¾-inch balls; roll in tomato-herb mixture. Place on plate; cover and chill up to 24 hours.
2. To serve, place each cheese ball in a nasturtium blossom. Drizzle cheese with a small amount of olive oil, avoiding the flower. Makes 12 poppers.
EACH POPPER *24 cal, 2 g fat, 2 mg chol, 22 mg sodium, 0 g carb, 0 g fiber, 1 g pro.*

HALE THE KALE SALAD

HANDS-ON TIME 30 min.
TOTAL TIME 1 hr.

- ½ cup uncooked farro
- ¼ cup whole almonds
- 1 tsp. extra-virgin olive oil
- ¼ tsp. garlic salt
- ¼ tsp. freshly ground black pepper
- 3 Tbsp. extra-virgin olive oil
- 3 Tbsp. lemon juice
- 1 clove garlic, minced
- ½ lb. dinosaur (Tuscan) kale, washed, rinsed, stemmed, and cut lengthwise into ¼-inch ribbons
- 3 small rainbow carrots, peeled
- ½ cup fresh blueberries
- ¼ cup shaved Kasseri or Havarti cheese

1. In saucepan combine farro and 1½ cups water. Bring to boiling; reduce heat. Cover; simmer 30 minutes or until tender. Drain; rinse with cold water until cool.
2. Preheat oven to 350°F. In a shallow baking pan toss almonds with 1 tsp. oil, garlic salt, and pepper. Roast 10 to 12 minutes or until toasted, stirring once. Remove from oven; cool.
3. For dressing, in a screw-top jar combine 3 Tbsp. oil, lemon juice, and garlic. Add salt and pepper. Cover; shake. In a bowl toss kale with 1 Tbsp. dressing. Using clean hands, work dressing into kale 15 seconds. Using vegetable peeler, cut ribbons from carrots. Add farro, carrots, nuts, berries, and cheese to kale in bowl. Add remaining dressing; toss. Makes 6 servings.
EACH SERVING *216 cal, 13 g fat, 5 mg chol, 123 mg sodium, 21 g carb, 5 g fiber, 6 g pro.*

PEPPERED ALMONDS

Photo on page 188.

TOTAL TIME 20 min.

- 2 cups whole raw almonds with skins
- 1 Tbsp. extra-virgin olive oil
- 1 Tbsp. cracked black pepper
- 1 tsp. kosher salt

Preheat oven to 350°F. In a shallow baking pan combine almonds, oil, pepper, and salt. Bake 10 to 12 minutes or until almonds are toasted, shaking pan once. Remove; cool. Store in an airtight container at room temperature up to 2 weeks. Makes 2 cups.
EACH ¼ CUP *224 cal, 20 g fat, 0 mg chol, 141 mg sodium, 8 g carb, 5 g fiber, 8 g pro.*

SPICED PESTO

Photo on page 188.

Unlike old-school pesto, you'll find no cheese and no nuts in Theo's version.

TOTAL TIME 10 min.

- 8 oz. fresh basil, washed and stemmed
- ½ cup extra-virgin olive oil
- 2 tsp. freshly grated nutmeg or 1 tsp. ground nutmeg
- 1 tsp. ground coriander
- 1 tsp. celery seed
- ½ tsp. fine sea salt

Place all ingredients in a food processor. Cover; process until combined. Transfer to a bowl; cover surface with plastic wrap. Chill up to 3 days. Makes 1¼ cups.
To serve as an appetizer Spoon over a slab of feta cheese, sprinkle with lemon zest, and drizzle with additional olive oil.
EACH TABLESPOON *52 cal, 6 g fat, 0 mg chol, 56 mg sodium, 0 g carb, 0 g fiber, 0 g pro.*

PEPPERED ALMONDS
Recipe on page 187

SPICED PESTO
Recipe on page 187

AVOCADO SOUP
Recipe on page 190

THEO TOPS VINEGAR-BRAISED SHORT RIB SANDWICHES WITH A SLATHER OF GARLIC SPREAD AND LOCAL BLUE CHEESE. "SATISFYING AFTER A DAY OF HARVESTING!"

AVOCADO SOUP

Photo on page 189-.

Cold soup is the perfect foil for summer. This one includes Theo's surprise addition of cumin and vanilla.

TOTAL TIME 30 min.

- 1   small fresh jalapeño chile pepper (tip, page 37)
- 2   medium avocados, halved, pitted, peeled, and chopped
- 2   cups reduced-sodium chicken broth
- 3   Tbsp. white balsamic vinegar
- 1   tsp. finely shredded lemon zest
- ½   tsp. ground cumin
- ½   tsp. vanilla
- 1   recipe Sesame Spice Mix

Preheat oven to 450°F. Place jalapeño on baking sheet lined with foil; roast 15 to 20 minutes or until skin is charred, turning occasionally. Wrap in foil; let stand 10 minutes. Stem, peel, and seed jalapeño. Place in blender with avocados, broth, vinegar, zest, cumin, and vanilla. Cover; blend until smooth. Serve at room temperature or cover and chill up to 24 hours. Top with Sesame Spice Mix. Makes 6 servings.

Sesame Spice Mix In a small skillet toast 1 Tbsp. sesame seeds, 1 tsp. coriander seeds, and 1 tsp. cumin seeds over medium heat 2 minutes. Remove; cool. Coarsely crush seeds; combine with 1 tsp. crushed red pepper and 1 tsp. coarsely ground black pepper. Store, covered, at room temperature up to 1 month.

EACH SERVING *101 cal, 7 g fat, 0 mg chol, 189 mg sodium, 8 g carb, 3 g fiber, 2 g pro.*

MONDO SHORT RIB SANDWICHES

"Better than a burger and more sophisticated than a BLT, this huge sandwich is all about comfort food and the perfect glass of California Malbec," Theo says.

HANDS-ON TIME 30 min.

TOTAL TIME 3 hr.

- 1   Tbsp. chopped dried tomatoes
- ½   tsp. garlic powder
- ½   tsp. dried oregano, crushed
- ½   tsp. dried dill weed
- ½   tsp. dried rosemary, crushed
- ½   tsp. kosher salt
- ½   tsp. black pepper
- 3   lb. beef short ribs with bone (about 6)
- 2   Tbsp. extra-virgin olive oil
- 1½ cups lower-sodium beef broth
- ½   cup fig-flavor balsamic vinegar or balsamic vinegar
- 1   large onion, halved and sliced
- 1   recipe Garlic Mash
- 6   round rolls, split and toasted
- 6   oz. blue cheese, softened
     Large basil leaves

1. In a bowl combine dried tomatoes, garlic powder, oregano, dill, rosemary, salt, and black pepper. Sprinkle short ribs with mixture.

2. Heat oil in a 5- to 6-qt. Dutch oven over medium-high heat. Add beef ribs, in batches if necessary, and cook about 8 minutes or until browned on all sides. Add broth and vinegar. Arrange onion over ribs in pot. Bring to boiling. Cover; reduce heat. Simmer about 2½ hours or until ribs are tender and meat pulls away from bone. Remove meat; discard bones. Meanwhile, prepare Garlic Mash.

3. Transfer meat and onion to cutting board; cover to keep warm. Skim fat from cooking liquid.

4. Thickly slice rib meat across the grain. Spread Garlic Mash on cut side of each roll bottom. Top with meat, a drizzling of pan juices, onion, blue cheese, and basil. Add roll tops. Serve with remaining pan juices for dipping. Makes 6 sandwiches.

Garlic Mash Preheat oven to 400°F. Slice off top third of three garlic bulbs; discard. Place bulbs on a piece of foil; drizzle with 1 tsp. extra-virgin olive oil each. Close foil around garlic to form a tight pouch. Place on a baking sheet and roast about 45 minutes or until tender; cool slightly. Remove garlic from foil; squeeze garlic cloves from skins and mash with a fork. Stir in ⅛ tsp. kosher salt and ⅛ tsp. smoked black pepper.

EACH SANDWICH *869 cal, 64 g fat, 135 mg chol, 869 mg sodium, 34 g carb, 2 g fiber, 36 g pro.*

MONDO SHORT RIB
SANDWICHES

THEO'S
CALITINI

PERFECT PICKLED
VEGGIES

THEO'S CALITINI

This California martini gets a spin on trendy shrub cocktails with vinegar ice cubes.

TOTAL TIME 3 hr., 10 min.

1   recipe Fruit Vinegar Cubes
    Ice cubes
¾   cup vodka or gin
4   cups tonic water, chilled
    Fresh mint leaves

Prepare and freeze Fruit Vinegar Cubes. In a large pitcher layer Fruit Vinegar Cubes, ice cubes, and vodka. Add tonic water and garnish with fresh mint. Makes 8 servings.
Fruit Vinegar Cubes Using 2 to 3 cups fruit-flavor vinegar (such as strawberry, orange, apple-ginger, or mango golden balsamic) pour 2 Tbsp. in each compartment of standard ice cube trays. Freeze about 3 hours or until firm.
EACH 6-OUNCE SERVING *322 cal, 0 g fat, 0 mg chol, 17 mg sodium, 53 g carb, 0 g fiber, 0 g pro.*

PERFECT PICKLED VEGGIES

Beautiful pickled vegetables contrast with the richness of braised sandwiches.

HANDS-ON TIME 20 min.
TOTAL TIME 2 hr., 20 min.

1½ to 2 lb. vegetables (such as peeled multicolor baby carrots, sweet onion, cucumber, and/or yellow summer squash) cut into 4- to 5-inch spears
⅛   tsp. salt
⅛   tsp. black pepper
    Dill weed sprigs
3½ to 4 cups fruit-flavor balsamic vinegar, such as mango, blood orange, apricot, or black currant*

Wash vegetables thoroughly; place in two 1-qt. glass canning jars. Add salt, black pepper, and a dill sprig to each jar. In a medium saucepan bring vinegar to a boil; immediately pour over vegetables. Cover; chill 2 hours to 5 days. Makes 12 servings.
EACH SERVING *28 cal, 0 g fat, 0 mg chol, 41 mg sodium, 6 g carb, 1 g fiber, 1 g pro.*
*If you can't find fruit-flavor balsamic vinegar, combine 3 cups white balsamic vinegar with 1 cup fruit juice or nectar.

HOW TO TASTE OLIVE OIL

When buying at Global Gardens farm stand or your favorite food shop, "ideally you choose extra-virgin olive oils by varietal," Theo says. The fruit affects the taste, color, and texture of extra-virgin oils, and whether they're delicate or intense. Follow Theo's tasting directions to find what you like best.

POUR A TABLESPOON INTO A SMALL CUP and warm it in the palm of your hand to help release the oil's aromas and flavors.

SIP AND LET THE OIL COAT YOUR MOUTH to the back of your tongue— "that's where the more sensitive taste buds live," Theo says. Let it linger a few seconds on your palate.

PAY ATTENTION TO THE "FINISH," that lasting essence of oil in your mouth and throat. It may be buttery, fruity, herbaceous, peppery, or bitter.

FOR MAKING DESSERTS, THEO RECOMMENDS USING A MILD EXTRA-VIRGIN OLIVE OIL, LIKE HER ARBEQUINA. ITS SUBTLE FLAVOR COMPLEMENTS THE DELICATE VANILLA IN THIS ZUCCHINI-OLIVE OIL CAKE.

ZUCCHINI-OLIVE OIL CAKE

No family celebration would be complete without their zucchini-olive oil cake. Adds Theo, "It's pure bliss to us and gets topped with olive leaves from our trees to remind us just how lucky we are!"

HANDS-ON TIME 30 min.
TOTAL TIME 2 hr.

- 2½ cups coarsely shredded unpeeled zucchini (1 large)
- 2⅓ cups sugar
- ¾ cup Arbequina olive oil or other extra-virgin olive oil
- 4 eggs
- ⅔ cup unsweetened vanilla almond milk
- 2 tsp. vanilla
- 4 cups cake flour
- 2½ tsp. baking powder
- 1 tsp. kosher salt
- 1 recipe Cream Cheese Frosting Fresh figs and olive leaves (optional)

1. Preheat oven to 350°F. Grease and flour three 8-inch round baking pans; set aside. Spread shredded zucchini on a plate. Blot dry with paper towels.

2. In a large mixing bowl whisk together sugar and oil. Add eggs, almond milk, and vanilla; whisk to combine. Add flour, baking powder, and salt; whisk to combine. Stir in zucchini. Pour into prepared pans (2 cups per pan). Bake 30 minutes or until a toothpick inserted near centers comes out clean. Cool in pans on wire rack 10 minutes. Remove from pans and cool completely.

3. To assemble, place one cake layer on a serving platter. Frost top lightly with some of the Cream Cheese Frosting. Repeat with cake layers and frosting. Frost tops and sides with remaining frosting. Garnish with fresh figs and olive leaves. Makes 16 servings.

Cream Cheese Frosting In a bowl beat 4 oz. cream cheese, softened; 2 Tbsp. butter, softened; 2 Tbsp. extra-virgin olive oil; and 1 tsp. vanilla on medium speed until light and fluffy. Gradually beat in 3 cups powdered sugar until spreading consistency. Makes about 2 cups frosting.

EACH SERVING *492 cal, 17 g fat, 57 mg chol, 284 mg sodium, 80 g carb, 1 g fiber, 5 g pro.*

ZUCCHINI-
OLIVE OIL CAKE

SPICY
WATERMELON
SALAD
Recipe on page 210

september

Expand your cooking repertoire with culinary lessons from chef Jacques Pépin and TV host Padma Lakshmi, and with eggplant recipes that are anything but routine.

199

205

207

at home with
JAQUES PÉPIN

In a special cooking session at his kitchen in Connecticut, cookbook author, artist, and PBS celebrity chef Jacques Pépin shares recipes that call for last-of-summer vegetables.

Jacques Pépin is known for his cooking skills and cookbooks (28 total), and for hosting 14 television series, including one with his close friend Julia Child. He launched his food career at age 13 as an apprentice at Le Grand Hôtel de l'Europe in Bourg-en-Bresse, France. This culinary legend has been painting for almost as long as he has been cooking, and has recently begun selling his paintings and prints.

GLAZED CARROTS WITH OLIVES

"I love the depth of flavor that olives bring to sweet carrots," Jacques says.

TOTAL TIME 20 min.

- 1   lb. carrots, trimmed, peeled, and cut into 2-inch lengths (halve large pieces)
- 1   Tbsp. unsalted butter
- 1   tsp. sugar
- ¼   tsp. salt
- ½   cup pitted Kalamata olives, halved, or oil-cured black olives, pitted
- 2   Tbsp. drained capers
- 2   tsp. minced fresh chives

Combine carrots, butter, sugar, salt, and ⅔ cup water in a large heavy skillet. Cover and cook over high heat about 8 minutes, until water is mostly gone and carrots are tender and glazed. (If any moisture remains in pan, cook uncovered 2 to 3 minutes to slowly evaporate water and glaze carrots.) Add olives and capers; cook 1 minute or until heated through. Sprinkle with chives. Makes 4 servings.

EACH SERVING *119 cal, 7 g fat, 8 mg chol, 725 mg sodium, 12 g carb, 3 g fiber, 1 g pro.*

"I LIKE CARROTS FRESH FROM THE GARDEN, BUT TINY CARROTS HAVEN'T HAD A CHANCE TO DEVELOP THEIR FLAVOR. LET CARROTS GROW TO DELICIOUS!"

THE ART OF PEELING Be efficient. Peel from tip of carrot to top in one single motion. Repeat. Rotate carrot with fingers as you peel, making sure fingers never get higher than cutting surface of carrot.

EQUAL SIZE MATTERS For even cooking it is important that vegetable pieces be the same size. Peel a strip off one side of each carrot so it won't roll, then line up carrots and cut to equal lengths. Halve thicker pieces.

THE MAGIC OF WATER Water is your secret ally and helps you build flavor and cook to perfect tenderness and doneness. Make sure the water doesn't evaporate too quickly. Slow is good.

LEEKS WITH TOMATOES & OLIVE OIL

"Save the water that you boil the leeks in for use in soups. It has a wonderfully intense flavor," Jacques says.

TOTAL TIME 30 min.

4   medium to large leeks (about 1¼ lb.), trimmed (leaving most of the green), split, and washed (tip, below right)
1   ripe tomato (about 7 oz.), peeled, halved, seeded, and cut into ¼-inch pieces
3   Tbsp. olive oil
1   Tbsp. red wine vinegar
1   Tbsp. Dijon-style mustard
1   tsp. Worcestershire sauce
½   tsp. salt
¼   tsp. freshly ground black pepper

1. Bring 2 cups water to a boil in a deep skillet. Add the leeks and bring back to a boil, then reduce the heat and boil gently, covered, 15 minutes or until tender. Drain, reserving liquid, if desired.

2. When they are cool enough to handle, squeeze the leeks to extract most of the remaining liquid (reserve it with the rest of the liquid). Cut the leeks into 2-inch pieces and arrange them in a gratin dish, mixing the white and green parts. Mix the tomato, oil, vinegar, mustard, Worcestershire, salt, and pepper. Spoon over leeks. Serve at room temperature. Makes 4 servings.

EACH SERVING *155 cal, 10 g fat, 0 mg chol, 412 mg sodium, 15 g carb, 2 g fiber, 2 g pro.*

"WHEN I WAS GROWING UP, LEEKS WERE THE POOR MAN'S ASPARAGUS—MILD-FLAVORED, BUT STILL ELEGANT."

THE WAY TO TRIM Trim off root end; remove outer leaves. Rotate leek and trim each leaf to the point where dark green shifts to lighter green. Cut leek lengthwise into quarters, from start of white part to tip.

DIVIDE AND WASH After leeks have been split lengthwise, but are still whole, gently spread the leaves open. Rinse thoroughly in water to remove any dirt and sand that collected in leaves as they grew.

CORN & SHALLOTS WITH SUN-DRIED TOMATOES

"Like most people, my wife and I usually eat local fresh sweet corn on the cob, cooked for a few seconds in boiling water," Jacques explains. *"But when the urge for a change hits during corn season, I remove the kernels for use in fritters and soup, or simply sauté them, as here."*

TOTAL TIME 20 min.

4	ears sweet corn, as young and fresh as possible, husked
1	Tbsp. peanut oil
1	Tbsp. unsalted butter
¼	cup chopped shallots
¼	cup diced (½ inch) sun-dried tomatoes in oil
½	tsp. freshly ground black pepper
¼	tsp. salt
¼	tsp. coarsely chopped fresh cilantro

Using a sharp knife or mandoline, slice the kernels off the ears of corn. (You should have about 3 cups kernels.) Heat the oil and butter in a large skillet until very hot. Add the shallots and sauté 30 seconds, then add the corn kernels and cook over high heat, tossing, about 2½ minutes. Add the tomatoes, pepper, salt, and cilantro, and cook 30 seconds longer. Mix well and serve. Makes 4 servings.

EACH SERVING *155 cal, 8 g fat, 8 mg chol, 179 mg sodium, 20 g carb, 3 g fiber, 4 g pro.*

KNIFE SKILLS Don't drag or push your knife through the corn kernels; use a long slicing motion. Start at the base of the blade, then slice up through corn and finish near tip of blade. Let the knife do the work.

"PEOPLE DON'T USUALLY EAT CORN IN FRANCE, BUT I HAVE ALWAYS LOVED IT. I GOT MY TASTE FOR IT FROM GAUDES, A SOUP IN THE FARMS OF BRESSE."

VELVET SPINACH

This side dish works overtime to dress up any presentation as well as add refreshing flavor. "I swirl it on the plate and top it with roasted chicken or vegetables," Jacques says. "Sometimes I serve it in a ramekin on the side."

TOTAL TIME 20 min.

1   lb. baby spinach
3   Tbsp. unsalted butter
¾   tsp. salt
¾   tsp. freshly ground black
     pepper

1. Bring 3 cups water to a boil in a very large skillet. Add the spinach and push it down into the water to wilt it. Bring the water back to a boil and boil the spinach, uncovered, about 1 minute.
2. Drain the spinach in a colander, reserving a little of the cooking water, and transfer to a blender. Add the butter, salt, and pepper, and blend until the spinach is finely pureed. If the mixture is too thick to process properly, add 1 or 2 Tbsp. of the reserved cooking water and process until smooth. Makes 4 servings.
EACH SERVING *104 cal, 9 g fat, 23 mg chol, 524 mg sodium, 4 g carb, 3 g fiber, 3 g pro.*

"SPINACH! SO SIMPLE; SO VIBRANT. THE BEST IS PREWASHED ORGANIC BABY SPINACH. IT IS JUST AS GOOD IN A SALAD AS IN OUR RECIPE."

START WITH A BOX Ready-to-use prewashed spinach is a great choice that saves time. Gently sort through it to remove any damaged leaves.

SHRINKING SPINACH Sometimes the trick is making spinach fit into the pan. If it overfills the pan, firmly press it down. It will shrink as it cooks.

new ways with
EGGPLANT

If parmigiana is the first (and only) thing that comes to mind when you think of this purple produce, prepare to expand your vocabulary.

Choose plump, firm eggplants that feel heavy for their size and have smooth, glossy skins and bright green stems. Eggplants are perishable, so store them whole and unwashed in the refrigerator crisper drawer. Use within four days of purchasing.

While the skin of small, young eggplants is edible, the skin on larger, more mature eggplants can become bitter. The flesh discolors rapidly after peeling, so if you opt to go without skin, remove it right before cooking.

Do all eggplants need to sweat—a technique using salt to extract moisture—to reduce bitterness? Most are fine to eat fresh, but sometimes older ones have a strong bitter taste. Lay slices or cubes on paper towels and sprinkle all sides with salt. Top with more paper towels and something (such as a plate) to weigh them down. Let stand 20 minutes, then rinse, pat dry, and use as desired.

LEMON GRILLED EGGPLANT SALAD

THAI EGGPLANT WITH BASIL & TOMATOES

GREEK EGGPLANT FRIES

SAY GOOD-BYE TO MUSHY EGGPLANT AND FALL IN LOVE WITH THIS VERSATILE VEGETABLE, LONG PRIZED FOR ITS BEAUTY.

LEMON GRILLED EGGPLANT SALAD

HANDS-ON TIME 20 min.
TOTAL TIME 50 min.

1 preserved lemon, halved
½ cup chopped fresh Italian parsley
¾ cup extra-virgin olive oil
¼ cup white wine vinegar
¼ tsp. ground black pepper
1 large eggplant (1½ lb.), sliced crosswise ½-inch thick
1 cup whole milk ricotta cheese
2 cups cooked Israeli couscous*

1. For dressing, juice preserved lemon; set aside juice. Remove and discard lemon pulp; chop rind. (You can substitute the juice and zest of 1 fresh lemon here.) In a bowl combine preserved lemon juice and rind, chopped parsley, ½ cup of the olive oil, vinegar, and pepper; set aside. Generously brush eggplant slices with remaining ¼ cup oil. Grill eggplant on rack of a covered grill directly over medium-high heat 5 to 7 minutes or just until tender, turning once. Transfer eggplant slices to a 2-qt. square baking dish. Pour dressing over slices; turn to coat. Let stand 30 minutes, gently turning slices halfway through.
2. Serve eggplant and dressing over ricotta cheese and couscous. Sprinkle with additional parsley.
*Tip Place ¾ cup uncooked Israeli couscous and 1¼ cups water in a medium saucepan. Bring to boiling; reduce heat. Simmer, covered, 10 minutes. Remove from heat. Let stand 2 minutes. Makes 4 servings.
EACH SERVING *637 cal, 49 g fat, 31 mg chol, 532 mg sodium, 38 g carb, 6 g fiber, 13 g pro.*

THAI EGGPLANT WITH BASIL & TOMATOES

HANDS-ON TIME 25 min.
TOTAL TIME 35 min.

½ cup reduced-sodium chicken broth
¼ cup reduced-sodium soy sauce
1 Tbsp. fish sauce
1 Tbsp. minced garlic (6 cloves)
1 tsp. cornstarch
2 Tbsp. coconut oil
1 large eggplant (1½ lbs.), coarsely chopped (7 cups)
12 oz. roma tomatoes, chopped
1 cup lightly packed basil leaves, chopped
1 to 2 fresh jalapeño chile peppers, seeded (if desired) and sliced (tip, page 37)
   Hot cooked rice noodles

1. In a small bowl combine the broth, soy sauce, fish sauce, garlic, and cornstarch. Set aside.
2. In an extra-large skillet heat coconut oil over medium-high heat. Add eggplant and cook 2 to 3 minutes or just until starting to brown, stirring frequently. Reduce heat to medium. Add tomatoes, basil, and chile peppers. Add broth mixture; cook and stir until bubbly. Cook and stir 2 minutes more. Serve over noodles. Makes 4 servings.
EACH SERVING *301 cal, 8 g fat, 0 mg chol, 1,059 mg sodium, 52 g carb, 7 g fiber, 7 g pro.*

GREEK EGGPLANT FRIES

HANDS-ON TIME 30 min.
TOTAL TIME 45 min.

   Nonstick cooking spray
3 oz. feta cheese, crumbled
1 5.3- to 7-oz. container plain Greek yogurt
2 Tbsp. finely chopped fresh oregano
2 Tbsp. water
1 Tbsp. lemon juice
1 large eggplant (1½ lb.), peeled if desired
1½ tsp. salt
¼ tsp. black pepper
½ cup all-purpose flour
3 eggs, lightly beaten
2 cups panko bread crumbs
⅔ cup grated Parmesan cheese
¾ cup purchased olive tapenade or bruschetta topper (optional)

1. Preheat oven to 450°F. Lightly coat two large baking sheets with cooking spray; set aside. In a small bowl combine crumbled feta, plain Greek yogurt, oregano, water, and lemon juice.
2. Cut the eggplant into 3- to 4-inch ½-inch wide sticks. Sprinkle with ½ tsp. of the salt and the pepper. Let stand 10 minutes. Blot dry with paper towels.
3. In a shallow dish combine flour and remaining 1 tsp. salt. Place eggs in another dish. In a third dish combine panko and Parmesan.
4. Working in batches, place eggplant sticks into flour, egg, then panko mixture; arrange on prepared baking sheets. Coat with nonstick cooking spray. Bake in batches 15 minutes or until browned and crisp. Top with yogurt and olive tapenade. Makes 8 servings.
EACH SERVING *187 cal, 7 g fat, 90 mg chol, 710 mg sodium, 21 g carb, 3 g fiber, 10 g pro.*

eat this now
SHAKSHUKA

Shak-what? Shakshuka (shahk-SHOO-kah) is the quintessential Israeli breakfast.

SHAKSHUKA

At its most basic, the dish is eggs cooked on a rich simmering tomato sauce with onions, peppers, and a cumin spice mixture. The genius of it is that you can skew the sauce in any direction your mood (or fridge) dictates. Brown mushrooms with the peppers or toss a handful of spinach into the sauce before adding eggs.

HANDS-ON TIME 15 min.
TOTAL TIME 45 min.

2   Tbsp. olive oil
1   large onion, chopped (1 cup)
1   large red sweet pepper, seeded
    and chopped
1   jalapeño chile pepper, stemmed,
    seeded, and chopped (tip, page 37)
3   cloves garlic, sliced
1   tsp. ground cumin
1   tsp. sweet paprika
1   tsp. ground turmeric
½   tsp. kosher salt
¼   tsp. freshly ground black pepper

1   28-oz. can whole plum tomatoes
    with juices, coarsely chopped
6   eggs
    Feta cheese, crumbled
    Fresh cilantro and/or oregano

1. In a large deep skillet heat oil over medium heat. Add onion, sweet pepper, jalapeño, garlic, cumin, paprika, turmeric, salt, and black pepper. Cook and stir 10 minutes or until vegetables are soft but not browned. Stir in undrained tomatoes. Bring to boiling; reduce heat. Simmer, uncovered, 10 minutes or until slightly thickened, stirring occasionally.
2. Crack eggs, one at a time, into a small dish and carefully pour into sauce. Cover; reduce heat. Cook 5 to 10 minutes or until whites are set and yolks are of desired doneness. Top with feta and cilantro and/or oregano. Makes 6 servings.
EACH SERVING *174 cal, 11 g fat, 192 mg chol, 478 mg sodium, 11 g carb, 4 g fiber, 9 g pro.*

THIS SKILLET DISH IS EASY TO CUSTOMIZE—CHANGE SPICES OR CHOP AND TOSS IN WHATEVER VEGETABLES YOU HAVE ON HAND.

PURE PADMA

On her Rooftop terrace, Top Chef host Padma Lakshmi entertains with ease, warmth, and color.

When TV star and cookbook author Padma Lakshmi bought her New York City condo, the centerpiece of its terrace was a hot tub with a built-in TV. "It was this weird '70s bachelor pad," she says. But not for long.

Out went the tub (and TV), and in went peach and crabapple trees, blueberry bushes, strawberry plants, "lots of funky herbs," and an arrangement of outdoor spaces that have transformed the 1,000-square-foot terrace into her favorite place to entertain. "It's inspired by nearly every secret garden I've ever read about," she says.

As host of Bravo's popular Top Chef, Padma judges the work of some of the nation's most talented up-and-coming restaurant chefs. And when she's not working and traveling, her favorite place to eat is right at home. She loves to cook—for herself and her 6-year-old daughter, Krishna, and for family and friends at weekend gatherings of all sizes. It might be a show-up-in-your-sneakers kind of cookout to get feedback on new recipes that she's testing, a standing-room-only dance party, or an elegant sit-down affair for a dozen guests under the moonlight.

"I am always aiming for something breezy and relaxed," she says. For a last-hurrah-of-summer party, she'll serve food buffet style and scatter large comfy pillows around the terrace, along with other textiles she has hunted

and gathered over the decades from India, Indonesia, and Morocco. As for the food, Padma strikes the perfect balance: deceptively simple crowd-pleasing seasonal recipes—each with its own easy and surprising twist that often involves adding tang (lots of citrus) and herbs and spices (such as kaffir, clove, dill, or cumin).

All this breeziness works because Padma has thought through every detail. The best way to make parties feel relaxed, she says, is to be fully engaged once the first guest arrives. That means she cooks almost everything ahead of time, leaving her at least a half hour to clean up, jump in the shower, and get dressed. Then she can focus on helping people interact and enjoy themselves.

"To me, being a great hostess is about more than just worrying about the menu and the decor," she says. "It's about being warm and engaged, being the person that isn't embarrassed to start a conversation. You have to take a person by the hand, walk him across the garden, and say, 'I want you to meet this person.'"

To get her gatherings started, she will leave some last-minute food prep, such as picking herbs, as an ice-breaking activity for guests. "Every meal is a celebration. I draw my inspiration from my friends, my travels, even colors and flavors, and let the menu bring them all together!" Padma says.

PADMA'S TRAVELS AND HER CHILDHOOD IN INDIA SPILL OVER INTO THE EVERYDAY MEALS SHE COOKS AND THE GATHERINGS SHE HOSTS. FOR PADMA, EATING CAN BE LIKE TRAVELING, BRINGING FLAVOR TO THE TABLE THROUGH NEW EXPERIENCES AS WELL AS MEMORIES.

SPICY WATERMELON SALAD

A simple watermelon and cucumber salad gets a punch from chiles and yuzu juice. "I think everything should have a little bit of sweet, a little bit of tart, a little bit of hot," Padma says. "The perfect bite should stimulate every part of your palate." Yuzu is a fragrant Asian citrus that can be purchased at Asian markets, larger supermarkets, or online.

TOTAL TIME 25 min.

4   cups watermelon, cut into 1-inch cubes
2   cups cucumber, peeled, seeded, and cut into ½-inch crescents
2   serrano chiles, thinly sliced (tip, page 37)
2   Tbsp. extra-virgin olive oil
1   Tbsp. yuzu juice or fresh lime juice
1   Tbsp. balsamic vinegar
1   tsp. lime zest
     Salt
     Black pepper
½   cup crumbled feta cheese
½   cup fresh mint leaves, torn

1. On a large platter arrange watermelon cubes surrounded by a ring of cucumber slices with curved sides out. Place serrano chiles on cucumber.
2. In a small bowl mix olive oil, yuzu juice, balsamic vinegar, lime zest, and salt and black pepper to taste with a fork.
3. Drizzle the dressing over salad. Top with feta and fresh mint just before serving. Makes 6 servings.
EACH SERVING *116 cal, 7 g fat, 11 mg chol, 217 mg sodium, 11 g carb, 1 g fiber, 3 g pro.*

BBQ CHICKEN WITH CHAATPATI CHUTNEY

Photo on page 212.

For Padma, chaatpati is a wonderful thing that she calls Indian umami. "This dark and gooey sludge became my first mother sauce of sorts because it instantly woke up any bland or boring ingredient and made it finger-sucking good," Padma says. Look for fresh curry leaves at Asian markets.

HANDS-ON TIME 20 min.
TOTAL TIME 1 hr., 5 min.

1   4- to 5-lb. chicken, cut into 8 pieces
1   Tbsp. canola oil
1   tsp. finely crushed black peppercorns
4   tsp. kosher salt
20   dates (about 4½ oz.), pitted and finely chopped (1 cup)
¼   cup natural tamarind concentrate or 2 Tbsp. Worcestershire sauce with 1 Tbsp. brown sugar
2   tsp. ground cumin
2   tsp. ground coriander
1   to 2 tsp. cayenne
     Fresh curry leaves (optional)

1. Prepare grill for medium indirect heat. Lightly season chicken with canola oil, black pepper, and 2 tsp. of the salt. Using a paring knife, make two slits in the meatiest part of each piece to better absorb the sauce.
2. For Chutney, in a 2-qt. saucepan bring 4 cups water to a boil. Add the dates, tamarind concentrate, cumin, coriander, cayenne, and remaining 2 tsp. salt; gently boil over medium heat, stirring frequently with a wooden spoon and mashing dates to create a thick pulpy mixture. Begin checking consistency at 30 minutes. (The finished chutney should look like a loose jam or thick barbecue sauce, and it will cook 30 to 50 minutes total.)

3. Meanwhile, grill chicken on rack of covered grill over indirect heat 35 to 45 minutes (175°F for wings, legs, and thighs), or 50 to 60 minutes (170°F for breasts). Brush with chutney; move chicken over direct heat and grill 1 to 2 minutes more or until chicken is lightly charred, turning frequently.
4. Transfer chicken to a serving platter. Top with fresh curry leaves, if desired. Pass remaining chutney. Makes 6 servings.
EACH SERVING *502 cal, 32 g fat, 153 mg chol, 730 mg sodium, 13 g carb, 1 g fiber, 39 g pro.*

PADMA'S GRILLED CORN

Photo on page 213.
For smoked paprika, chile peppers are slow-dried over a wood fire before being ground.

TOTAL TIME 10 min.

6   ears fresh sweet corn, shucked
3   lemons, halved
2   tsp. fleur de sel or kosher salt
2   tsp. smoked paprika

Heat grill to medium-hot. Grill corn on covered rack directly over heat 6 to 8 minutes or until corn starts to blacken. Rub each ear with lemon half. Stir together the fleur de sel and smoked paprika. Evenly, pinch by pinch with your fingers, sprinkle approximately ½ tsp. onto each ear of corn. Serve warm. Makes 6 servings.
EACH SERVING *90 cal, 1 g fat, 0 mg chol, 795 mg sodium, 23 g carb, 5 g fiber, 4 g pro.*

SPICY
WATERMELON
SALAD

**BBQ CHICKEN
WITH CHAATPATI
CHUTNEY**
Recipe on page 210

PADMA'S
GRILLED CORN
Recipe on page 210

HEIRLOOM
TOMATO
SALAD

HEIRLOOM TOMATO SALAD

Seasoning the tomatoes first— with salt, a drizzle of olive oil, and lemon—brings out fresh flavor. Padma then adds her unique touches to this version of an heirloom tomato salad: cool dill, cilantro, and peanuts spiced with sharp white pepper. "When I started making this salad, I thought of one I love from South India that's made with boiled peanuts," she says. Look for heirloom tomatoes at farmers markets or the produce section of large supermarkets.

TOTAL TIME 20 min.

4	large heirloom tomatoes (about 3 lb.), cut into ½-inch slices or wedges
3	to 4 Tbsp. extra-virgin olive oil
2	Tbsp. fresh lemon juice
	Fleur de sel or salt
½	cup packed fresh dill weed
½	cup packed fresh cilantro
1	cup raw peanuts
½	tsp. white pepper

1. Arrange tomatoes on a platter and drizzle with oil, lemon juice, and salt.
2. Wash and drain herbs, then dry between paper towels. Heat an iron wok on the stove top until hot. Dry-roast raw peanuts, 2 to 4 minutes over medium heat, so they cook on all sides. In the last minute of cooking, add ¾ tsp. fleur de sel and white pepper.
3. Chop herbs and combine with roasted peanuts. Sprinkle peanut and herb mixture over tomatoes. Serve topped with additional herbs. Makes 6 servings.
EACH SERVING *242 cal, 19 g fat, 0 mg chol, 359 mg sodium, 13 g carb, 5 g fiber, 8 g pro.*

PADMA'S PARTY PUNCH

PADMA'S PARTY PUNCH

"It is important to me to create a colorful atmosphere for entertaining and relaxing at home with friends," Padma says. Her signature punch is the result of much experimentation— grapefruit, tangerine, and lime juices combined with vodka, soda water, and citrus-flavor soda. An ice ring of edible flowers decorates and cools the punch.*

TOTAL TIME 20 min.

1½	cups fresh grapefruit juice
1½	cups fresh tangerine juice
1½	cups vodka
⅓	cup pickled jalapeño juice
⅓	cup fresh lime juice
12	to 15 kaffir lime leaves or strips of lime peel
1½	cups citrus-flavor soda, such as Fresca
	Edible orchids or other flowers

In a large serving or punch bowl mix grapefruit juice, tangerine juice, vodka, jalapeño juice, lime juice, and kaffir lime leaves. Stir together until combined; stir in soda. Garnish with orchids. Makes 6½ cups.
EACH 4-OZ. SERVING *84 cal, 0 g fat, 0 mg chol, 93 mg sodium, 6 g carb, 0 g fiber, 0 g pro..*

"MOST OF ALL, REMEMBER TO COOK WITH YOUR HEART, BECAUSE COOKING IS A CELEBRATION, AND FOOD IS LOVE."

PEACHES IN RED WINE

BRAISED PLUM GRANITA

Padma cooks juicy plums to concentrate flavor before turning them into an ice granita. "I mix red and black plums to get the color I like. Leaving the skin on while cooking intensifies the tang and color. It's decadent topped with whipped cream," *Padma says.*

HANDS-ON TIME 1 hr., 10 min.
TOTAL TIME 6 hr.

- 6 ripe plums or wild garden plums just about to fall off the tree
- 1 cup sugar
- 2 to 3 whole cloves
- 1½ cups water
- 1 cup red Burgundy wine
- ½ cup cold heavy cream
- 1½ tsp. sugar

1. Remove the pits and chop the plums into very small bits, saving as much of the juice as you can and retaining the skin.
2. In a deep saucepan heat the plums, sugar, and cloves over medium heat, turning often to coat plums well. After about 5 minutes, slowly add the water, ¼ cup at a time; reduce heat to low. Simmer 15 minutes, stirring occasionally.
3. Add wine and simmer another 20 minutes. If the mixture is too thick and pastelike, add additional water, 1 Tbsp. at a time. Pour the mixture into a 13×9-inch baking dish; cool. Cover with plastic wrap and freeze 4 to 6 hours.
4. Remove dish from freezer. With a long fork, scrape frozen surface until little pebbles form. Using a hand mixer, beat the mixture gently and quickly so it doesn't melt too much; refreeze.
5. Whip the cream in a bowl with a hand mixer. When it starts to thicken add sugar and beat until firm. Right before serving, repeat fork process and spoon granita into chilled glasses. Top with whipped cream. Makes 5 cups.
EACH ½-CUP SERVING *159 cal, 4 g fat, 14 mg chol, 4 mg sodium, 26 g carb, 1 g fiber, 1 g pro.*

PEACHES IN RED WINE

"This is an ideal recipe to marinate ahead and serve during peach season," *Padma says.*

HANDS-ON TIME 10 min.
TOTAL TIME 2 hr., 10 min.

- 3 cinnamon sticks
- 5 ripe peaches, peeled, pitted, and quartered
- 1½ cups Recioto red dessert wine or port
  Fresh herbs or edible flowers

Place cinnamon sticks in a bowl and place peaches on top. Pour in wine, making sure to cover all the fruit. Marinate in refrigerator at least 2 hours. Serve topped with fresh herbs or flowers. Makes 6 servings.
EACH SERVING *144 cal, 0 g fat, 0 mg chol, 2 mg sodium, 20 g carb, 2 g fiber, 1 g pro.*

BRAISED
PLUM
GRANITA

SLOW COOKER
PUMPKIN-
BLUEBERRY BREAD
Recipe on page 244

october

When cool weather calls for roasting, bring out the best in squash for both savory and sweet recipes. Boldly spice up weeknight meals and take a nod from Gesine Bullock-Prado and her fall-inspired menu.

227

229

235

how to cook
PAELLA

Spain's famous culinary creation is the definitive choose-your-own adventure, with adaptations to please the palate or the season.

**CHICKEN, SHRIMP &
CHORIZO PAELLA**
Recipe on page 222

PAELLA (pah-AY-uh) is endlessly adaptable; all versions share a basic blueprint: short-grain rice with a flavor base of olive oil, onions, tomatoes, and garlic cooked in a wide, round vessel (paellera, which gives the dish its name). There's saffron and often smoked paprika, along with a jumble of meat, seafood, and/or vegetables. Ultimately this dish is about the rice: Cooked al dente, it's tender while retaining some bite. The final dish is dry on top with a chewy, caramelized crust on the bottom—so prized it has a name: soccarat. In Spain, paella is served straight from the pan, everyone working from the crisp edges to the moist center. It's a true one-dish showstopper.

PAELLA BASICS

RICE This is the star of the show. Short-grain Spanish rices such as bomba, Valencia, and Calasparra are ideal because they have a high starch content to absorb lots of liquid while retaining shape and texture. Italian arborio rice (used for risotto) is a suitable substitution.

SOFRITO A staple in Spanish cooking, sofrito is an aromatic mix of tomatoes, onions, garlic, and olive oil cooked down to the consistency of paste. Many paellas call for paprika, which gives rice a rich smokiness.

SAFFRON Paella isn't paella without saffron, which gives rice its bright yellow color. Although expensive, a tiny bit goes a long way. Steeping the threads in warm water is essential to allow flavor to bloom.

CHICKEN, SHRIMP & CHORIZO PAELLA

If you want to try your hand at paella but aren't ready to invest in a paella pan, use a 12-inch skillet instead. Prepare as directed except use 1½ cups rice and 4 cups chicken broth.

HANDS-ON TIME 25 min.
TOTAL TIME 1 hr.

½	tsp. saffron threads, crushed
2	Tbsp. olive oil
1	lb. skinless, boneless chicken thighs, cut into 2-inch pieces
4	oz. cooked, smoked Spanish-style chorizo sausage, sliced
1	medium onion, chopped
4	cloves garlic, minced
1	cup coarsely grated tomatoes (about 1 lb.)
1	Tbsp. smoked sweet paprika
6	cups reduced-sodium chicken broth
½	tsp. salt
2	cups short grain Spanish rice, such as bomba, Calasparra, or Valencia
12	large shrimp, peeled and deveined
8	oz. frozen peas, thawed
	Chopped green olives (optional)
	Chopped Italian parsley

1. In a small bowl combine saffron and ¼ cup hot water; let stand 10 minutes.

2. Meanwhile, in a 15-inch paella pan heat oil over medium-high heat. Add chicken to pan. Cook, turning occasionally, until chicken is browned, about 5 minutes. Add chorizo. Cook 1 minute. Transfer all to a plate. Add onion and garlic to pan. Cook and stir 2 minutes. Add tomatoes and paprika. Cook and stir 5 minutes or until tomatoes are thickened and almost pastelike.

3. Return chicken and chorizo to pan. Add broth, saffron mixture, and salt; bring to boiling over high heat. Add rice to pan, stirring once to evenly distribute. Cook, without stirring, until rice has absorbed most of the liquid, about 12 minutes. (If the pan is bigger than the burner, rotate every few minutes to ensure the rice cooks evenly.) Reduce heat to low. Cook, without stirring, 5 to 10 minutes more until all liquid is absorbed and rice is al dente. Top with shrimp and peas. Turn heat to high. Cook without stirring, 1 to 2 minutes more (edges should look dry and a crust should form on bottom). Remove. Cover pan with foil. Let rest 10 minutes before serving. Top with olives, if desired, and parsley. Makes 6 to 8 servings.

EACH SERVING *577 cal, 17 g fat, 322 mg chol, 927 mg sodium, 63 g carb, 5 g fiber, 41 g pro.*

1 BROWN THE MEAT The goal is to brown the pieces and get crispy bits stuck to the pan (flavor!). Remove and set aside to return to the pan later.

2 SLOW DOWN Don't rush the sofrito step—cooking the mixture develops intense flavor. Cook until thick and darkened; it should look like tomato paste.

3 DEVELOP A FILM As the rice absorbs the liquid, a film will develop over the top. This film traps steam so the rice cooks evenly.

4 DO NOT STIR Unlike risotto, leave the paella alone once the rice is added. To make sure the rice cooks evenly, rotate the pan every few minutes.

5 CRANK THE HEAT The socarrat, or crust, develops as the rice cooks, but a little blast of heat at the end ensures a crisp brown layer on the bottom.

6 LET IT REST Allow 10 minutes to rest under foil before serving. The rice will continue to absorb any remaining moisture as it stands.

PERSONAL PAN PAELLA Switch up the meat, seafood, and veggies to customize paella to your liking. Below is inspiration.

KALE & MUSHROOM

Inspired by clean-out-the-fridge night, paella can be a tasty vegetarian option when you swap vegetable broth for chicken broth. Add a chopped poblano pepper and mushrooms along with the rice, sprinkle on a bunch of sautéed kale at the end and, if you please, top the dish with a few fried eggs.

MIXED SEAFOOD

To wow company, the seafood trio of squid, mussels, and clams exclaims special occasion. Opt for fish stock, toss in a chopped sweet pepper with the rice, and scatter green onions and cherry tomatoes over the top for a colorful finish.

PORK & BUTTERNUT

Paella adapts to suit any season. Try this fall favorite: Pork tenderloin assumes the protein role, canned chickpeas are stirred in with the rice, and roasted butternut squash makes its way in during the last couple minutes of cooking. Toasted hazelnuts and sage leaves seal the autumnal deal.

eat this now
SAVORY OATS

The influence of creamy Asian rice dishes such as congee, takes familiar porridge to spunky, savory, and intriguing.

SESAME-GINGER OATS WITH MUSHROOMS & CHARRED GREEN ONIONS

Oats are negotiable in this savory porridge; other grains make a hearty base too. Try quinoa, buckwheat, or barley.

HANDS-ON TIME 15 min.
TOTAL TIME 45 min.

- 1 cup reduced-sodium chicken broth or water*
- ½ cup steel-cut oats
- 2 tsp. toasted sesame oil
- 1 cup assorted mushrooms, chopped or sliced
- 1 tsp. minced fresh ginger
- 2 green onions, cut into 1- to 2-inch pieces
- 1 tsp. reduced-sodium soy sauce
- Crushed red pepper

1. In a small saucepan bring broth to boiling. Stir in oats. Reduce heat to medium-low. Cook, uncovered, 25 to 30 minutes or until oats are tender and mixture is thickened and creamy, stirring occasionally.
2. Meanwhile, in an 8-inch skillet, heat 1 tsp. of the oil over medium heat. Add the mushrooms and ginger. Cook and stir 3 to 4 minutes or until tender. Transfer to a bowl. Add remaining oil to skillet. Increase heat to medium-high. Add green onions. Cook 1 to 2 minutes or until charred. Remove from heat.
3. Stir mushrooms into oats. Top with soy sauce, green onions, and crushed red pepper. Makes 1 serving.
*For creamier consistency, add up to 1 cup more broth or water.
EACH SERVING *474 cal, 15 g fat, 0 mg chol, 748 mg sodium, 65 g carb, 12 g fiber, 21 g pro.*

new ways with ACORN SQUASH

This autumn staple pairs well with bold flavors from around the world.

Find acorn squash in green, gold, and white varieties, choosing those that feel heavy for their size. The heavier the squash, the more edible flesh it contains.

Use a sharp heavy-duty chef's knife to slice a squash. To halve lengthwise, carefully pierce squash near the stem with the knife tip until it penetrates the tough skin through to the center. Cut all the way around to the stem on the opposite side, then pull halves apart.

Don't ditch the seeds! Toast them for a crunchy snack or a topping for soups and salads. See recipe, page 227.

WARM INDIAN-
SPICED ACORN
SQUASH SALAD

CHORIZO-
STUFFED
SQUASH

COCONUT ACORN
SQUASH & CARROT
SOUP

BECAUSE OF ITS HARD PROTECTIVE SHELL, ACORN SQUASH GETS A GOLD STAR FOR SHELF LIFE. IT WILL KEEP FRESH UP TO TWO MONTHS IN A COOL, DARK PLACE.

CHORIZO-STUFFED SQUASH

HANDS-ON TIME 25 min.
TOTAL TIME 1 hr., 5 min.

1   Tbsp. olive oil
2   medium acorn squash
1   tsp. chili powder
½   tsp. salt
1   small poblano chile pepper (tip, page 37)
1   Anaheim chile pepper (tip, page 37)
4   oz. cooked Spanish chorizo, chopped
½   cup golden raisins
2   oz. Cotija cheese, chopped
2   tsp. chopped fresh oregano

1. Preheat oven to 400°F. Drizzle a shallow baking pan with oil. Cut squash in half lengthwise. Remove seeds. Sprinkle squash with chili powder and salt. Place halves, cut sides down, in pan. Bake 15 minutes. Add whole chile peppers to pan. Bake 10 to 15 minutes more or just until squash is tender. Remove and cover with foil; let stand 10 minutes or until cool enough to handle.
2. Scoop out squash flesh, leaving ¼-inch shells. Place halves in baking pan, cut sides up. Coarsely chop flesh; place in a large bowl. Stem, seed, and chop chile peppers; add to bowl. Stir in chorizo, raisins, cheese, and chopped oregano. Spoon into squash halves. Bake 8 to 10 minutes or until heated through. Makes 4 servings.
EACH SERVING *426 cal, 19 g fat, 39 mg chol, 873 mg sodium, 56 g carb, 7 g fiber, 14 g pro.*

WARM INDIAN-SPICED ACORN SQUASH SALAD

TOTAL TIME 30 min.

2   small acorn squash
¼   cup olive oil
    Salt and black pepper
½   tsp. garam masala
¼   cup pomegranate juice
2   Tbsp. red wine vinegar
1   Tbsp. honey
3   cups torn mustard greens or kale (3 oz.)
½   cup pitted, halved dates
    Pomegranate seeds

1. Preheat oven to 425°F. Slice squash into ½-inch rings or wedges. Arrange on a shallow baking pan. Drizzle with 1 Tbsp. oil and sprinkle with salt and pepper. Roast 20 minutes or until tender and starting to brown. Remove from oven. Sprinkle with garam masala.
2. In a large bowl whisk together remaining 3 Tbsp. oil, the pomegranate juice, vinegar, and honey. Add greens and dates; toss to coat.
3. Toss salad with squash. Sprinkle with pomegranate seeds. Makes 4 servings.
EACH SERVING *294 cal, 14 g fat, 0 mg chol, 267 mg sodium, 44 g carb, 6 g fiber, 3 g pro.*

COCONUT ACORN SQUASH & CARROT SOUP

HANDS-ON TIME 25 min.
TOTAL TIME 1 hr., 5 min.

1   medium acorn squash
1   Tbsp. butter
1   cup shredded carrot
½   cup chopped sweet onion
1   Tbsp. grated fresh ginger
1   13- to 14-oz. can unsweetened coconut milk
1½ cups water
½   tsp. salt
    Fried onions, basil leaves, and/or Toasted Squash Seeds (optional)

1. Preheat oven to 400°F. Cut squash in half lengthwise; remove seeds. Arrange squash halves, cut sides down, in a foil-lined shallow baking pan. Bake, uncovered, 40 minutes or until tender. Scoop flesh from squash; discard skin.
2. In a large saucepan melt butter over medium heat. Add carrot, onion, and ginger. Cook and stir 3 to 4 minutes or until tender. Add squash flesh, coconut milk, the water, and salt. Bring to boiling; reduce heat. Simmer, covered, 10 minutes, stirring occasionally.
3. Use an immersion blender to puree soup (or puree soup in a blender in batches). Ladle into bowls and, if desired, top with fried onions, basil leaves, and/or Toasted Squash Seeds. Makes 4 servings.
EACH SERVING *252 cal, 18 g fat, 8 mg chol, 388 mg sodium, 20 g carb, 3 g fiber, 2 g pro.*
Toasted Squash Seeds Preheat oven to 400°F. Rinse seeds and pat dry with paper towels. In a small bowl mix seeds with ½ tsp. vegetable oil. Spread in a single layer in a shallow baking pan. Sprinkle lightly with salt. Roast 5 to 8 minutes or until toasted, stirring once.

FAST & FRESH

Easy, delicious recipes for a better dinner tonight.

GARLIC-ROASTED SALMON & BRUSSELS SPROUTS

GARLIC-ROASTED SALMON & BRUSSELS SPROUTS

The secret to really good Brussels sprouts is caramelization. Roasting on high heat brings out sweetness while browning the edges to crunchy deliciousness. For a simple one-pan meal, tuck salmon fillets into the pan halfway through cooking. Dry Chardonnay added to the pan keeps the fish moist and complements the rich salmon.

TOTAL TIME 45 min.

- 14 large cloves garlic, divided
- ¼ cup extra-virgin olive oil
- 2 Tbsp. finely chopped fresh oregano
- 1 tsp. salt
- ¾ tsp. ground pepper, divided
- 6 cups Brussels sprouts, trimmed and halved or sliced (about 1¼ lb.)
- 2 lb. wild-caught salmon fillet, skinned, cut into 6 portions
- ½ cup white wine, preferably Chardonnay
  Lemon wedges

1. Preheat oven to 450°F.
2. Mince 2 garlic cloves and combine in a small bowl with oil, 1 Tbsp. of the oregano, ½ tsp. of the salt, and ¼ tsp. of the pepper. Halve the remaining garlic and toss with Brussels sprouts and 3 Tbsp. of the seasoned oil in a large roasting pan. Roast, 15 minutes, stirring once.
3. Brush fish with the remaining seasoned oil. Season with remaining salt and pepper. Remove pan from oven, stir vegetables, and place salmon on top. Drizzle wine over the sprouts. Bake 10 to 15 minutes more or just until salmon is cooked through. Sprinkle with remaining oregano and serve with lemon wedges. Makes 6 servings.
EACH SERVING *368 cal, 19 g fat, 83 mg chol, 477 mg sodium, 11 g carb, 3 g fiber, 33 g pro.*

HARISSA-RUBBED STEAK & CARROT SALAD

HARISSA-RUBBED STEAK & CARROT SALAD

Spice is the easy way to give ordinary steak and carrots major personality. Versatile harissa, a Tunisian chile paste, delivers a kick to the steak while a blend of cumin, cinnamon, and paprika makes warm carrot salad spicy-sweet.

TOTAL TIME 35 min.

- 2 Tbsp. lemon juice
- 1 Tbsp. extra-virgin olive oil
- 2 cloves garlic, minced
- 1½ tsp. ground cumin
- ½ tsp. ground cinnamon
- ½ tsp. paprika
- ¾ tsp. kosher salt
- 3 cups thinly sliced carrots (about 1 lb.)
- 1 to 1¼ lb. skirt steak, trimmed and cut into 4 portions
- 4 tsp. harissa
- 1 Tbsp. chopped fresh parsley or cilantro

1. Preheat grill to medium-high.
2. Whisk lemon juice, oil, garlic, cumin, cinnamon, paprika, and ½ tsp. of the salt in a microwave-safe medium bowl. Add carrots; stir to coat. Cover and microwave 2 minutes on high or until carrots are crisp-tender. Uncover. (Alternatively, steam carrots over 1 inch of boiling water in a large saucepan fitted with a steamer basket 2 to 3 minutes or until crisp-tender. Toss carrots with spice mixture.)
3. Rub both sides of steak with harissa and sprinkle with the remaining ¼ tsp. salt. Grill steak 1½ to 3 minutes per side for medium. Transfer to a clean cutting board, let rest 5 minutes, then thinly slice across the grain. Serve with spiced carrots; top with parsley or cilantro. Makes 4 servings.
EACH SERVING *267 cal, 14 g fat, 73 mg chol, 400 mg sodium, 11 g carb, 3 g fiber, 25 g pro.*

PASTA WITH
BRAISED
RADICCHIO

CELERY & PARMESAN MINESTRONE

Minestrone is the ultimate recipe to cook with what's on hand. Adding grated Parmigiano-Reggiano into tomato-laced broth adds a salty, almost meaty richness. Another tip: Save Parm rinds and store them in the freezer. Toss them into the pot any time you make soups and sauces for a similar flavor boost.

HANDS-ON TIME 35 min.
TOTAL TIME 45 min.

2	Tbsp. extra-virgin olive oil
2	cups diced celery
½	cup diced carrot
½	cup diced onion
1	clove garlic, chopped
1	tsp. celery seeds
½	tsp. ground pepper
4	cups reduced-sodium chicken broth or vegetable broth
⅓	cup whole wheat orzo or other small pasta
1	14.5-oz. can diced tomatoes
1¾	cups cooked chickpeas or cannellini beans or one 15-oz. can, rinsed
½	cup chopped celery leaves, divided
¼	cup packed grated Parmigiano-Reggiano cheese, plus more for serving

1. Heat oil in a large saucepan or soup pot over medium heat. Add celery, carrot, onion, garlic, celery seeds, and pepper. Cook 10 minutes or until vegetables are tender, stirring occasionally.
2. Add broth and bring to a boil. Add pasta and cook, uncovered, until pasta is tender, 8 to 10 minutes. Add tomatoes, chickpeas (or beans), half the celery leaves, and ¼ cup cheese. Cook over medium heat 3 to 5 minutes or until steaming hot. Ladle into bowls and top with remaining celery leaves and, if desired, a light dusting of cheese. Makes 6 servings.
EACH SERVING *209 cal, 7 g fat, 3 mg chol, 607 mg sodium, 28 g carb, 8 g fiber, 10 g pro.*

PASTA WITH BRAISED RADICCHIO

The characteristic bitterness of radicchio mellows when braised in garlicky prosciutto-enriched broth, for a rich, tender accompaniment to pasta. Chioggia (the round, tight, red cabbage variety) is the most common type of radicchio in grocery stores. Treviso (similarly red with white veins and oblong) also appears during fall and winter. They can be used interchangeably.

TOTAL TIME 35 min.

1	Tbsp. extra-virgin olive oil
3	cloves garlic, slivered
¼	tsp. crushed red pepper
2	oz. thinly sliced prosciutto, cut into 2½-inch matchsticks
2	large heads radicchio, cored and sliced
	Black pepper
1	14.5-oz. can reduced-sodium chicken broth
1	lb. whole wheat linguine or spaghetti
½	cup freshly grated Parmesan cheese

1. Bring a large pot of water to boil.
2. Heat oil in a large nonstick skillet over medium-low heat. Add garlic and crushed red pepper. Cook and stir 30 to 60 seconds or until tender and fragrant but not brown. Add prosciutto and cook and stir 2 to 3 minutes or until lightly browned. Increase heat to medium and gradually add radicchio, turning with tongs. Season with pepper.
3. Pour in broth and bring to a simmer. Reduce heat to low and simmer, uncovered, 10 minutes or until radicchio is desired doneness, stirring occasionally,
4. Meanwhile, cook pasta in boiling water 8 to 10 minutes (or according to package directions) just until tender. Drain and transfer to a serving bowl. Add the sauce and ¼ cup cheese; toss to coat. Serve immediately; pass remaining cheese separately. Makes 4 servings.
EACH SERVING *349 cal, 8 g fat, 12 mg chol, 431 mg sodium, 59 g carb, 7 g fiber, 16 g pro.*

CELERY & PARMESAN
MINESTRONE

**ROASTED
CHICKEN WITH
GRAPES**
Recipe on page 235

GRAND FINALE

Cookbook author Gesine Bullock-Prado bids farewell to Vermont's harvest season with a simple feast inspired by her German roots and nature's final fruits.

Dusky red plums cling on the branch as Gesine Bullock-Prado starts her ritual to mark the end of fall harvest, picking those last plums and pears from the trees and pulling the final sun-ripened grapes from the vines. "It's the beginning of peak leaf season when the air is first turning crisp, and the fact that all of this goodness dovetails with oktoberfest is cause for one last hurrah," she says.

To celebrate, Gesine and her husband, Ray, will gather friends at Freegrace, the 222-year-old tavern and stagecoach stop they've made their home. The 6-acre Vermont farm features a centuries-old barn, ancient corncrib, sweet little chicken coop, and a stable that houses ducks and geese. "The landscape here reminds me of Bavaria, where I spent much of my childhood, and the house came with a history of conviviality that I was so drawn to," Gesine says. Entertaining reveals her roots. "My family's house in Germany was always full of family and friends. My grandmother nurtured everyone with her food."

Although inspired by Gesine's favorite German comfort foods, the menu represents both Bavaria and the Green Mountains of Vermont—two places she loves most.

BAVARIAN PRETZELS
Recipe on page 239

NÜRNBERG
BRATS

HELGA'S
POTATO
SALAD

ROASTED
CHICKEN
WITH
GRAPES

BRAISED
CABBAGE WITH
BRUSSELS
SPROUTS &
SQUASH

GESINE'S MENU HONORS HER MOM'S GERMAN COOKING AND THE SEASON. BRATWURST FROM HER MOTHER'S HOMETOWN, NÜRNBERG, ROUND OUT THE SPREAD.

HELGA'S POTATO SALAD

"I have spent years with my sister trying to deconstruct my mother's potato salad recipe, hoping to perfect it," Gesine Bullock-Prado says. "I add dressing to the potatoes while they're warm so they absorb all the yummy goodness."

HANDS-ON TIME 30 min.
TOTAL TIME 1 hr.

3   lb. whole tiny new potatoes or fingerling potatoes
½   cup mayonnaise
½   cup white wine vinegar
½   cup canola oil
¼   cup cornichon pickle juice
1   Tbsp. Maggi seasoning sauce*
1   shallot, finely chopped
10 cornichons, finely chopped
4   slices bacon, crisp-cooked, drained, and crumbled
2   hard-cooked eggs, peeled, brined in beet juice,** and sliced
    Snipped fresh chives

1. In a large pot cook potatoes in boiling water 15 minutes or just until fork-tender. Drain; let potatoes stand 15 minutes or until cool enough to handle.
2. Peel and slice potatoes into thin rounds; place in large bowl.
3. In a small bowl whisk mayonnaise, vinegar, oil, cornichon juice, and Maggi seasoning. Pour over hot potatoes along with shallot and cornichons; gently stir to coat. Cover and refrigerate until completely cool or up to 3 days. Season with kosher salt and pepper. Serve topped with bacon, eggs, and chives. Makes 24 servings.
*Note Maggi seasoning sauce is like a wheat version of soy sauce. Look for it in international sections of supermarkets, Asian markets, or online.
**Tip In a bowl combine 2 peeled hard-cooked eggs and liquid from a 16-oz. jar pickled beets. Cover; chill 2 to 3 hours, turning occasionally.
EACH SERVING *126 cal, 9 g fat, 19 mg chol, 164 mg sodium, 9 g carb, 1 g fiber, 2 g pro.*

ROASTED CHICKEN WITH GRAPES

"We roast this chicken in a German white wine, like a Gewürztraminer," Gesine says.

HANDS-ON TIME 20 min.
TOTAL TIME 2 hr., 20 min.

2   whole roasting chickens (3 to 3½ lb. each)
6   thick slices bacon, chopped
1   tsp. paprika
    Kosher salt and black pepper
2   lemons, halved
4   cups seedless red and/or green grape bunches
1   medium yellow onion, halved and sliced
1   shallot, finely chopped
2   cloves garlic, minced
8   oz. button mushrooms, sliced
1   Tbsp. tomato paste
1   cup white wine
¼   cup heavy whipping cream
2   sprigs fresh thyme and/or rosemary

1. Preheat oven to 350°F. Remove neck and gizzards from chickens. Rinse chickens and pat dry. Tuck wings under and secure drumsticks.
2. In a large skillet cook bacon until browned and crisp. Remove; drain on paper towels, reserving drippings. Cover and chill. Combine 2 Tbsp. drippings (or melted butter) and paprika; brush over chickens. Sprinkle with kosher salt and pepper. Place chickens in 7- to 8-qt. oval Dutch oven or roasting pan. Arrange lemons around chicken. Roast chicken, uncovered, 1½ hours.
3. Using a turkey baster, remove ⅔ cup pan juices; skim off fat and set aside for sauce. Tuck bunches of grapes around chickens in pan. Return to oven; roast 20 to 30 minutes or until chickens are done (at least 175°F in the thighs).
4. Meanwhile, for sauce, in skillet cook and stir onion, shallot, and garlic in 2 Tbsp. drippings about 4 minutes or until softened. Add mushrooms; cook and stir about 5 minutes or until browned. Add tomato paste; cook and stir to combine.

Add wine and ½ cup reserved pan juices; cook and stir until thickened and bubbly. Stir in cream and herb sprigs. Boil gently, uncovered, about 5 minutes or until thickened. Stir in bacon. Serve chickens with grapes and lemons. Pass the sauce. Makes 10 to 12 servings.
EACH SERVING *581 cal, 42 g fat, 142 mg chol, 186 mg sodium, 13 g carb, 1 g fiber, 35 g pro.*

BRAISED CABBAGE WITH BRUSSELS SPROUTS & SQUASH

"You can't be German and not serve rotkohl (red cabbage) with a meal," Gesine says.

HANDS-ON TIME 25 min.
TOTAL TIME 50 min.

1   Tbsp. olive oil
12 oz. Brussels sprouts, trimmed and halved
1½ lb. butternut squash, peeled, seeded, and cut into ¾-inch cubes
1   1½-lb. head red cabbage, cored and cut into ½-inch strips
1   large sweet onion, finely chopped (1 cup)
¾   cup white balsamic vinegar
½   cup vegetable broth
5   cloves garlic, minced
1   Tbsp. mustard seeds
1   tsp. caraway seeds
½   tsp. kosher salt
½   tsp. black pepper
1   medium red cooking apple, cored and thinly sliced

1. In a large Dutch oven heat olive oil over medium-high heat. Add Brussels sprouts and cook about 5 minutes or until browned, stirring once.
2. Add squash, cabbage, onion, vinegar, broth, garlic, seeds, salt, and pepper. Bring to boiling; reduce heat. Cover and simmer 20 to 25 minutes or until desired doneness, stirring occasionally. Stir in sliced apple. Makes 12 servings.
EACH SERVING *108 cal, 2 g fat, 0 mg chol, 153 mg sodium, 23 g carb, 4 g fiber, 3 g pro.*

SQUASH CARPACCIO
WITH GOAT CHEESE
& FIGS
Recipe on page 239

BRAISED CABBAGE
WITH BRUSSELS
SPROUTS & SQUASH
Recipe on page 235

APPLE CIDER
COCKTAIL

SPICY SUGARED
ALMONDS

SQUASH CARPACCIO WITH GOAT CHEESE & FIGS

Photo on page 236.

"Don't be afraid of this salad," Gesine says. "It's so easy to just peel the length of the squash until you get these nice ribbons. Don't try to be perfect. It's about flavor, not looks."

HANDS-ON TIME 20 min.
TOTAL TIME 50 min.

1   lb. zucchini, trimmed
1   lb. yellow summer squash, trimmed
1½ tsp. kosher salt
¼   cup olive oil
1   Tbsp. lemon juice
¼   tsp. black pepper
2   oz. goat cheese, crumbled
4   fresh figs, stemmed and quartered

Using a mandoline or vegetable peeler, cut zucchini and yellow summer squash lengthwise into thin long strips. Place the long strips in a large shallow bowl and sprinkle evenly with salt; toss to coat. Cover and chill squash 30 to 60 minutes. Transfer squash strips to a colander and rinse with water; pat dry with paper towels. Return to bowl and toss with oil, lemon juice, salt, and pepper. Arrange squash on a platter with goat cheese and figs. Makes 10 servings.

EACH SERVING *99 cal, 7 g fat, 4 mg chol, 324 mg sodium, 7 g carb, 2 g fiber, 2 g pro.*

SPICY SUGARED ALMONDS

TOTAL TIME 15 min.

1   Tbsp. sugar
¼   tsp. ground cinnamon
¼   tsp. cayenne pepper
1½ cups sugar
½   cup plus 2 Tbsp. water
2½ cups whole almonds

1. In a small bowl stir together 1 Tbsp. sugar, cinnamon, and cayenne pepper; set aside.
2. In a 4-quart saucepan combine 1½ cups sugar and the water. Stir over medium-high heat until sugar is dissolved and mixture boils. Add almonds and stir constantly over medium-high heat until water evaporates and sugar starts to dry and turn gray. (Sugar mixture will start to foam then start to dry and look like sand.

This takes 5 to 6 minutes.) Continue stirring constantly for 2 to 3 minutes or until sugar starts to melt and caramelize, coating about half the almonds in a reddish-brown sugar mixture and the rest in a glossy sugar mixture. Sprinkle cinnamon mixture over almonds, stirring constantly, and immediately transfer to baking sheet lined with parchment paper, spreading almonds to separate. Cool, then break apart. Store almonds in airtight container up to 2 weeks. Makes 4½ cups.

EACH ¼-CUP SERVING *183 cal, 10 g fat, 0 mg chol, 1 mg sodium, 22 g carb, 3 g fiber, 4 g pro.*

APPLE CIDER COCKTAIL

"My cider is made from apples that are grown on the farm," Gesine says. "The cider is so rich it almost tastes buttery. I mix it with my favorite local gin and a bit of lemon for tartness."

TOTAL TIME 5 min.

2   cups seedless green grapes
2   cups apple cider
1   cup barrel-aged artisan gin
¾   cup lemon juice
½   cup ginger liqueur
1   Tbsp. orange bitters
1   cup Vermont hard cider or other hard cider
    Ice cubes
    Apple slices

In a pitcher use a muddler or wooden spoon to muddle grapes. Add apple cider, gin, lemon juice, ginger liqueur, and orange bitters. Cover and chill 1 to 24 hours. Just before serving, strain and add hard cider. Serve with ice and garnish each drink with an apple slice. Makes about 7 cups.

EACH 8-OZ. COCKTAIL *180 cal, 0 g fat, 0 mg chol, 14 mg sodium, 22 g carb, 1 g fiber, 0 g pro.*

BAVARIAN PRETZELS

Photo on page 233.

"Baking is my ultimate outlet," Gesine says. These pretzels are served with German Nürnberger bratwurst that she orders online (germandeli.com).

HANDS-ON TIME 30 min.
TOTAL TIME 5 hr., 30 min.

3½ cups all-purpose flour
1   Tbsp. barley malt syrup or packed brown sugar
1   package active dry yeast
1½ tsp. fine sea salt or kosher salt
1¼ cups lukewarm water (105°F to 115°F)
    Nonstick cooking spray
¼   cup baking soda
1   egg
1   to 2 tsp. kosher or pretzel salt

1. In a mixer bowl combine flour, malt syrup, yeast, and salt. Whisk to combine. Add the water; mix with mixer fitted with a dough hook 8 to 10 minutes or until dough is smooth and shiny.* Transfer to large bowl coated with cooking spray; mist top of dough with cooking spray. Cover with plastic wrap; let stand in warm place until double in size (1 to 1½ hours).
2. Line a baking sheet with parchment paper; coat with cooking spray. On work surface coated with cooking spray roll dough into a 12-inch-long log; cut into six equal portions. Shape each portion into a small round and place on prepared baking sheet. Cover with plastic wrap; let rest 10 minutes.
3. Roll and stretch each portion into an 18- to 20-inch rope, middle thicker than ends. Shape into a U; cross ends twice, leaving 3-inch ends. Press ends into base of U. Return to baking sheet. Wrap with plastic wrap; freeze 2 hours to 1 week.
4. Before baking, make sure pretzels are frozen solid. Bring 2 cups water to boiling and pour into bowl just large enough to hold one pretzel. Add baking soda and stir until soda is dissolved. Let come to room temperature. Dip each frozen pretzel into baking soda mixture for 5 seconds. Turn; soak 5 seconds more. Lift pretzel and let excess water drip back into bowl. Return pretzel to baking sheet. Cover loosely with waxed paper coated with cooking spray; let rest in warm place 1 to 2 hours or until puffy.
5. Preheat oven to 400°F. Whisk together egg with 1 Tbsp. water; brush on pretzels. Sprinkle with salt. Bake 25 to 30 minutes or until deep golden brown. Cool on racks. Makes 6 pretzels.
*Hand method Combine first five ingredients in bowl. Turn out onto floured surface. Knead 8 to 10 minutes or until smooth and shiny. Continue as directed.
EACH PRETZEL *291 cal, 2 g fat, 31 mg chol, 963 mg sodium, 58 g carb, 2 g fiber, 9 g pro.*

WHAT'S ZWETSCHGENDATSCHI?
IT'S A PLUM TART THAT'S "BUTTERY,
RICH, AND BEAUTIFULLY SWEET—
AND TART," ACCORDING TO GESINE.

GESINE'S PLUM TART

"I include Italian plums," says Gesine, who created this tart as a nod to her mother's favorite dessert. As the tart bakes, the plums run red and dye the buttery, rich crust.

HANDS-ON TIME 30 min.
TOTAL TIME 3 hr.

	Nonstick cooking spray for baking
1	egg
1	egg yolk
3	Tbsp. sweetened condensed milk*
1½	tsp. vanilla
2¼	cups all-purpose flour
1	cup cornstarch
½	cup sugar
½	tsp. kosher salt
1¼	cups very cold unsalted butter (2½ sticks)
2¼	lb. assorted plums, pitted and cut into ¼-inch-thick wedges
	Honey (optional)

1. Preheat oven to 350°F. Line a 15×10-inch baking pan with parchment paper; coat with cooking spray and set aside. In a small bowl whisk together egg, yolk, sweetened condensed milk, and vanilla.
2. In a large bowl stir together flour, cornstarch, sugar, and salt. Using the largest holes on a box grater, grate butter onto flour mixture. Use your fingertips to massage butter into flour mixture until it resembles cornmeal. Pour egg mixture over flour mixture and stir to moisten. Gently knead until dough comes together.
3. Transfer dough to prepared pan; pat evenly into bottom and up sides. Prick dough all over with a fork.
4. Arrange plums in rows over dough in pan, overlapping as necessary. Bake about 40 minutes or until crust is deep golden brown and fruit is tender and bubbly. Cool in pan on wire rack. If desired, drizzle with honey before serving. Makes 24 servings.
EACH SERVING *197 cal, 10 g fat, 42 mg chol, 57 mg sodium, 24 g carb, 1 g fiber, 2 g pro.*
*Tip Refrigerate remaining sweetened condensed milk up to 2 weeks. Drizzle it over ice cream or stir it into malts or smoothies.

PUMPKIN TIME

Fall holidays are an excuse to indulge pumpkin cravings that we've resisted the rest of the year. These four recipes take afternoon coffee breaks to the ultimate level of pumpkin spice nirvana.

PUMPKIN
PAN PIE

PUMPKIN PAN PIE

Transform pumpkin pie into an anytime treat with this super easy pat-in-the-pan crust and stir-together filling. For sweetened whipped cream, combine 1 cup whipping cream, 2 Tbsp. sugar, and ½ tsp. vanilla in a chilled mixing bowl. Beat with a mixer on medium speed until soft peaks form.

HANDS-ON TIME 30 min.
TOTAL TIME 1 hr., 10 min.

1   recipe Pastry for Double-Crust Pie
1   15-oz. can pumpkin (1¾ cups)
¾   cup packed brown sugar
1¼   tsp. pumpkin pie spice
½   tsp. salt
4   eggs, lightly beaten
1½   cups half-and-half
     Whipped cream

1. Preheat oven to 400°F. Line a 15×10-inch baking pan with foil. Prepare Pastry for Double-Crust Pie. Pat onto bottom and up sides of prepared pan. Do not prick pastry. Line pastry with a double thickness of foil. Bake 10 minutes; remove foil.
2. Meanwhile, in a bowl combine pumpkin, brown sugar, spice, and salt. Stir in eggs just until combined. Gradually stir in half-and-half. Spread over partially baked piecrust.
3. Bake 30 minutes or until a knife inserted near center comes out clean. Cool on a wire rack. Cover and chill within 2 hours. Serve with whipped cream and sprinkle with additional pumpkin pie spice. Makes 16 servings.
Pastry for Double-Crust Pie In a bowl stir together 2½ cups all-purpose flour and 1 tsp. salt. Using a pastry blender, cut in ½ cup shortening and ¼ cup cut-up butter or shortening until pea size. Sprinkle 1 Tbsp. ice water over part of the mixture; toss gently with a fork. Push moistened pastry to side of bowl. Repeat moistening flour mixture, gradually adding ice water (½ to ⅔ cup total) until pastry begins to come together. Gather pastry into a ball, kneading gently until it holds together.
PER SERVING *249 cal, 13 g fat, 63 mg chol, 273 mg sodium, 28 g carb, 1 g fiber, 5 g pro.*

SPICED PUMPKIN
COFFEE CREAMER

SPICED PUMPKIN COFFEE CREAMER

Skip coffee shop lines and customize your coffee at home.

TOTAL TIME 10 min.

2   cups heavy cream, half-and-half, or dairy or nondairy milk
1   14-oz. can sweetened condensed milk
3   Tbsp. canned pumpkin
1   tsp. pumpkin pie spice
1   tsp. vanilla

1. In a 1-qt. canning jar combine all ingredients; seal. Store in refrigerator up to 2 weeks. Shake before serving. Makes 3½ cups.
PER TBSP. *54 cal, 4 g fat, 14 mg chol, 13 mg sodium, 4 g carb, 0 g fiber, 1 g pro.*

Chocolate Coffee Creamer Prepare as directed, except omit pumpkin and pumpkin pie spice. Add 3 Tbsp. chocolate-flavor syrup.
Amaretto Coffee Creamer Prepare as directed, except omit pumpkin, pumpkin pie spice, and vanilla. Add 1 tsp. almond extract and ½ tsp. ground cinnamon.
Caramel Coffee Creamer Prepare as directed, except omit pumpkin and pumpkin pie spice. Add ¼ cup caramel-flavor ice cream topping.
French Vanilla Coffee Creamer Prepare as directed, except omit pumpkin and pumpkin pie spice. Substitute 2 tsp. vanilla bean paste for the vanilla.
Hazelnut Coffee Creamer Prepare as directed, except omit pumpkin, pumpkin pie spice, and vanilla. Add 2 tsp. hazelnut extract.

SLOW COOKER PUMPKIN-BLUEBERRY BREAD

GLAZED PUMPKIN-PECAN CAKES

If you have fewer than 10 mini fluted tube pans, bake the cakes in batches. While each batch bakes, cover and chill the remaining batter.

HANDS-ON TIME 30 min.
TOTAL TIME 1 hr., 10 min.

1   orange
2   eggs, lightly beaten
1   cup granulated sugar
1   cup water
¾   cup canned pumpkin
¼   cup vegetable oil
2   tsp. vanilla
1   cup all-purpose flour
1   cup whole wheat flour
2½   tsp. baking powder
2   tsp. pumpkin pie spice
½   tsp. salt
¾   cup finely chopped pecans, toasted (tip, page 37)
1   cup powdered sugar

1. Preheat oven to 325°F. Generously grease and flour ten 3¾- to 4-inch fluted individual tube pans or one 10-inch fluted tube pan. Remove 2 tsp. zest and squeeze juice from orange; set juice aside for glaze.
2. In a bowl combine orange zest, eggs, sugar, the water, pumpkin, oil, and vanilla. Stir in flours, baking powder, pumpkin pie spice, and salt until combined.
3. Sprinkle 1 Tbsp. pecans in each prepared individual pan and top with about ⅓ cup batter. Or sprinkle all the pecans in 10-inch pan and top with all of the batter. Bake 30 to 35 minutes for mini cakes, 45 to 50 minutes for 10-inch cake, or until a wooden skewer comes out clean. Cool on wire rack 10 minutes for mini cakes or 20 minutes for large cake. Remove from pan(s); cool completely on wire rack.
4. Meanwhile, for glaze, in a medium bowl stir together powdered sugar and enough orange juice (3 to 4 tsp.) to reach drizzling consistency.
5. Drizzle cake(s) with glaze and, if desired, sprinkle with additional pumpkin pie spice. Makes 10 mini cakes.
PER MINI CAKE *341 cal, 13 g fat, 37 mg chol, 255 mg sodium, 54 g carb, 3 g fiber, 5 g pro.*

SLOW COOKER PUMPKIN-BLUEBERRY BREAD

Prepare to satisfy afternoon cravings for sweets by freezing individual portions of this hearty bread.

HANDS-ON TIME 15 min.
TOTAL TIME 2 hr., 45 min.

     Nonstick cooking spray
2   eggs, lightly beaten
1½   cups sugar
¾   cup canned pumpkin
½   cup half-and-half
½   cup vegetable oil
2   cups all-purpose flour
2   tsp. baking soda
1½   tsp. pumpkin pie spice
½   tsp. salt
¾   cup fresh blueberries
1   Tbsp. all-purpose flour
½   cup chopped pecans
     Maple syrup (optional)

1. Coat a 4-qt. oval slow cooker with nonstick cooking spray; line bottom and sides with parchment paper. In a medium bowl combine eggs, sugar, pumpkin, half-and-half, and oil.
2. In a large bowl stir together flour, soda, pumpkin pie spice, and salt. Add pumpkin mixture all at once to flour mixture; stir just until combined. Toss blueberries with 1 Tbsp. flour; fold into batter. Spoon into cooker.
3. Cover and cook on high 1 hour. If possible, give crockery liner a half-turn. Sprinkle bread with pecans. (Carefully lift lid so condensation from lid does not drip onto bread.) Cover and cook on high 1 to 1½ hours more or until a toothpick comes out clean.
4. Turn off cooker. Remove lid. Completely cover opening of cooker with paper towels; replace lid. Cool 30 to 45 minutes. If desired, serve with maple syrup. Makes 8 servings.
PER SERVING *486 cal, 22 g fat, 52 mg chol, 486 mg sodium, 68 g carb, 3 g fiber, 6 g pro.*

GLAZED PUMPKIN-
PECAN CAKES

SWEET POTATO PIE
Recipe on page 270

november

Thanksgiving evokes memories of mouthwatering feasts with family or friends. Whether you're the host or the guest bringing a dish to share, these delicious recipes will add to your special gathering.

252

259

264

BETTER BAKING
for the Holidays

Cookbook author Genevieve Ko has a unique approach to baking: Pack in the good stuff—whole grains, fruits and vegetables, healthy fats—not just to feel good about indulging but also to make desserts more delicious. These recipes from her new book, *Better Baking,* satisfy holiday baking needs and many a sweet tooth.

JEWELED APRICOT-ALMOND BUNDT

JEWELED APRICOT-ALMOND BUNDT

This rich, tender cake features the delicious combination of sweet almond paste and dried apricots.

HANDS-ON TIME 30 min.
TOTAL TIME 1 hr., 45 min. (plus cooling)

Nonstick baking spray
1¼ cups unbleached all-purpose flour
1¼ cups white whole wheat flour
1 tsp. baking powder
¼ tsp. baking soda
½ tsp. salt
7 oz. almond paste, chopped or broken into chunks (⅔ cup packed)
1½ cups sugar
1 cup dried California (tart) apricots
10 Tbsp. unsalted butter, softened
5 large eggs, at room temperature
1 tsp. pure almond extract
1 tsp. pure lemon extract
1 cup plain whole-milk yogurt
Powdered sugar

1. Position a rack in the center of the oven; preheat to 325°F. Coat a 10-inch Bundt pan with baking spray.
2. In a medium bowl whisk together ¾ cup of the all-purpose flour and the next four ingredients (through salt). In a food processor pulse almond paste with sugar until finely ground; transfer to another bowl. In the food processor combine apricots and remaining ½ cup all-purpose flour; pulse until chopped.
3. Add butter to almond mixture. Beat with an electric mixer on medium-high speed until pale and fluffy. Scrape bowl. Turn speed to medium. Add eggs one at a time, beating until smooth and scraping bowl after each. Beat in extracts. Scrape bowl. Turn speed to low. Add flour mixture in thirds, alternating with the yogurt in two additions, mixing until each is incorporated before adding the next. Add apricot mixture. Mix just until evenly distributed and all traces of flour have disappeared. Transfer to prepared pan and smooth top.
4. Bake 1¼ hours or until a skewer inserted in domed part of cake comes out clean.
5. Cool in pan on a wire rack 10 minutes. Invert onto rack, lift off pan; cool completely. Dust with powdered sugar before serving. Makes 16 servings.
EACH SERVING *318 cal, 13 g fat, 79 mg chol, 156 mg sodium, 46 g carb, 2 g fiber, 6 g pro.*

CINNAMON-TOAST GRAHAM CRACKERS

CINNAMON-TOAST GRAHAM CRACKERS

Whole wheat graham and pastry flours give these crackers an unmistakable snap.

HANDS-ON TIME 30 min.
TOTAL TIME 50 min.

1 cup whole wheat graham flour
¾ cup whole wheat pastry flour
¼ cup ground flaxseeds
¼ tsp. ground cinnamon
½ tsp. salt
½ tsp. baking soda
¼ cup packed light brown sugar
¼ cup grapeseed oil or other neutral oil
1 Tbsp. apple cider vinegar
2 Tbsp. granulated sugar
¼ tsp. cinnamon
Pinch of salt

1. In a medium bowl whisk together the first six ingredients (through baking soda). In a large bowl whisk together brown sugar, oil, vinegar, and 3 Tbsp. water until smooth. Add dry ingredients to wet ingredients. Gently stir just until all traces of flour disappear. If dry ingredients are not evenly moistened, stir in 1 Tbsp. water. Cover bowl. Let stand 15 minutes.

2. Meanwhile, position a rack in the center of the oven and preheat to 350°F.
3. Place dough on a sheet of parchment that fits the baking sheet. Cover dough with a large sheet of plastic wrap; roll into a 14×12-inch rectangle, occasionally replacing plastic wrap.
4. In a small bowl mix granulated sugar, ¼ tsp. cinnamon, and pinch of salt. Sprinkle over dough. Use a pizza wheel or sharp knife to trim edges; leave scraps on parchment. Cut rectangle into 1×2-inch rectangles. Prick dough with a fork. Slide parchment with dough onto baking sheet.
5. Bake 17 to 20 minutes or until edges are dark golden brown and center is dry and set. Cool completely on sheet on a wire rack. Break into crackers along cut lines. Store at room temperature up to 5 days or in the freezer up to 2 months. Makes 66 crackers.
EACH CRACKER *26 cal, 1 g fat, 0 mg chol, 30 mg sodium, 4 g carb, 1 g fiber, 0 g pro.*

**MAPLE-PEAR
CHEESECAKE TART
WITH GINGER-
COOKIE CRUST**
Recipe on page 252

APPLESAUCE
GRANOLA WITH
WALNUTS, SESAME
& FLAX
Recipe on page 252

APPLESAUCE GRANOLA WITH WALNUTS, SESAME & FLAX

Photo on page 251.

"If you want a cookielike texture, grind the oats in a food processor or blender. But I like them whole," Genevieve says. "If you want something that feels more like traditional granola, use rye flakes, which are thick and toothsome, or multigrain cereal with its mix of nubby grains."

HANDS-ON TIME 20 min.
TOTAL TIME 1 hr. 5 min.

½	cup unsweetened applesauce
½	cup runny mild honey
2	Tbsp. toasted walnut oil or other nut oil or neutral oil
1	tsp. pure vanilla
½	tsp. ground cinnamon
¼	tsp. ground cardamom
¼	tsp. salt
3	cups dry multigrain hot cereal, old-fashioned rolled oats, rye flakes, or a combination
1½	cups walnuts, chopped
3	Tbsp. ground flaxseeds
1	Tbsp. sesame seeds

1. Position a rack in center of oven and preheat to 325°F. Line a 15×10-inch pan with parchment paper.
2. In a large bowl whisk together the first seven ingredients (through salt). Fold in remaining ingredients until evenly coated. Pour onto the prepared pan and spread in an even layer.
3. Bake 20 minutes or until golden. Using a large spatula, stir granola. Bake 25 to 30 minutes more or until golden brown.
4. Cool completely on a wire rack. (To avoid breaking up clumps, do not stir.) Store at room temperature up to 5 days or in the freezer up to 4 months. Makes 18 servings.
EACH SERVING *178 cal, 9 g fat, 0 mg chol, 34 mg sodium, 22 g carb, 4 g fiber, 4 g pro.*

MAPLE-PEAR CHEESECAKE TART WITH GINGER-COOKIE CRUST

Photo on page 250.

"I love the combination of pears and ginger. The fruit and creamy maple filling also makes a delicious dessert on its own," Genevieve says. "If you like, omit the crust and bake in an 11-inch quiche dish."

HANDS-ON TIME 35 min.
TOTAL TIME 1 hr. 20 min. plus cooling

8	graham crackers, broken
1	7-oz. bag Tate's Gluten-Free Ginger Zinger cookies*
4	Tbsp. unsalted butter, melted and cooled
4	oz. cream cheese, softened
¼	cup sugar
2	large eggs, at room temperature
½	cup sour cream
¼	cup pure maple syrup
1	Tbsp. lemon juice
½	tsp. pure vanilla
3	very ripe small Anjou pears (1¾ lb.)

1. Position a rack in center of oven and preheat to 350°F. Coat an 11-inch fluted tart pan with removable bottom with nonstick cooking spray and place on a 15×10-inch pan.
2. In a food processor pulse graham crackers until ground into fine crumbs. Add cookies; pulse until finely ground. Scrape the bowl sides, add butter, and pulse until all crumbs are evenly moistened. Transfer to the tart pan. Press evenly and firmly into bottom and up the sides. (To ensure a flat bottom, press crust with the bottom of a dry measuring cup.)
3. Bake 10 to 15 minutes or until crust is golden brown and set. Cool completely in the pan on a wire rack.
4. Meanwhile, for the filling, in a food processor combine cream cheese and sugar. Process until smooth and fluffy. Scrape bowl; add eggs. Pulse until smooth, scraping bowl occasionally. Add remaining ingredients except for pears. Pulse until smooth, scraping bowl occasionally.

5. Cut one pear in half from top to bottom. Remove stem and use a teaspoon to scoop out the core. Place one pear half, cut side down, on a cutting board. Cut crosswise into ¼-inch slices, keeping shape intact. Slide the knife under the sliced pear, cup your hand over pear, and push forward to fan slices slightly. Lift the pear on the knife and slide into the tart shell, with the stem end in the center and bottom end against the edge. Repeat with remaining pears, alternating positions of pear ends in the shell and spacing them evenly.
6. Carefully pour filling into the shell, starting in the center and letting it run toward the edges.
7. Bake 40 to 45 minutes or until the filling is golden, puffed, and set.
8. Cool completely in the pan on a wire rack. Makes 12 servings.
*Alternately, use 1 cup gingersnap crumbs, 2 Tbsp. sugar, and ¼ cup chopped candied ginger, and increase butter to 6 Tbsp.
EACH SERVING *283 cal, 13 g fat, 67 mg chol, 172 mg sodium, 39 g carb, 2 g fiber, 3 g pro.*

PUMPKIN CINNAMON SPIRALS

The spirals are best the day they're made but will keep in the freezer up to two weeks. To reheat, wrap the frozen spirals in heavy foil and bake at 300°F for 20 to 30 minutes or until heated through.

HANDS-ON TIME 25 min.
TOTAL TIME 45 min.

1	15-oz. can pure pumpkin puree
¼	cup plus 2 Tbsp. granulated sugar
1½	tsp. ground cinnamon
2	cups unbleached all-purpose flour, plus more for rolling
1	cup whole wheat pastry flour
4½	tsp. baking powder
¼	tsp. salt
8	Tbsp. cold unsalted butter, cut into ½-inch cubes
½	cup raisins (optional)
½	cup plain yogurt
¼	cup powdered sugar

1. Position a rack in center of oven and preheat to 375°F. Line a 15×10-inch pan with parchment paper.

2. Place 2 Tbsp. of the pumpkin in a small bowl. In another small bowl stir together 2 Tbsp. of the sugar and 1 tsp. of the cinnamon.

3. In a large bowl whisk together both flours, baking powder, salt, and remaining ¼ cup sugar and ½ tsp. cinnamon. Add butter. Toss to coat, then cut it in with a pastry cutter or your fingertips until small crumbs form. Add remaining pumpkin. Fold with a fork just until dough comes together in large clumps. Gather dough in the bowl. Gently knead to bring it into a ball.

4. Turn dough out onto a lightly floured work surface. With a lightly floured rolling pin, roll into an 8×16-inch rectangle. Spread reserved pumpkin over dough. Sprinkle cinnamon-sugar mixture over pumpkin. Sprinkle with raisins, if desired.

5. Starting from a long side, roll dough into a log. Use a serrated knife to cut into sixteen 1-inch slices. Place cut sides up on prepared pan, spacing 1 inch apart.

6. Bake 20 to 22 minutes or until golden brown. Cool on parchment paper on a wire rack.

7. For glaze, in a small bowl stir together yogurt and powdered sugar. Drizzle over spirals. Let stand until set. Makes 16 servings.

EACH SERVING *176 cal, 6 g fat, 16 mg chol, 181 mg sodium, 27 g carb, 2 g fiber, 3 g pro.*

"CINNAMON ROLLS OFTEN FAIL TO LIVE UP TO THEIR INTOXICATING SCENT, BUT THESE TASTE EVEN BETTER THAN THEY SMELL," GENEVIEVE SAYS.

PUMPKIN CINNAMON SPIRALS

crank up the
HEAT

Roasting vegetables in a high-temp oven caramelizes their natural sugars to bring out deeper, complex flavors.

ROASTED
CABBAGE
WITH PEARS

CRISPY
PARMESAN-
ROASTED
BUTTERNUT
SQUASH

ROASTED CABBAGE WITH PEARS

HANDS-ON TIME 15 min.
TOTAL TIME 50 min.

1   1½-lb. head savoy, green, or red cabbage, trimmed and cut into 8 wedges
¼   cup olive oil
    Salt and black pepper
3   Bosc or Anjou pears, halved lengthwise
2   Tbsp. fresh lemon juice
¾   cup chopped walnuts, toasted (tip, page 37)
½   cup crumbled blue cheese (2 oz.)

1. Preheat oven to 425°F. Place cabbage in a 15×10-inch baking pan. Drizzle with oil and sprinkle with salt and pepper.

2. Roast 35 to 40 minutes or until tender, turning cabbage once and adding pears the last 10 to 15 minutes of roasting.
3. Drizzle lemon juice over cabbage and pears; sprinkle with walnuts and cheese. Makes 4 servings.
EACH SERVING *364 cal, 25 g fat, 11 mg chol, 529 mg sodium, 32 g carb, 10 g fiber, 10 g pro.*

CRISPY PARMESAN-ROASTED BUTTERNUT SQUASH

HANDS-ON TIME 20 min.
TOTAL TIME 45 min.

    Nonstick cooking spray
1   1½-lb. butternut squash, peeled, seeded, and cut into ¾-inch pieces or precut fresh butternut squash

2   Tbsp. olive oil
    Salt and black pepper
⅓   cup grated Parmesan cheese
¼   tsp. dried thyme, sage, or basil, crushed

1. Preheat oven to 425°F. Spray a 15×10-inch baking pan with cooking spray. Place squash in prepared pan. Drizzle with oil and sprinkle with salt and pepper; toss to coat.
2. Roast 15 minutes. Stir squash; roast 5 minutes more. Stir in cheese and thyme. Roast 5 minutes or until squash is tender. Makes 5 servings.
PER ½-CUP SERVING *154 cal, 9 g fat, 6 mg chol, 267 mg sodium, 18 g carb, 3 g fiber, 3 g pro.*

new ways with
SWEET POTATOES

Every Thanksgiving table needs a wild card. Roast, pickle, and shred your way to a decidedly unexpected addition.

Two common types of sweet potatoes are found in the states. The firm type has a light tan skin and flaky, dry flesh. When cooked, the flesh becomes a little waxy but remains relatively firm.

The second type has a reddish-brown skin and moist flesh (shown here and used in these recipes). The flesh turns soft and fluffy when cooked. Grocery stores frequently label these as yams.

PICKLED
SWEET
POTATOES

HONEY-HOISIN
SWEET POTATOES

SWEET POTATO-
POMEGRANATE
SLAW

THE NAMES SWEET POTATO AND YAM TEND TO BE USED INTERCHANGEABLY. BUT YOU'VE LIKELY NEVER EATEN A YAM, WHICH COMES FROM A DIFFERENT BOTANICAL GROUP THAN A SWEET POTATO AND IS RARELY SOLD IN THE UNITED STATES.

HONEY-HOISIN SWEET POTATOES

HANDS-ON TIME 15 min.
TOTAL TIME 45 min.

- ¼ cup hoisin sauce
- 2 Tbsp. honey
- 1 Tbsp. olive oil
- ½ tsp. salt
- 4 small sweet potatoes, halved lengthwise
  Nonstick cooking spray
- 2 Tbsp. lime juice
- ⅓ cup chopped cashews
- 1 green onion, chopped
  Lime wedges

1. Preheat oven to 425°F. Line a baking pan with foil. Coat foil with cooking spray. In a small bowl stir together hoisin, honey, olive oil, and salt. Halve sweet potatoes. Brush the cut sides with 2 Tbsp. of the hoisin mixture. Place potatoes, cut sides down on prepared baking pan. Roast 25 to 30 minutes or until tender.
2. Add lime juice to remaining hoisin mixture; spoon over cooked sweet potatoes. Top with cashews and green onion. Serve with lime wedges. Makes 8 servings.
EACH SERVING *183 cal, 5 g fat, 0 mg chol, 316 mg sodium, 34 g carb, 4 g fiber, 3 g pro.*

PICKLED SWEET POTATOES

HANDS-ON TIME 25 min.
TOTAL TIME 1 hr., 25 min. (includes cooling)

- 1¼ cups rice vinegar
- 1¼ cups water
- ¼ cup sugar
- 1 Tbsp. salt
- 2 chopped and seeded Anaheim chile peppers (tip, page 37)
- 1 cup thinly sliced red onion
- 2 large peeled sweet potatoes

In a large nonreactive saucepan combine vinegar, the water, sugar, and salt. In a large heatproof bowl combine chiles and red onion. Using a mandoline, slice potatoes about 1/16 inch thick; add to vinegar mixture. Bring to boiling; reduce heat. Simmer, uncovered, 2 minutes. Pour vinegar mixture over onion mixture. Let stand 1 hour before serving, or cover and refrigerate up to 1 week. Makes 8 servings.
EACH SERVING *109 cal., 0 g fat, 0 mg chol, 180 mg sodium, 25 g carb, 3 g fiber, 2 g pro.*

SWEET POTATO-POMEGRANATE SLAW

TOTAL TIME 30 min.

- ½ cup balsamic vinegar
- ½ cup olive oil
- ½ tsp. salt
- ½ tsp. black pepper
- 2 lb. sweet potatoes, peeled
- ½ cup chopped salted and roasted pistachios
- ½ cup pomegranate seeds
- ½ cup fresh cilantro leaves

For dressing, in a large bowl whisk together the vinegar, oil, salt, and pepper. Using a food processor, shred potatoes. Place potatoes in a colander; rinse thoroughly with cold water. Transfer to paper towels; pat completely dry. Add to the bowl with the dressing. Add pistachios, pomegranate seeds, and cilantro. Toss to coat evenly. Makes 8 servings.
EACH SERVING *260 cal, 17 g fat, 0 mg chol, 154 mg sodium, 24 g carb, 4 g fiber, 3 g pro.*

FAST & FRESH

Easy, delicious recipes for a better dinner tonight.

ROASTED CAULIFLOWER WITH GARAM MASALA

ROASTED CAULIFLOWER WITH GARAM MASALA

Use any combination of colorful cauliflower—purple, yellow, green, and/or white—in this sweet and nutty Indian-inspired dish. Serve as a vegetarian main or as a side with grilled chicken. Garam masala is an aromatic blend of spices used widely in Indian cooking. Although there is no definitive recipe, most blends include a combination of coriander, black pepper, cumin, cardamom, and cinnamon.

HANDS-ON TIME 15 min.
TOTAL TIME 40 min.

- 2 small or 1 large head yellow, purple, green, and/or white cauliflower
- 2 Tbsp. extra-virgin olive oil
- ½ tsp. garam masala
- ¼ tsp. kosher salt
- ¼ tsp. black pepper
- ¼ cup sliced almonds
- ¼ cup golden raisins or currants
- 1 cup basmati rice
  Mango chutney (optional)
- ½ cup fresh mint leaves

1. Preheat oven to 400°F. Cut cauliflower into florets; toss with the olive oil, garam masala, salt, and pepper. Spread in a 15×10-inch baking pan. Stir in almonds. Roast 25 to 30 minutes or until lightly browned and tender, stirring once. Remove pan from oven. Stir in raisins. Cool slightly.
2. Meanwhile, cook basmati rice according to package directions. Serve roasted cauliflower over rice. Drizzle with additional extra-virgin olive oil and, if desired chutney. Top with mint just before serving. Makes 4 servings.
EACH SERVING *312 cal, 10 g fat, 0 mg chol, 206 mg sodium, 51 g carb, 4 g fiber, 7 g pro.*

BACON & PEAR AUTUMN SALAD

BACON & PEAR AUTUMN SALAD

Bacon drippings give this salad irresistible smokiness while slightly wilting the greens.

TOTAL TIME 25 min.

- 8 slices smoked peppered bacon
- 1 Tbsp. extra-virgin olive oil
- 2 shallots, thinly sliced
  Salt
- 2 Tbsp. red wine vinegar
- 6 cups torn fresh kale, Swiss chard, and/or beet greens
  Black pepper
- 1 cup cooked, cooled grain, such as barley or farro
- 2 pears, cored and thinly sliced
- 4 oz. Gouda cheese, cubed

1. In a large skillet cook bacon until crisp; remove to paper towels to drain, reserving 1 Tbsp. drippings in skillet. Add the olive oil to skillet; add shallots and a pinch of salt. Cook over medium heat 3 to 4 minutes or until shallots are soft and golden brown, stirring occasionally. Stir in vinegar; remove from heat. Scrape up browned bits from bottom of skillet.
2. Place greens in a large bowl. Pour warm dressing over; toss to coat. Season to taste with salt and pepper. Cut bacon into 1-inch pieces. Add bacon, grain, and pears to greens; toss to coat. Top with cheese. Makes 6 servings.
EACH SERVING *257 cal, 14 g fat, 34 mg chol, 421 mg sodium, 23 g carb, 5 g fiber, 12 g pro.*

STRIPED BASS EN BRODO

SEARED STEAK & PEPPERS WITH CILANTRO CHIMICHURRI

Get delicious crust on the steak and char on the vegetables in a heavy skillet. If you prefer to grill, that works, too. Place steak on a rack directly over medium heat. Cover and grill 17 to 21 minutes. Add the peppers and onions in a grill basket the last 5 to 8 minutes.

HANDS-ON TIME 20 min.
TOTAL TIME 40 min.

1½ to 1¾ lb. beef flank steak
½ tsp. salt
½ tsp. black pepper
2 Tbsp. plus 2 tsp. olive oil
2 fresh poblano chile peppers, stemmed, seeded, and cut into ¾-inch strips (tip, page 37)
1 large red onion, cut into ½-inch wedges
1 medium yellow sweet pepper, cut into ¾-inch strips
1 cup loosely packed cilantro leaves, coarsely chopped
1 fresh jalapeño chile pepper, seeded and finely chopped (tip, page 37)
2 Tbsp. fresh lime juice
1 tsp. dried oregano, crushed
1 clove garlic, minced

1. Season steak with salt and black pepper. Heat a heavy 12-inch skillet over medium-high heat. Add 1 Tbsp. olive oil. Add poblano peppers, onion, sweet pepper, and a large pinch of salt. Cook 5 minutes without stirring. Cook 5 minutes more or until vegetables are lightly charred and tender, stirring once. Remove from skillet; keep warm.
2. Add remaining 1 Tbsp. oil to the skillet. Add steak. Cook 12 to 15 minutes or until medium rare (145°F), turning once. Transfer steak to a cutting board. Cover; let stand 5 minutes.
3. For Cilantro Chimichurri, in a small bowl combine cilantro, jalapeño, lime juice, oregano, garlic, and a pinch of salt. Stir in 2 tsp. oil. Slice steak; serve with pepper-onion mixture and chimichurri. Makes 4 servings.
EACH SERVING *402 cal, 22 g fat, 111 mg chol, 312 mg sodium, 13 g carb, 2 g fiber, 38 g pro.*

STRIPED BASS EN BRODO

Cooking en brodo (Italian for in broth) is an easy way to infuse a piece of fresh fish with aromatic flavor. Here, striped bass cooks in a wine-base broth rich with tomatoes, shallots, and thyme.

TOTAL TIME 25 min.

½ cup dry white wine
¼ cup water
¼ cup extra-virgin olive oil
2 medium tomatoes, sliced
2 shallots, sliced ¼ inch thick
6 fresh thyme sprigs
¼ tsp. kosher salt
1 lb. skinless striped bass, red snapper, or halibut fillets, cut into 4 pieces

1. In a large skillet combine wine, the water, and oil. Add tomatoes, shallots, thyme sprigs, and salt. Bring to boiling; reduce heat. Simmer, uncovered, 3 to 5 minutes or until tomatoes soften.
2. Place fish fillets in skillet, spooning some of the broth over the fish. Reduce heat to medium-low. Cook, covered, 8 to 10 minutes or until fish flakes when tested with a fork. Using a slotted spoon, lift fish and tomatoes into shallow bowls. Discard thyme. Ladle broth and shallots into each bowl. Top with additional fresh thyme. Makes 4 servings.
EACH SERVING *272 cal, 16 g fat, 91 mg chol, 155 mg sodium, 5 g carb, 1 g fiber, 21 g pro.*

SEARED STEAK &
PEPPERS WITH
CILANTRO
CHIMICHURRI

FLASH-ROASTED
TURKEY
Recipe on page 264

LET'S TALK TURKEY

& Stuffing & Potatoes & Cranberries & Pie

Chef and cookbook author Ian Knauer founded The Farm Cooking School in New Jersey. Here he shares step-by-step instructions for making his favorite Thanksgiving menu.

Ian Knauer says "The stakes are never higher than they are for the Thanksgiving meal." If you are among the ranks of the panicked, relax with these lessons from Ian's Thanksgiving class. "I created this class to help ease fear and bolster confidence."

Ian and co-instructor Shelley Wiseman dispel the turkey myth that home cooks have believed for generations: Low and slow is the only way to go.

"Think about it this way," Ian says. "An oven is a dehydrating environment. Water makes a turkey moist, and the longer the turkey stays in the oven, the more moisture is going to escape. So if you roast it on high, for less time, the turkey will retain more moisture, the skin will get crisper, and you'll have room in your oven for other things."

As the turkey roasts, a sage-loaded compound butter beneath the skin soaks into the meat. The addition of fat is imperative because turkeys are low in fat. The butter delivers a rich juiciness while the skin turns a beautiful caramel color in the high heat.

Here's Ian's caveat: Use a 12- to 16-lb. bird with this method. If you need more meat, don't buy a 30-lb. turkey, buy two smaller ones. "I promise you'll be happier with a pair of moist birds rather than one big dry one," Ian says.

SAUSAGE-CRANBERRY STUFFING AND CRANBERRY-ORANGE RELISH
Recipes on page 265

"THE MOST IMPORTANT PART OF PREPPING A TURKEY IS GETTING SOME FAT BENEATH THE SKIN. I RECOMMEND SOFTENED BUTTER PACKED WITH A MIX OF FRESH HERBS."

FLASH-ROASTED TURKEY

Co-instructor Shelly Wiseman tosses halved Italian onions and lemons with olive oil then roasts them in a separate pan with the turkey the last 30 minutes. Use the combo to garnish the turkey platter.

HANDS-ON TIME 25 min.
ROAST TIME 2 hr.
STAND TIME 30 min.

- 2 large cloves garlic, peeled and minced
- 1 tsp. kosher salt
- ¾ cup unsalted butter, softened
- ¼ cup chopped fresh herbs, such as sage, parsley, thyme, and chives
- ½ tsp. black pepper
- 5 Tbsp. all-purpose flour
- 1 10- to 12-lb. turkey*
- 3 large onions
- 1 large carrot, peeled and quartered
- 1 stalk celery, quartered
- 1 bouquet garni (3 sprigs parsley, 3 sprigs thyme, and 1 bay leaf tied into a bundle with 100% cotton kitchen string)
- 2 cups dry white wine

1. Preheat oven to 450°F. Place rack in lower third of oven. In a small bowl mash garlic with salt to make a paste. Add butter, herbs, and pepper; mash with a fork. Put one-third of the compound butter in a separate bowl; stir in flour. Cover and chill for thickening gravy.
2. Remove neck and giblets from turkey; set aside. Discard the liver. Pat turkey dry. Working from large cavity end, use your fingers to gently loosen breast skin and leg skin nearest breast. Push remaining compound butter under the loosened skin. Massage to spread butter evenly. Season inside of turkey with salt and pepper. Quarter two of the onions; finely chop the third. Insert one quartered onion into cavity. Season outside of turkey with salt and pepper. Fold neck skin under body, tuck wing tips under breast, and tie drumsticks together with 100% cotton kitchen string.

3. Place turkey on a rack in a roasting pan; pour 2 cups water into the pan. Tent turkey with foil. Roast 2 hours or until an instant-read thermometer inserted in thigh registers at least 175°F, rotating pan and adding 1 cup water to pan after 1 hour. Remove from oven. Carefully tilt turkey so juices inside turkey run into pan. Discard onion from cavity. Transfer turkey to a platter; loosely cover with foil. Let stand 30 minutes. Remove and discard string.
4. Meanwhile, for turkey stock, place neck and giblets in a large saucepan. Add second quartered onion, the carrot, celery, and bouquet garni; fill with cold water (about 4 cups). Bring to boiling, skim foam from surface; reduce heat. Simmer, covered, 1 hour. Strain, discarding solids. Measure 3 cups.

5. For gravy, strain pan juices through a fine-mesh sieve into bowl. Let stand 5 minutes; skim off and reserve fat. Place roasting pan across two burners and cook remaining chopped onion in ¼ cup of reserved fat over medium heat 5 minutes or until golden, scraping up browned bits. Add wine; bring to boiling. Boil gently 8 to 12 minutes or until liquid is almost evaporated. Add turkey stock and pan juices; return to boiling. Whisk chilled herb-butter into boiling liquid until thickened. Simmer, uncovered, 5 minutes, whisking occasionally. Season with salt and pepper. Slice turkey; serve with gravy. Makes 10 to 12 servings.
* For a 14- to 16-lb. turkey, roast 3 to 3½ hours or until thigh is 175°F.
EACH SERVING *634 cal, 31 g fat, 267 mg chol, 706 mg sodium, 7 g carb, 71 g pro.*

SAUSAGE-CRANBERRY STUFFING

Photo on page 263.

HANDS-ON TIME 20 min.
TOTAL TIME 1 hr.

12 oz. crusty country bread, cut or torn into 1-inch pieces (8 cups)
1½ lb. bulk pork sausage
¼ cup unsalted butter
1 cup chopped onion
3 stalks celery, sliced ¼-inch thick (1½ cups)
4 cloves garlic, minced
1 cup dried cranberries
2 Tbsp. chopped fresh sage or 1 Tbsp. dried sage, crushed
1 Tbsp. chopped fresh thyme or 2 tsp. dried thyme, crushed
½ tsp. kosher salt
½ tsp. black pepper
1½ to 2 cups reduced-sodium chicken broth

1. Position rack in middle of oven; preheat to 375°F. Spread bread in a shallow baking pan. Bake about 20 minutes or until bread is dry and a light golden color, stirring once.
2. In a large skillet cook sausage over medium heat until no longer pink, stirring to break up meat. Using a slotted spoon, transfer to an extra-large bowl; reserve drippings in skillet.
3. Add butter to drippings in skillet. Add onion and cook 7 minutes or until softened, scraping up brown bits from bottom of skillet. Add celery and garlic; cook and stir 2 minutes. Transfer to bowl with sausage. Stir in bread, cranberries, sage, thyme, salt, and pepper.
4. Butter a 3-qt. baking dish. Transfer stuffing to baking dish; drizzle with broth. Cover with foil; bake 20 minutes. Uncover; bake 20 to 25 minutes more or until bread is golden and stuffing is heated through. Stir before serving. Makes 12 servings.
EACH SERVING *291 cal, 15 g fat, 46 mg chol, 634 mg sodium, 25 g carb, 2 g fiber, 12 g pro.*

CRANBERRY-ORANGE RELISH

Photo on page 263.

Let your food processor make quick work of chopping this all-fresh version of a Thanksgiving staple.

TOTAL TIME 15 min.

1 orange
1 12-oz. pkg. cranberries, thawed if frozen
1 Gala, Fuji, or Red Delicious apple, cored, peeled, and chopped
¼ cup sugar
¼ tsp. ground allspice
1 Tbsp. sugar (optional)

1. Cut peel and white pith from orange; cut orange segments free from the membrane. Discard any seeds.
2. In a food processor pulse orange segments, cranberries, apple, the ¼ cup sugar, and the allspice until coarsely chopped. Transfer relish to a bowl and, if desired, stir in 1 Tbsp. sugar. Cover and chill up to one week. Makes 10 to 12 servings.
EACH SERVING *51 cal, 0 g fat, 0 mg chol, 1 mg sodium, 13 g carb, 2 g fiber, 0 g fiber, 0 g pro.*

SHAVED BRUSSELS SPROUTS SALAD

Photo on page 266.

Brussels sprouts are mixed up fresh and crunchy in this salad—it's one dish you don't have to cook. "When everything doesn't have to be piping hot, you can relax," Ian says.

TOTAL TIME 30 min.

1½ lb. fresh Brussels sprouts, with stems intact and wilted leaves discarded
1 cup walnuts, lightly toasted (tip, page 37)
½ cup olive oil
⅓ cup fresh lemon juice
¼ tsp. black pepper
2 oz. shaved Pecorino Romano cheese

1. Holding each Brussels sprout at the stem end, cut into very thin slices using a mandoline slicer. Toss in a bowl to separate layers.
2. Lightly crush the toasted walnuts with your hands and add to Brussels sprouts. In a small bowl whisk together oil, lemon juice, and pepper. Drizzle over salad and toss to coat. Serve topped with the shaved cheese. Makes 12 servings.
EACH SERVING *176 cal, 16 g fat, 5 mg chol, 81 mg sodium, 6 g carb, 3 g fiber, 5 g pro.*

"NEVER PUT STUFFING INSIDE THE TURKEY," IAN SAYS. "TO GET STUFFING TO A SAFE TEMPERATURE YOU WOULD OVERCOOK THE TURKEY. PLUS, YOU NEVER GET THAT CRISP EDGE TO THE BREAD THAT YOU ACHIEVE WHEN YOU BAKE IT IN A BAKING DISH."

SAUERKRAUT &
APPLES

TWICE-BAKED
CRÈME
FRAÎCHE
POTATOES

SHAVED BRUSSELS
SPROUTS SALAD
Recipe on page 265

CELERY ROOT
PUREE

"WHAT HAPPENS WHEN A POTATO MARRIES CELERY AND THEY HAVE A BABY? YOU GET BEAUTIFUL, DELICIOUS CELERY ROOT. PUREE IT FOR A SILKY, CREAMY SIDE THAT WILL UPSTAGE MASHED POTATOES ON ANY TABLE—I PROMISE YOU."

SAUERKRAUT & APPLES

For the Knauer family's sauerkraut recipe—a nod to Pennsylvania Dutch tradition—Ian uses bagged ready-made kraut to save time and adds chopped sweet apples to balance the acidity. Because the recipe involves slicing and chopping, he teaches students the proper methods. "For this dish, rather than lengthwise, I slice the onions crosswise, against the fiber, which helps them break down and become more melty during the cooking process," Ian says.

HANDS-ON TIME 20 min.
TOTAL TIME 1 hr., 20 min.

2   Tbsp. unsalted butter
1   large onion, thinly sliced (1 cup)
4   lb. refrigerated sauerkraut, rinsed and drained
2   Gala, Fuji, or Red Delicious apples, cored and thinly sliced
1   cup dry white wine
3   to 4 Tbsp. packed dark brown sugar
½   tsp. kosher salt
½   tsp. black pepper
1   recipe Topping (optional)

1. In a 4- to 5-qt. heavy pot melt butter over medium-high heat. Add onion and cook 6 minutes or until golden, stirring occasionally. Stir in sauerkraut, apples, and wine. Bring to boiling. Reduce heat; simmer, covered, 1 hour or until sauerkraut is very tender, stirring occasionally.
2. Stir in 3 Tbsp. brown sugar, salt, and pepper. Stir in additional brown sugar, salt, and pepper to taste. Makes 8 to 10 servings.
EACH SERVING *150 cal, 3 g fat, 8 mg chol, 849 mg sodium, 24 g carb, 7 g fiber, 2 g pro.*

Topping Core and chop one Gala, Fuji, or Red Delicious apple. In a small skillet cook apple in 2 Tbsp. butter just until softened. Sprinkle over sauerkraut dish with 1 Tbsp. snipped fresh dill weed.

TWICE-BAKED CRÈME FRAÎCHE POTATOES

Ian recommends making these potatoes a day ahead, then chilling and reheating them in a 375°F oven about 45 minutes.

HANDS-ON TIME 20 min.
TOTAL TIME 1 hr., 45 min.

8   6- to 8-oz. russet potatoes
2   tsp. vegetable oil
1   8-oz. container crème fraîche
½   cup chopped mixed fresh herbs, such as chives, sage, thyme, savory, and/or marjoram
¼   cup half-and-half
3   Tbsp. unsalted butter, softened
    Kosher salt
    Black pepper

1. Position rack in center of oven; preheat to 375°F. Line a baking sheet with foil. Pierce potatoes in several spots with a fork. Rub oil over potatoes. Place directly on center oven rack. Place foil-lined baking sheet on rack below potatoes. Bake 45 minutes or until very tender. Transfer to a wire rack; cool 10 minutes.
2. Use oven mitts to hold a hot potato. With a serrated knife horizontally cut off top quarter of the potato. Using a spoon, scoop out potato, leaving a ¼-inch shell; transfer flesh to a large bowl. Repeat with remaining potatoes. Mash the potato in bowl until smooth. Stir in crème fraîche, herbs, half-and-half, and butter. Season with kosher salt and pepper.
3. Spoon or pipe mashed potato into shells. Place on 15×10-inch baking pan. Bake 30 minutes or until heated through. Makes 8 servings.
EACH SERVING *303 cal, 17 g fat, 39 mg chol, 21 mg sodium, 31 g carb, 2 g fiber, 4 g pro.*

CELERY ROOT PUREE

"The best mashed potatoes you'll ever eat are celery root," Ian says. "Try this recipe, and you'll use it the rest of your life."

HANDS-ON TIME 15 min.
TOTAL TIME 30 min.

3   lb. celery root, peeled and cut into ½-inch cubes (8 cups)
4   small cloves garlic, peeled
2   tsp. kosher salt
1   cup heavy cream
½   cup unsalted butter
    Black pepper
    Celery root leaves (optional)

1. In a large saucepan combine celery root, garlic, and salt. Add enough water to cover. Bring to boiling. Reduce heat; simmer, covered, 12 to 15 minutes or until very tender; drain.
2. In a food processor puree cooked celery root and garlic with cream and butter until smooth. Season to taste with additional salt and pepper. If desired, top with additional butter and celery root leaves. Makes 8 servings.
EACH SERVING *277 cal, 23 g fat, 64 mg chol, 672 mg sodium, 17 g carb, 3 g fiber, 4 g pro.*

ALL-BUTTER
PIECRUST
Recipe on page 270

**BRANDIED SOUR
CHERRY & PEAR PIE,
SWEET POTATO PIE
AND BANANA PIE**
Recipes on page 270

ALL-BUTTER PIECRUST

Photo on page 268.

"If you don't use all three of these baked crusts, freeze the extras to use later," Ian says.

HANDS-ON TIME 20 min.
TOTAL TIME 1 hr., 20 min

3¾ cups all-purpose flour
1½ tsp. kosher salt
3 sticks (1½ cups) cold unsalted butter, cut into ½-inch pieces
¾ to 1 cup cold water

1. Preheat oven to 375°F. In a large bowl whisk together flour and salt. Using a pastry blender or your fingers, work butter into flour mixture until butter is peasize. Stir in ¾ cup of the water, a few tablespoons at a time. Squeeze a small handful of dough. If dough is still crumbly, stir in the remaining water, 1 Tbsp. at a time.
2. Turn out dough on a work surface; divide into fourths. Push each quarter of dough with the palm of your hand away from the mound. Gather the dough into a ball, divide into thirds, wrap in plastic wrap, and press each into a round disk. Chill 30 to 60 minutes.
3. Using a floured rolling pin on a generously floured surface, roll one portion of dough into a 12-inch circle. Transfer to a 9-inch pie plate and trim to ½ inch beyond edge of pie plate. Fold extra dough under, even with the pie plate edge; press it together. Flute as desired. Prick the bottom and sides of dough several times with a fork.
4. Line dough with a double thickness of foil; fill with pie weights or dried beans. Bake 20 minutes or until sides are golden and firm. Remove weights and foil; bake 10 to 15 minutes more or until the bottom is golden. Cool completely on wire rack. Makes three 9-inch piecrusts.

SWEET POTATO PIE

Ian prefers this dessert over traditional pumpkin pie. "Roasting the sweet potatoes concentrates their flavor," he says.

HANDS-ON TIME 25 min.
TOTAL TIME 2 hr., 25 min.

1 baked All-Butter Piecrust (above)
1¼ lb. sweet potatoes
1 cup whipping cream
¾ cup packed brown sugar
½ cup whole milk
2 eggs
1 tsp. ground cinnamon
Pinch kosher salt

1. Prepare the All-Butter Piecrust as directed, except after removing foil and weights, bake 5 minutes more or until set but not browned. Preheat oven to 400°F. Prick the sweet potatoes all over with a fork, wrap them in foil, and roast in the oven 60 to 70 minutes or until tender. Reduce oven to 375°F.
2. Let sweet potatoes cool. Peel and place in a bowl. Mash with a potato masher. (You should have about 2 cups.) In a food processor combine mashed sweet potatoes and remaining ingredients. Cover and process just until smooth. Pour filling into piecrust. Cover edges of pie with foil. Bake 30 minutes. Remove foil and bake 30 to 40 minutes more or until evenly puffed and a knife inserted near center comes out clean. Cool on a wire rack. Makes 12 servings.
EACH SERVING *294 cal, 16 g fat, 75 mg chol, 147 mg sodium, 34 g carb, 2 g fiber, 4 g pro.*

BRANDIED SOUR CHERRY & PEAR PIE

Photo on page 269.

Ian's riff on classic mincemeat pie contains a big splash of brandy to marry the medley of sour cherries and pears.

HANDS-ON TIME 1 hr.
TOTAL TIME 2 hr.

1½ lb. firm ripe pears (about 3)
2 cups dried tart red cherries (10 oz.)
½ cup brandy
3 Tbsp. sugar
2 Tbsp. cornstarch
1 baked All-Butter Piecrust (recipe, left)

Peel, halve, and core pears. Cut pears into a 1¼-inch dice, then combine with cherries, brandy, sugar, cornstarch, and ½ cup water in a heavy 3-qt. pot. Bring to boiling. Reduce heat; simmer, uncovered, about 10 minutes or until thick, stirring frequently. Transfer filling to a shallow dish; cool and chill. Before serving, spoon filling into piecrust. Makes 12 servings.
EACH SERVING *278 cal, 8 g fat, 20 mg chol, 88 mg sodium, 44 g carb, 3 g fiber, 2 g pro.*

BANANA PIE

Photo on page 269.

Ian refers to this as Elvis Pie. "Elvis loved peanut butter and bananas, and I love Elvis," Ian explains. Ease Thanksgiving Day stress by prepping the pudding filling the day before and assembling the pie at the last minute.

HANDS-ON TIME 30 min.
TOTAL TIME 2 hr,. 30 min.

5 egg yolks
3 cups whole milk
⅔ cup granulated sugar
⅓ cup cornstarch
½ tsp. kosher salt
2 tsp. vanilla
4 medium ripe bananas
1 baked All-Butter Piecrust (recipe, left)
1 cup heavy cream
2 Tbsp. powdered sugar
1 Tbsp. creamy peanut butter
Chopped peanuts

1. For pudding, in a large bowl prepare an ice bath. In a small bowl whisk the yolks lightly. In a large saucepan whisk together the milk, granulated sugar, cornstarch, and salt. Cook and stir until thickened, whisking constantly.
2. Pour about half the hot milk mixture in a thin stream into the egg yolks, whisking constantly. Return all to saucepan. Cook and stir over medium-high heat 3 minutes or until thickened and bubbly. Remove from heat, whisk in 1 tsp. of the vanilla; set pan in the ice bath. Stir occasionally until cool. Transfer to a bowl; cover surface with plastic wrap. Refrigerate until completely cooled or up to 24 hours.
3. To assemble, slice bananas; arrange a layer of slices in bottom of baked All-Butter Piecrust. Cover with a layer of pudding; repeat with remaining banana slices and pudding.
4. For topping, whisk the cream, powdered sugar, peanut butter, and remaining vanilla until stiff peaks form. Pile the topping onto the filling and sprinkle with some peanuts. Makes 10 servings.
EACH SERVING *442 cal, 25 g fat, 151 mg chol, 281 mg sodium, 47 g carb, 2 g fiber, 8 g pro.*

SWEET POTATO PIE

ENCORE!

Transform leftovers from the Thanksgiving feast into mouthwatering (upscale) diner food.

TURKEY CRANBERRY SANDWICHES

Sometimes it's the day-after sandwich that makes the production involved in roasting a 14-lb. turkey worth it.

TOTAL TIME 20 min.

1   cup halved and sliced red onion
1   Tbsp. vegetable oil
1   cup leftover cranberry sauce
¼   cup bottled barbecue sauce
2   Tbsp. finely chopped chipotle chile pepper in adobo sauce (tip, page 37)
3   cups shredded cooked turkey
    Pretzel buns or ciabatta rolls, split and, if desired, toasted
6   leaves Bibb lettuce
    Sliced mozzarella cheese
    Sliced fresh jalapeño peppers (tip, page 37) (optional)

1. In large saucepan cook and stir onion in hot oil over medium-high heat 4 minutes or until tender. Stir in cranberry sauce, barbecue sauce, and chipotle. Add turkey; toss to coat. Heat through.
2. Line bottom half of buns with lettuce. Top with turkey mixture and cheese. Add bun tops. Serve with additional cranberry sauce and, if desired, sliced jalapeño peppers. Makes 6 servings.
EACH SERVING *561 cal, 15 g fat, 84 mg chol, 716 mg sodium, 73 g carb, 3 g fiber, 34 g pro.*

CHEESY TOTS

HANDS-ON TIME 20 min.
TOTAL TIME 40 min.

2½ cups leftover mashed potatoes or sweet potatoes
¼ cup finely shredded Parmesan or sharp cheddar cheese
1 egg
2 Tbsp. all-purpose flour
2 Tbsp. chopped fresh chives
½ tsp. kosher salt
1¼ cups panko bread crumbs
¼ cup butter
½ cup sour cream
1 tsp. sriracha sauce

1. Place a 15×10-inch baking pan in oven. Preheat oven to 425°F. Meanwhile, microwave leftover potatoes in a medium bowl 30 seconds on 100% power (high); stir to soften. Stir in the cheese, egg, flour, chives, and salt. Place panko in a shallow bowl. Using a small cookie scoop, drop potato mixture into panko, a few at a time. Roll to coat with panko and shape as desired. Add butter to preheated pan. Return to oven 1 to 2 minutes or until melted. Tilt pan to distribute butter. Arrange potatoes in prepared pan.
2. Bake 8 minutes. Turn; bake 8 minutes more or until golden. For dipping sauce, combine sour cream and sriracha. Makes 8 servings.
EACH SERVING *207 cal, 12 g fat, 55 mg chol, 423 mg sodium, 19 g carb, 1 g fiber, 4 g pro.*

GREEN BEAN FRITTATA

TOTAL TIME 25 min.

- 4 slices bacon
- 8 eggs
- ¼ tsp. kosher salt
- ¼ tsp. black pepper
- 2 cups leftover green bean casserole
- 1 cup shredded sharp cheddar cheese
  Vegetable oil
- ½ cup thinly sliced sweet onion
- ¼ cup milk
- ⅓ cup all-purpose flour

1. In skillet cook bacon over medium heat until browned and crisp. Remove; drain on paper towels, reserving drippings. Crumble bacon; set aside.
2. In a large bowl whisk eggs with salt and pepper. Stir in green bean mixture, bacon, and half the cheese. Pour into skillet with bacon drippings; cook over medium heat. As mixture sets, run a spatula around edge of skillet, lifting egg mixture so uncooked portion flows underneath. Continue cooking and lifting until almost set. Top with remaining cheese; cover.
3. Meanwhile, in a medium saucepan heat ½ inch oil over medium-high heat. Dip onion slices in milk, letting excess drip off. Toss slices in flour; shake off excess. Cook coated onion slices in batches in hot oil 3 minutes or until golden and slightly crisp. Using a slotted spoon, transfer onion slices to paper towels to drain. Top frittata with fried onion. Makes 6 servings.

EACH SERVING *476 cal, 37 g fat, 301 mg chol, 633 mg sodium, 16 g carb, 2 g fiber, 21 g pro.*

SALMON HASH

TOTAL TIME 25 min.

- 3 Tbsp. vegetable oil
- 1 large red sweet pepper, cut into 1-inch pieces
- 2 stalks celery, cut into 1-inch pieces
- 1 large onion, coarsely chopped
- 4 cups leftover stuffing
- 4 oz. smoked salmon (not lox-style), flaked into 1-inch chunks
- 4 eggs
  Chopped fresh sage or parsley
  Leftover gravy, warmed (optional)

1. Heat 2 Tbsp. oil in a 12-inch skillet over medium heat. Add sweet pepper, celery, and onion. Cook and stir 5 to 6 minutes or until tender. Stir in stuffing; cook 5 minutes. Stir and cook 3 to 4 minutes or until heated through and browned. Stir in salmon; heat through. Remove from skillet; cover and keep warm.
2. Wipe out skillet. Heat remaining oil over medium heat. Add eggs; cook sunny-side up 4 minutes or until done. Serve over hash with herb and, if desired, gravy. Makes 4 servings.
EACH SERVING *618 cal, 41 g fat, 193 mg chol, 1,243 mg sodium, 45 g carb, 4 g fiber, 18 g pro.*

PUMPKIN PIE SHAKE

TOTAL TIME 5 min.

- 1 cup cinnamon or vanilla ice cream
- ⅛ leftover pumpkin pie
- ¼ cup milk
  Whipped cream
  Ground cinnamon

In a blender combine ice cream, pie, and milk. Cover and blend until almost smooth. Serve topped with whipped cream and cinnamon. If desired, garnish with a sliver of pie. Makes 2 servings.
EACH SHAKE *348 cal, 18 g fat, 75 mg chol, 248 mg sodium, 39 g carb, 1 g fiber, 7 g pro.*

eat this now:
GOCHUJANG

Meet Korean gochujang, a thick paste made with red chiles, glutinous rice, fermented soybeans, and salt.

GOCHUJANG SPICED NUTS

Every now and then an ingredient comes along and changes our kitchens forever. With a healthy dose of heat, a touch of sweetness, and a whole lot of umami, gochujang adds savory depth to dips, marinades, soups, stews, stir-fries, and beyond.

TOTAL TIME 30 min.

2	Tbsp. honey
1	Tbsp. coconut oil
1	Tbsp. gochujang chile paste
1	tsp. salt
3	cups assorted raw nuts

1. Preheat oven to 325°F. Line a shallow baking pan with parchment paper.
2. In a medium saucepan melt honey and coconut oil over medium heat. Remove from heat; stir in gochujang and salt. Add nuts, stirring to coat evenly. Transfer to prepared pan. Bake 15 to 20 minutes or until nuts are toasted, stirring once. Break nuts apart; cover and store at room temperature. Makes 3 cups.
EACH ¼-CUP SERVING *232 cal, 19 g fat, 0 mg chol, 224 mg sodium, 11 g carb, 2 g fiber, 7 g pro.*

HOLIDAY COOKIES
Recipes begin on page 289

december

Get in the holiday mood with festive cookies from famed author Dorie Greenspan. Then smile through the season with exceptional dishes suited for drop-in company and healthful recipes for colorful chard.

280

284

287

CRANBERRY,
MAPLE & RYE SOUR

WHIPPED GOAT
CHEESE & GREEN
OLIVE DIP

CRISPY BLACK-EYED
PEAS WITH OLD BAY

Drop-ins
WELCOME

You're gift-wrapping, baking, and going in 18 different holiday directions. Then suddenly: Ding-dong. Here's how to entertain on the fly with advice and a few back-pocket recipes from cookbook author Julia Turshen.

CRANBERRY, MAPLE & RYE SOUR

Mix drinks in a large measuring cup to easily serve several guests at one time (plus you don't have to own a cocktail shaker). This cocktail also features bitters to add a touch of warmth and spice.

TOTAL TIME 10 min.

3   Tbsp. rye, bourbon, or whiskey
2   Tbsp. fresh lemon juice
2   Tbsp. unsweetened cranberry juice
1   Tbsp. maple syrup
    Few dashes Angostura bitters
    Crushed ice
2   Tbsp. seltzer
    Fresh cranberries (optional)

In a large measuring cup whisk rye, lemon juice, cranberry juice, maple syrup, and bitters. Fill a highball glass with crushed ice; pour in rye mixture. Top with seltzer; stir. Garnish with cranberries, if desired. Serve immediately. Makes 1 serving.
EACH SERVING *175 cal, 0 g fat, 0 mg chol, 4 mg sodium, 20 g carb, 0 g fiber, 0 g pro.*

WHIPPED GOAT CHEESE & GREEN OLIVE DIP

This delicious dip takes little time to make and uses ingredients you may already have in your fridge. Serve with sliced radishes (or other cut-up vegetables), and/or toasted pita wedges. Just brush the wedges with olive oil, sprinkle with sea salt, and toast in the oven.

TOTAL TIME 15 min.

½   cup green olives, pitted
8   oz. plain goat cheese
½   cup full-fat plain Greek yogurt
2   Tbsp. fresh lemon juice
2   Tbsp. extra-virgin olive oil
1   small clove garlic, minced
½   tsp. salt

In a food processor pulse olives until roughly chopped; set aside half. To remaining olives in food processor, add remaining ingredients. Process 1½ minutes or until smooth and slightly aerated, scraping sides as necessary. Transfer to a serving bowl; drizzle with additional olive oil, if desired, and top with reserved olives. Serve immediately. Makes 1¾ cups dip.
EACH 2-TBSP. SERVING *95 cal, 8 g fat, 14 mg chol, 222 mg sodium, 1 g carb, 0 g fiber, 4 g pro.*

CRISPY BLACK-EYED PEAS WITH OLD BAY

Oven-roasted beans are an unexpected alternative to mixed nuts. You can also use black beans or chickpeas. For black beans, roast about 25 minutes and sprinkle with smoked paprika, chickpeas about 35 minutes and dust with curry powder.

HANDS-ON TIME 15 min.
TOTAL TIME 45 min.

1   15-oz. can black-eyed peas, rinsed
    and drained
2   Tbsp. extra-virgin olive oil
½   tsp. salt
1   tsp. Old Bay seasoning

1. Preheat oven to 400°F. Place black-eyed peas in an even layer on a clean dish towel; cover with another towel; pat dry. Uncover and let air-dry for 10 minutes.
2. Transfer peas to a 15×10-inch baking pan. Drizzle with olive oil and sprinkle with salt. Spread in a single layer. Roast 30 minutes or until peas are slightly cracked, browned, and crisp, stirring occasionally.
3. Sprinkle hot peas with the seasoning; stir well. Serve warm or at room temperature. Makes about 1 cup.
EACH ¼-CUP SERVING *129 cal, 7 g fat, 0 mg chol, 479 mg sodium, 12 g carb, 3 g fiber, 4 g pro.*

"EMBRACE SIMPLE FOOD AND TECHNIQUES. THE MORE YOU CAN RELAX, THE BETTER EVERYTHING TASTES," SAYS JULIA.

PECORINO IS A FAMILY OF HARD ITALIAN CHEESES MADE FROM SHEEPS MILK AND COMES IN A VARIETY OF STYLES, DEPENDING ON HOW LONG IT'S BEEN AGED.

ROASTED BROCCOLI WITH PECORINO & PISTACHIOS

Roasted vegetables are easy sides and in this recipe you can swap in just about any vegetable—squash, cauliflower, Brussels sprouts, or carrots.

HANDS-ON TIME 10 min.
TOTAL TIME 40 min.

1   to 1½ lb. broccoli, cut into small florets
2   Tbsp. extra-virgin olive oil
½   tsp. salt
1   Tbsp. fresh lemon juice
3   Tbsp. shelled pistachios, lightly toasted and roughly chopped (tip, page 37)
3   Tbsp. finely grated pecorino cheese

1. Preheat oven to 425°F. Line a 15×10-inch baking pan with parchment paper.
2. Place broccoli on prepared baking sheet. Drizzle with olive oil and sprinkle with salt. Roast 30 minutes or until tender and well browned, stirring occasionally. Transfer to serving platter.
3. Drizzle lemon over broccoli; top with pistachios and pecorino. Makes 4 servings.
EACH SERVING *148 cal, 11 g fat, 4 mg chol, 257 mg sodium, 10 g carb, 4 g fiber, 6 g pro.*

SPAGHETTI WITH SHEET-PAN SCAMPI

Scampi under the broiler is an impressive meal for company and requires minimal effort. This no-mess sheet-pan method also works well for chopped chicken breast or thigh.

HANDS-ON TIME 15 min.
TOTAL TIME 20 min.

2   lb. shrimp, peeled and deveined
6   Tbsp. unsalted butter, melted
¼   cup oil-packed dried tomatoes, drained and roughly chopped
4   to 6 large cloves garlic, sliced
1   tsp. salt
½   tsp. crushed red pepper (optional)
¼   cup dry white wine or chicken broth
1   lemon, zested and juiced
    Large handful fresh Italian parsley, finely chopped
8   oz. dried spaghetti, cooked al dente
    Lemon wedges

1. Preheat broiler. Place shrimp on a 15×10-inch baking pan; drizzle with half the melted butter. Scatter the tomatoes and garlic over shrimp. Sprinkle with salt and crushed red pepper (if desired); toss to coat; spread shrimp in an even layer. Pour the wine over shrimp.
2. Broil shrimp 4 to 5 inches from heat for 5 to 7 minutes or until pink and firm to the touch, turning shrimp once.
3. Drizzle remaining butter and the lemon juice over hot shrimp. Sprinkle with lemon zest and parsley. Toss to combine.
4. Spoon scampi and sauce over spaghetti. Toss to coat. Serve immediately with lemon wedges. Makes 4 servings.
EACH SERVING *594 cal, 20 g fat, 411 mg chol, 777 mg sodium, 49 g carb, 4 g fiber, 54 g pro.*

ROASTED BROCCOLI WITH PECORINO & PISTACHIOS

SPAGHETTI WITH SHEET-PAN SCAMPI

ROASTED
BOURBON
CHERRIES

ONE-BOWL
CHOCOLATE
& ORANGE
CAKE

VERSATILE ONE-BOWL CHOCOLATE AND ORANGE CAKE, A WELCOME AFTERNOON SNACK WITH COFFEE OR TEA, CAN ALSO BE TOPPED WITH WHIPPED CREAM AND RASPBERRIES FOR A SPECIAL HOLIDAY DESSERT.

ONE-BOWL CHOCOLATE & ORANGE CAKE

This moist cake freezes well. When company arrives, wrap wedges in foil and warm in the oven.

HANDS-ON TIME 20 min.
TOTAL TIME 1 hr., 20 min.

1¼ cups all-purpose flour, plus 1 Tbsp.
1 cup granulated sugar
¾ cup Dutch-processed cocoa powder, sifted if lumpy
1 tsp. baking soda
1 tsp. baking powder
Large pinch ground cloves
½ cup unsalted butter (1 stick), melted and cooled
2 eggs, lightly beaten
2 tsp. orange zest
¾ cup freshly squeezed orange juice
1 cup buttermilk
1 tsp. vanilla
1 cup semisweet chocolate chips or chunks
Powdered sugar

1. Preheat oven to 350°F. Spray the bottom and sides of one 9×2-inch round cake pan with baking spray. Line the bottom of the cake pan with a circle of parchment paper. Spray parchment with baking spray.
2. In a large mixing bowl stir together the 1¼ cups flour, the sugar, cocoa powder, baking soda, baking powder, cloves, and ½ tsp. salt. Add melted butter, eggs, orange zest and juice, buttermilk, and vanilla; whisk the mixture until batter is smooth. Toss chocolate chips with remaining 1 Tbsp. flour. Using a rubber spatula, fold chocolate chips into the batter. Transfer batter to the prepared cake pan.
3. Bake 1 hour or until cake is firm to the touch. Cool in pan on wire rack. Run a table knife around edge of pan. Invert. Peel off parchment; invert cake. Sprinkle with powdered sugar. Makes 8 to 10 servings.
EACH SERVING *439 cal, 21 g fat, 79 mg chol, 344 mg sodium, 64 g carb, 4 g fiber, 7 g pro.*

ROASTED BOURBON CHERRIES

Because fruit compote will keep in the refrigerator up to 2 weeks, it's an ideal dish to keep on hand to jazz up a bowl of vanilla ice cream, pound cake, or One-Bowl Chocolate & Orange Cake (left). Or serve it alongside cheese during happy hour. Roasting the cherries concentrates flavor.

HANDS-ON TIME 10 min.
TOTAL TIME 35 min.

1 12-oz. bag frozen pitted tart red or dark sweet cherries
3 Tbsp. packed light brown sugar
3 Tbsp. bourbon
½ tsp. ground ginger
Pinch kosher salt
1 tsp. vanilla

1. Preheat oven to 400°F. In a small roasting dish stir together cherries, brown sugar, bourbon, ginger, and salt.
2. Roast 25 minutes or until cherries have released a lot of liquid and compote is fragrant, stirring occasionally. Stir in vanilla. Let cool. Transfer to a clean jar and refrigerate up to 2 weeks. Serve at room temperature or warm gently in a saucepan over low heat. Makes 1½ cups.
EACH 2-TBSP. SERVING *54 cal, 0 g fat, 0 mg chol, 16 mg sodium, 11 g carb, 0 g fiber, 0 g pro.*

a new (old) TRADITION

Bring a new dish to your Hanukkah table, even though it's centuries old. Cookbook author Amelia Saltsman adds more fun to the feast with a rediscovery of zengoula—crispy, sugar-syrup-soaked funnel cakes.

ZENGOULA WITH LEMON SYRUP

"The batter should not be ice cold when it's fried, or it will bring down the temperature of the oil and you won't get that beautiful golden color and crispiness," Amelia says. "I recommend taking the batter out of the fridge about an hour before frying. It will thin a little bit, making it easier to shape."

HANDS-ON TIME 1 hr.
TOTAL TIME 8 hr.

½   pkg. active dry yeast (1⅛ tsp.)
1¼ cups warm water (100°F to 110°F)
1   cup unbleached all-purpose flour
¾   cup cornstarch
½   tsp. salt
2   to 3 lemons
1   cup sugar
    Vegetable oil for deep-frying

1. For batter, in a small bowl stir together yeast and ¼ cup of the warm water. Let stand in a warm place 10 minutes or until mixture bubbles.

2. In a bowl use a fork to combine flour, cornstarch, and salt. Stir in ½ cup of the warm water and the yeast mixture. Slowly stir in enough of the remaining ½ cup warm water until dough is lump-free and has the consistency of thick pancake batter. Cover batter with plastic wrap and refrigerate 6 to 24 hours. (Batter will be loose and spongy with a yeasty aroma.)

3. For the lemon syrup, use a five-hole zester to remove long strands of zest from one lemon. Halve and squeeze enough of the remaining lemons to yield ⅓ cup juice. In a small saucepan combine lemon juice, zest, sugar, and ½ cup water; bring to boiling over medium heat. Cook 1 minute or until sugar is dissolved and clear, stirring frequently. Pour into a pie pan; cool. (Syrup can be made a day ahead. Cover and refrigerate.)

4. For zengoula, scrape batter into a large resealable plastic bag set in a bowl. Let batter stand 1 hour before frying. Pour vegetable oil into a 4- or 5-qt. pot, wok, or electric fryer, filling it half full. Heat the oil to 375°F. Snip ¼ inch off the bottom corner of bag. Roll bag closed, forcing batter to corner.

5. Test the temperature of the oil by piping a bit of batter into the hot oil. The oil should bubble around batter immediately. If it doesn't, continue heating. When it bubbles, pipe the batter into the hot oil, creating 3- to 4-inch coils or squiggles. (Don't crowd the pan.)

Fry zengoula for 4 to 5 minutes or until golden and crisp, turning once. Use a slotted spoon to transfer zengoula to a plate lined with paper towels; drain briefly. Drop into the syrup, turning to coat evenly. Arrange them in a single layer on a tray lined with parchment paper; cool. Repeat with remaining batter, skimming loose bits out of the oil between batches.

6. Pile the warm zengoula on a platter and pour the remaining lemon syrup over the top. Serve the same day. Makes 20 servings.

EACH SERVING *274 cal, 22 g fat, 0 mg chol, 60 mg sodium, 20 g carb, 0 g fiber, 1 g pro.*

new ways with
SWISS CHARD

Hearty enough for stir-fries yet tender enough for salads, this colorful green is also a nutritional powerhouse.

Stem colors differs by variety and includes red, white, yellow, and pink. All are interchangeable in recipes, and you might find them labeled as chard, Swiss chard, or rainbow chard (several kinds bundled together).

Look for crisp stalks and firm emerald green leaves free of holes and blemishes. Rinse in cold water, wrap with a damp paper towel, and place in a perforated plastic bag. Chard lasts up to three days in the refrigerator.

SMOKED
SALMON
& CHARD
GRATIN

CHARD, BEET
& MUSHROOM
STIR-FRY

SAVORY
CHARD PIE

THERE'S RARELY A REASON TO TOSS ASIDE CHARD STEMS. EVEN THICK STEMS CAN BE TRIMMED FROM THE LEAVES AND CHOPPED FOR GRATINS, STIR-FRIES, AND HUMMUS—OR THINLY SLICED AND PICKLED.

SAVORY CHARD PIE

HANDS-ON TIME 20 min.
TOTAL TIME 45 min.

1   14.1-oz. pkg. rolled refrigerated unbaked piecrust (2 piecrusts)
6   to 8 cups coarsely chopped chard with stems
2   tsp. coarse cornmeal
4   oz. garlic-and-herb-flavor goat cheese
4   large dates, pitted and chopped
3   oz. thinly sliced ham, pancetta, or prosciutto
½   tsp. salt
½   tsp. black pepper

1. Preheat oven to 375°F. Let piecrusts stand according to package directions. In a large bowl massage chard for 30 seconds. (Chard will reduce to about 3 cups.)
2. Unroll piecrusts onto a lightly floured surface. Cut each crust in half. Roll or press each half with your hands until wide enough to trace around an 8-inch plate with a small knife. Discard scraps or reserve for another use. Transfer rounds to a baking sheet sprinkled with cornmeal.
3. Layer the chard, goat cheese, dates, and ham in the center of each round. Fold edges over the filling, pleating as necessary and leaving center of filling exposed. Sprinkle with salt and pepper. Bake 25 to 30 minutes or until golden. Makes 4 servings.
EACH SERVING *601 cal, 37 g fat, 42 mg chol, 1,119 mg sodium, 57 g carb, 2 g fiber, 13 g pro.*

SMOKED SALMON & CHARD GRATIN

HANDS-ON TIME 30 min.
TOTAL TIME 50 min.

2   bunches chard (12 oz.), stems and leaves sliced
1   small bulb fennel, trimmed, cored, and sliced
1   Tbsp. olive oil
2   Tbsp. all-purpose flour
½   tsp. black pepper
1½ cups milk
6   oz. Gruyère or Swiss cheese, shredded (1½ cups)
2   oz. smoked salmon (not lox-style), skin removed and flaked
1   cup coarse soft bread crumbs
2   Tbsp. butter, melted
1   Tbsp. snipped fresh dill weed

1. Preheat oven to 375°F. In a large oven-going skillet cook and stir chard and fennel in hot oil over medium heat for 8 minutes or until nearly tender. Sprinkle with flour and black pepper and stir to coat. Gradually stir in the milk and simmer, uncovered, 2 minutes or until slightly thickened. Stir in cheese until melted. Stir in smoked salmon. Remove from heat.
2. In a small bowl combine bread crumbs, butter, and dill weed; sprinkle over gratin. Bake 20 minutes or until crumbs are toasted. Cool slightly before serving. Makes 4 servings.
EACH SERVING *392 cal, 26 g fat, 73 mg chol, 744 mg sodium, 19 g carb, 3 g fiber, 22 g pro.*

CHARD, BEET & MUSHROOM STIR-FRY

TOTAL TIME 30 min.

8   oz. golden beets (about 3 small), peeled, quartered and thinly sliced
2   Tbsp. coconut oil
8   oz. mushrooms, quartered
4   cloves garlic, thinly sliced
2   Tbsp. grated fresh ginger
1   bunch chard, stems and leaves coarsely chopped (6 oz.)
⅓   cup reduced-sodium chicken broth or vegetable broth
½   tsp. salt
½   tsp. black pepper
½   cup coarsely chopped fresh cilantro
    Hot cooked polenta or rice

1. In an extra-large skillet cook beets in hot oil over medium-high heat for 5 minutes or just until tender. Add mushrooms, garlic, and ginger. Cook and stir 4 minutes or until mushrooms are golden. Stir in chard and broth. Bring to boiling; reduce heat. Simmer, uncovered, 1 to 2 minutes or until chard is tender.
2. Remove from heat and stir in salt, pepper, and cilantro. Serve over polenta and sprinkle with additional cilantro. Makes 4 servings.
EACH SERVING *180 cal, 7 g fat, 0 mg chol, 476 mg sodium, 24 g carb, 4 g fiber, 6 g pro.*

ITALIAN TORTA
SBRISOLONA

FRENCH
SNACKLETTES
Recipe on page 290

SPANISH
ROUSQUILLES
Recipe on page 290

MOROCCAN
SEMOLINA COOKIES
Recipe on page 290

FRENCH BRETON
GALETTES
Recipe on page 291

What's new, COOKIE?

Plenty! Prolific cookbook author and cookie master Dorie Greenspan shares her latest recipes and baking tips to spice up this year's holiday cookie plates.

CHRISTMAS SPICE COOKIES

CHRISTMAS SPICE COOKIES

HANDS-ON TIME 20 min.
TOTAL TIME 1 hr., 35 min.

- 1   cup unsalted butter (2 sticks), cut into chunks, at room temperature
- ⅔   cup sugar
- ½   tsp. fine sea salt
- ½   tsp. ground cinnamon
- ½   tsp. ground ginger
- ⅛   tsp. ground cloves
- ⅛   tsp. ground allspice
- 1   large egg white, at room temperature
- 1½ tsp. vanilla
- 2   cups all-purpose flour
       Decorating sugar

1. In a large mixing bowl beat the butter, sugar, salt, cinnamon, ginger, cloves, and allspice with an electric mixer on medium speed for 3 minutes or until creamy. Reduce speed to low and beat in the egg white then vanilla. (Dough might appear curdled.) Add flour in three additions, beating on low after each until mixture is almost combined (scrape down bowl); mix until combined. Shape dough into a disk.
2. Place the dough between two sheets of parchment paper; roll ¼ inch thick.

Slide dough, still between the paper, onto a baking sheet; freeze at least 1 hour or refrigerate at least 3 hours.
3. Place rack in center of oven. Preheat oven to 350°F. Line a baking sheet with parchment paper; set aside. Peel top sheet of parchment off dough. Flip dough onto a clean sheet of parchment paper. Peel off remaining sheet of parchment. Using a 2- to 3-inch cutter, cut out cookies. (Reroll and chill scraps.) Place cutouts 1½ inches apart on the prepared baking sheet. Sprinkle edges of cookie cutouts with decorating sugar.
4. Bake 15 to 20 minutes (rotate sheet front to back after 10 minutes) or until cookies feel firm. Cool on baking sheet 5 minutes; transfer to wire rack to cool. Cut out and bake scraps on cooled baking sheet. Makes 14 to 18 cookies.
EACH COOKIE *225 cal, 13 g fat, 35 mg chol, 85 mg sodium, 24 g carb, 1 g fiber, 2 g pro.*

ITALIAN TORTA SBRISOLONA

HANDS-ON TIME 20 min.
TOTAL TIME 1 hr.

- ¾   cup all-purpose flour
- ½   cup almond flour
- ⅓   cup yellow cornmeal

- ⅓   cup sugar
- ½   tsp. fleur de sel or ¼ tsp. fine sea salt
- ½   tsp. ground cinnamon
- 5½ Tbsp. cold unsalted butter, cut into small chunks
- 1   large egg yolk, lightly beaten
- ⅓   cup blanched whole almonds, very coarsely chopped
       Coarse red decorating sugar (optional)

1. Place rack in center of oven. Preheat oven to 325°F. Lightly butter an 8-inch square baking pan.
2. In a food processor add the all-purpose and almond flours, cornmeal, sugar, salt, and cinnamon; pulse to blend. Scatter with chunks of butter; process in long pulses until the mixture resembles coarse cornmeal, scraping bottom of bowl once or twice if needed. Pour in the egg yolk, and process in long pulses until mixture is moist (it will look like grainy, thick, wet sand). Continue processing until dough holds together when pinched.
3. Place dough in a bowl. Stir in the almonds. Squeeze dough into small streusel-like morsels, dropping the pieces into the prepared pan. Gently pat the pieces down.
4. Bake 34 to 38 minutes or until the top is a deep golden brown. Sprinkle with decorating sugar, if desired. Cool in pan 3 minutes. Run a table knife around edges of torta; turn out onto wire rack. Invert onto a cutting board. Cut into pieces, and return to rack to cool. If desired, leave uncut and serve as a break-apart sweet. Makes 16 bars or about 32 chunks.
EACH BAR *124 cal, 8 g fat, 22 mg chol, 76 mg sodium, 12 g carb, 1 g fiber, 2 g pro.*

"NO MATTER WHERE WE'RE FROM, COOKIES HOLD THE POWER TO TAKE US HOME," DORIE SAYS. "THEY'RE OUR MEMORIES ROLLED INTO SOMETHING SWEET, REMINDING US OF OUR GRANDMOTHERS AND OUR ROOTS."

SPANISH ROUSQUILLES

Photo on page 288.

HANDS-ON TIME 40 min.
TOTAL TIME 1 hr., 15 min.

1½   cups all-purpose flour
½   cup powdered sugar
1½   tsp. anise seeds (optional)
½   tsp. baking soda
½   tsp. fine sea salt
¼   cup cold unsalted butter (½ stick),
     cut into small chunks
2   cold large egg yolks (save one for
     the glaze)
2   Tbsp. orange flower water, milk, or
     white wine
2   tsp. honey
¾   cup powdered sugar
2   Tbsp. egg white

1. Place rack in center of oven. Preheat oven to 325°F. Line a baking sheet with parchment paper.
2. In a food processor pulse to blend flour, sugar, anise seeds (if desired), baking soda, and salt. Drop in pieces of cold butter; process in long pulses until mixture is grainy. In a small bowl combine yolks, orange flower water, and honey; add to processor in small amounts, pulsing after each addition and then until mixture turns to moist curds, scraping bottom of bowl as needed.
3. Transfer dough to counter; knead lightly until dough holds together. Place between two pieces of parchment paper; roll ¼ inch thick.
4. Peel top sheet of parchment off dough. Flip dough onto clean parchment paper; remove remaining parchment paper. Using a 1¾-inch-diameter round cutter, cut out as many circles as you can. Transfer to a baking sheet (they won't spread much). Use a ¾-inch-diameter round cookie cutter to remove centers. Shape scraps into a disk; roll and cut. (Gather, roll, and cut scraps once more.)
5. Bake cookies for 18 to 20 minutes (rotate front to back after 10 minutes) or until golden and firm enough to lift. Place baking sheet on wire rack; dust cookies with powdered sugar or let cool to glaze.
6. For glaze, in a small saucepan bring powdered sugar and 3 Tbsp. water to boiling. Boil at a moderate rate until candy thermometer registers 235°F to 240°F, or soft-ball stage (about 4 minutes). In small bowl whisk egg white 1 to 2 minutes or until soft peaks form.
7. Anchor bowl of egg white on a silicone potholder or dish towel; in a slow, steady stream whisk egg white into hot sugar syrup. Using a pastry brush, brush each cookie with glaze. Allow glaze to set at room temperature. Makes 30 cookies.
EACH COOKIE *66 cal, 2 g fat, 16 mg chol, 60 mg sodium, 11 g carb, 0 g fiber, 1 g pro.*

FRENCH SNACKLETTES

Photo on page 288.

HANDS-ON TIME 35 min.
TOTAL TIME 50 min.

1   cup sliced, slivered, or whole
     almonds (blanched or unblanched)
½   cup sugar
¾   cup all-purpose flour
⅓   cup unsweetened cocoa powder
½   tsp. fine sea salt or ¾ tsp. fleur de sel
¼   tsp. ground cinnamon
7   Tbsp. cold unsalted butter, cut into
     small chunks
½   cup mini chocolate chips or very
     finely chopped semisweet or
     bittersweet chocolate

1. Position racks to divide oven in thirds; preheat to 325°F. Line two baking sheets with parchment paper.
2. In a food processor process almonds and sugar until almonds are mostly ground, scraping bowl occasionally to ensure no thick layer on the bottom. Add flour, cocoa, salt, and cinnamon; pulse to combine. Scatter bits of cold butter over mixture and process in long pulses to moist curds and crumbs, scraping as needed, and checking dough often to see whether it holds together (might take a couple of minutes). Add chocolate; process for a couple pulses until combined. Shape the dough into a ball.
3. For each cookie, squeeze about 1 teaspoon of dough into a nugget, pyramid, or random shape. Place on baking sheets with a little space between.
4. Bake cookies 15 minutes (rotate sheets top to bottom and front to back after 8 minutes). Cookies will be very soft, and will firm as they cool. Cool on baking sheets 5 minutes; gently transfer cookies to wire racks to cool. Makes 60 cookies.
EACH COOKIE *45 cal, 3 g fat, 4 mg chol, 19 mg sodium, 5 g carb, 0 g fiber, 1 g pro.*

MOROCCAN SEMOLINA COOKIES

Photo on page 288.

HANDS-ON TIME 40 min.
TOTAL TIME 55 min.

2   cups almond flour
1¾   cups plus 2 Tbsp. semolina flour
1½   tsp. baking powder
¼   tsp. fine sea salt
¾   cup granulated sugar
1   lemon
2   large eggs, at room temperature
¼   cup mild-flavor oil, such as canola
1   tsp. vanilla
1   tsp. orange flower water (optional)
     Powdered sugar

1. Position racks to divide oven in thirds. Preheat oven to 350°F. Line two baking sheets with parchment paper.
2. In a bowl combine almond and semolina flours, baking powder, and salt.
3. Add granulated sugar to a large mixing bowl. Finely zest lemon over the sugar, then rub ingredients together until sugar is moist and fragrant. Add eggs; beat with an electric mixer on medium speed 3 minutes. With mixer running, pour in the oil and beat 3 minutes. Beat in vanilla and, if desired, orange flower water. Add half the dry ingredients, beating on low just until combined. Repeat with remaining dry ingredients (dough will be thick).
4. Sift some powdered sugar into a small bowl. Shape level tablespoons of dough into balls; roll in powdered sugar. Place 2 inches apart on prepared baking sheets. Gently press your thumb in the center of each ball.
5. Bake 14 to 16 minutes (rotate pans top to bottom and front to back after 8 minutes) or until golden on bottom and firm to the touch (they'll puff and crack on top). Transfer to wire racks to cool. If desired, top cooled cookies with additional powdered sugar and lemon zest. Makes about 38 cookies.
EACH COOKIE *99 cal, 5 g fat, 10 mg chol, 40 mg sodium, 12 g carb, 1 g fiber, 3 g pro.*

FRENCH BRETON GALETTES

Photo on page 288.

HANDS-ON TIME 20 min.
TOTAL TIME 3 hr., 30 min.

2¼ cups all-purpose flour
2½ tsp. baking powder
1 cup unsalted butter (2 sticks), cut into chunks, at room temperature
1 cup sugar
1¼ tsp. fleur de sel or ¾ tsp. fine sea salt
2 large egg yolks, at room temperature
¾ cup thick fruit jam or marmalade

1. In a medium bowl combine flour and baking powder. In a large mixing bowl beat butter, sugar, and salt with an electric mixer on medium-low speed until smooth. Add egg yolks, one at a time, beating until combined. Add dry ingredients all at once and beat on low speed until combined, scraping bowl as needed. (Dough will be thick and will almost clean sides of bowl.)
2. Turn dough out onto work surface; divide in half. Shape each into a 6-inch log. Wrap with plastic wrap; freeze at least 1 hour or refrigerate at least 2 hours.
3. Center rack in oven; preheat to 325°F. Lightly butter or spray two 12-cup muffin pans. Using a thin sharp knife, cut one log into 18 ⅓-inch slices. Place in muffin cups. Slice enough of remaining log to fill both muffin pans now, or cut and bake it later.
4. Bake cookies for 18 to 20 minutes (rotating muffin pans front to back after 10 minutes) or until edges of cookies are golden brown. (Cookies dip in the center as they bake, forming a raised edge.)
5. Remove cookies from oven; press a cork into the center of each. (Make sure indent goes almost to bottom of cookie.) Cool cookies in pans; remove once they're room temperature. Repeat with remaining dough, using cool muffin pans.
6. For filling, in a small bowl stir together the jam and 1 Tbsp. water. Microwave until mixture boils. Spoon jam into each indentation level with the top of galette. Refrigerate 30 minutes or until filling is set. Serve at room temperature. Makes 36 cookies.

EACH COOKIE *117 cal, 5 g fat, 24 mg chol, 115 mg sodium, 16 g carb, 0 g fiber, 1 g pro.*

KERRIN'S MULTIGRAIN CHOCOLATE CHIP COOKIES

HANDS-ON TIME 30 min.
TOTAL TIME 1 hr., 50 min.

½ cup all-purpose flour
½ cup whole wheat flour
½ cup buckwheat flour
½ tsp. baking powder
½ tsp. baking soda
7 Tbsp. unsalted butter, cut into chunks, at room temperature
⅔ cup packed light brown sugar
½ cup sugar
⅛ tsp. fine sea salt
1 large egg, at room temperature
1 large egg yolk, at room temperature
¼ cup kasha (buckwheat groats; Dorie prefers Wolff's medium granulation) or finely chopped toasted nuts
6 oz. bittersweet chocolate, coarsely chopped
Flaky sea salt or fine sea salt

1. In a bowl whisk together the three flours, baking powder, and baking soda. In a large bowl beat butter, sugars, and salt with an electric mixer on medium speed for 5 minutes. Add egg and beat 1 minute; add the yolk and beat 1 minute more. Add dry ingredients all at once and beat on low speed until almost all the dry ingredients are combined. Add kasha and beat a few seconds. Add chocolate and beat on low just until all is combined. Shape into a ball; wrap in plastic wrap. Chill at least 1 hour.
2. Place rack in center of oven. Preheat oven to 375°F. Line a baking sheet with parchment paper. Using a medium cookie scoop, scoop level portions of dough (or rounded tablespoonfuls) and place 2 inches apart on prepared baking sheet. Sprinkle evenly with flaky salt.
3. Bake 8 to 9 minutes (rotate pan front to back after 4 minutes) or just until edges of cookies start to brown. (Cookies should look underbaked.) Let cool on baking sheet 2 minutes. Transfer cookies to a wire rack to cool. Cookies will firm as they cool. Repeat with remaining cookie dough. Makes 25 cookies.

EACH COOKIE *137 cal, 6 g fat, 24 mg chol, 75 mg sodium, 20 g carb, 1 g fiber, 2 g pro.*

KERRIN'S MULTIGRAIN CHOCOLATE CHIP COOKIES

FRUIT AND WALNUT BREAD BARS
Recipe on page 292

FRUIT AND WALNUT BREAD BARS

Photo on page 292.

HANDS-ON TIME 15 min.
TOTAL TIME 1 hr., 30 min.

- 1   cup all-purpose flour
- 1¼ tsp. baking powder
- 3   large egg whites, at room temperature
- ¼   tsp. salt
- ½   cup sugar
- 1   cup coarsely chopped walnuts
- 1   cup plump, moist* mixed dried fruit (candied red or green cherries, crystallized ginger, papaya, cherries, pineapple, apricots, figs, and/or other favorites), snipped, cut, or chopped into bite-size pieces

1. Place rack in center of oven. Preheat oven to 350°F. Lightly butter an 8-inch square baking pan.

2. In a bowl stir together the flour and baking powder. In a mixing bowl beat egg whites and salt with an electric mixer on medium until stiff peaks form. Gradually beat in the sugar; continue to beat until peaks are firm and glossy. Using a spatula, gently fold in the flour mixture, followed by the walnuts and candied fruit. (The fruit and nuts are heavy and bulky, so no matter how gentle your touch the meringue will deflate.) Transfer batter to pan and smooth the top.

3. Bake 30 to 32 minutes (rotate pan front to back after 15 minutes) or until bread feels set yet still has some give all over and a skewer inserted in center comes out clean. (Bars will not brown; they will be a warm ivory color, like nougat.) Cool in pan on a wire rack 5 minutes. Run a table knife around edges, unmold, and turn over to cool at room temperature. Cut into 2×1-inch bars. Makes 32 bars.

EACH BAR *65 cal, 2 g fat, 0 mg chol, 47 mg sodium, 10 g carb, 1 g fiber, 1 g pro.*

*Tip If fruit isn't moist, place in a bowl and cover with very hot tap water. Let plump 5 minutes; drain and pat dry.

MS. CORBITT'S PECAN CAKE FINGERS

HANDS-ON TIME 30 min.
TOTAL TIME 1 hr., 20 min.

- ¾   cup plus 2 Tbsp. all-purpose flour
- ½   tsp. baking powder
- ¼   tsp. fine sea salt
- 1½ cups finely chopped pecans, toasted (tip, page 37)
- 2   cups plus 2 Tbsp. packed light brown sugar
- 3   large egg whites, at room temperature
- 2   tsp. vanilla
- 2   cups powdered sugar
- ½   cup unsalted butter (1 stick), cut into chunks
- ½   tsp. vanilla
       Pecan halves (optional)

1. Place rack in center of oven . Preheat oven to 275°F. Put a dab of butter (to act like glue) in middle of 13×9-inch baking pan or quarter-sheet pan, line with parchment or wax paper, and generously butter the paper.

2. In a bowl combine the flour, baking powder, and salt. Put pecans in a small bowl or on a piece of parchment paper. Pour ¼ cup of the flour mixture over the nuts; toss to combine. Push the brown sugar through a strainer into a bowl or onto a piece of parchment paper; discard any hard lumps of sugar that remain in the strainer. (Or stir brown sugar in a bowl to crush any lumps.)

3. In a large mixing bowl beat the egg whites with an electric mixer on medium-high speed until soft peaks form. With mixer running, very gradually add the brown sugar, then beat on high speed 1 minute more. (You'll have a shiny, marshmallowy, cafe-au-lait-color meringue.) Beat in the 2 tsp. vanilla.

4. Gently fold the flour mixture into meringue in three additions. (Don't worry about getting the last portion of flour thoroughly mixed because you have more folding to do.) Gently fold in the flour-coated pecans in three batches. (The meringue will deflate, but the shine lingers.) Spread batter evenly into prepared pan.

5. Bake 50 to 55 minutes or until the top is dry, dull, and pale. (It won't spring back when lightly pressed.) Transfer to a cooling rack and cool 3 minutes. Run a table knife around edges to release cake; turn onto wire rack to unmold. (If cake doesn't release immediately, run your knife around edges again, turn cake over, and give the pan and wire rack a little shake.) Gently remove paper; invert the cake onto another wire rack to cool. Transfer cooled cake to a cutting board. Using a long, thin knife, cut the cake into 3×1-inch fingers.

6. For icing, pour powdered sugar into a medium heatproof bowl. In a small saucepan heat butter over medium heat until it boils. (Swirl pan occasionally so you can see beneath the foam.) Cook the butter until it turns a cozy shade of brown. (You'll see dark spots in the butter. The more color you get, the more flavor you'll get. Just don't take it so far that the butter burns.) Pour the butter and brown bits over the powdered sugar; add the ½ tsp. vanilla. Working with a flexible spatula, stir and mash butter into sugar until you have a firm mixture. (It will look more like something you'd mold than spread.)

7. Press some icing onto center of cookie, spreading to cover the cookie. After you cover the cookie with icing, use the spatula to press and smooth the top. Press pecan halves into the icing, if desired. Leave cookies at room temperature 1 hour or until icing firms. Makes 36 bars.

EACH BAR *143 cal, 6 g fat, 7 mg chol, 31 mg sodium, 22 g carb, 1 g fiber, 1 g pro.*

MS. CORBITT'S PECAN CAKE FINGERS

CHOCOLATE & OLIVE COOKIES

HANDS-ON TIME 30 min.
TOTAL TIME 1 hr., 30 min.

1¼ cups all-purpose flour
¼ cup cornstarch
¼ cup unsweetened cocoa powder
½ cup unsalted butter (1 stick), cut into chunks, at room temperature
2 Tbsp. extra-virgin olive oil, preferably a fruity one
⅓ cup sugar
½ tsp. fine sea salt
¼ tsp. black pepper
1 large egg yolk
⅓ cup chopped pitted oil-cured black olives

1. Sift flour, cornstarch, and cocoa powder together into a bowl. In a large mixing bowl beat the butter, olive oil, sugar, salt, and pepper with an electric mixer 2 minutes or until smooth. Add yolk; beat for another minute, scraping down bowl as needed. Add dry ingredients all at once, beating on low speed until you have moist curds. (You are done mixing when you can squeeze some of the curds and they hold together easily.) Using a flexible spatula, stir in the olives.
2. Turn out dough, and knead briefly to bring it together; divide in half. Roll each half into an 8- to 8½-inch log. Wrap with plastic wrap; refrigerate at least 2 hours or freeze at least 1 hour.
3. Position racks to divide oven in thirds; preheat to 325°F. Line two baking sheets with parchment paper. Working with one log at a time, use a thin sharp knife to cut dough into ¼-inch-thick slices. Place slices 1 inch apart on prepared baking sheets.
4. Bake 15 to 17 minutes (rotate baking sheets top to bottom and front to back after 8 minutes) or until just firm to the touch. Cool on baking sheets 3 minutes. Carefully transfer to wire racks to cool. Makes 48 cookies.
EACH COOKIE *36 cal, 2 g fat, 7 mg chol, 25 mg sodium, 4 g carb, 0 g fiber, 0 g pro.*

FENNEL & ORANGE SHORTBREAD

HANDS-ON TIME 20 min.
TOTAL TIME 1 hr., 45 min.

1 cup all-purpose flour
2 Tbsp. cornstarch
2 Tbsp. sugar
 Finely grated zest of 1 orange or tangerine
1¾ tsp. fennel seeds, crushed
½ cup unsalted butter (1 stick), cut into chunks, at room temperature
1 Tbsp. powdered sugar
½ tsp. fleur de sel or ¼ tsp. fine sea salt
 Fleur de sel or kosher salt

1. Place rack in center of oven. Preheat oven to 350°F.
2. In a bowl combine flour and cornstarch. In a large mixing bowl combine sugar and orange zest; rub together until sugar is moist. Toss in the fennel seeds; rub into the sugar. Add the butter, powdered sugar, and salt; beat with an electric mixer on medium speed for 3 minutes or until mixture is smooth, scraping down bowl as needed. Add dry ingredients all at once, beating on low speed until dough resembles a crumble topping that holds together when pinched. (The first 3 minutes dough will look like oatmeal.)
3. Gently knead dough until ball comes together. Shape into a disk; place between sheets of parchment paper. Roll into an 8-inch circle. Lift off the top sheet and slide the dough, still on the bottom sheet, onto a baking sheet. Use a fork to prick all the way through the dough in a spoke pattern to form 12 wedges. Sprinkle with fleur de sel.
4. Bake 20 minutes (rotate baking sheet front to back after 10 minutes) or just until edges are lightly browned. Cool on baking sheet 5 minutes. Using a knife or pizza wheel, cut along fork marks. Cool on baking sheet. Makes 12 wedges.
EACH WEDGE *123 cal, 8 g fat, 20 mg chol, 148 mg sodium, 12 g carb, 0 g fiber, 1 g pro.*

PUFFED GRAIN & MISO COOKIES

HANDS-ON TIME 20 min.
TOTAL TIME 35 min.

 Nonstick cooking spray
3¼ cups puffed rice cereal
1 cup salted peanuts, coarsely chopped
¾ cup puffed whole grain cereal or puffed barley cereal
⅓ cup plump dried cranberries, goji berries, or raisins, coarsely chopped (optional)
¼ cup white sesame seeds
1 tsp. fleur de sel or ½ tsp. fine sea salt
⅓ cup plus 2 Tbsp. brown rice syrup
2 Tbsp. light-color miso paste
2 tsp. olive oil
1 tsp. toasted sesame oil

1. Position racks to divide oven in thirds. Preheat oven to 325°F. Lightly coat 2½-inch muffin cups with cooking spray.
2. In an extra-large bowl toss together puffed rice, peanuts, puffed whole grain, dried fruit (if desired), sesame seeds, and the salt.
3. In a small saucepan bring rice syrup just to a boil over low heat (or boil in a microwave). Remove syrup from heat; let stand 2 minutes. Add miso and both oils; whisk to blend. (It's OK if miso doesn't dissolve completely, leaving little strands.)
4. Pour the warm liquid over the dry ingredients. Using a silicone spatula, stir for a few minutes until all is moistened. Fill each muffin cup with 2 Tbsp. of the mixture; press flat with the bottom of a jar. Bake 15 to 18 minutes (rotate muffin pans front to back after 8 minutes) or until cookies are golden brown. Transfer to wire racks and cool completely before unmolding. Makes 36 to 40 cookies.
EACH COOKIE *56 cal, 3 g fat, 0 mg chol, 125 mg sodium, 6 g carb, 1 g fiber, 1 g pro.*

"DON'T CHEAT THE COOL DOWN. IT'S TEMPTING TO GRAB A JUST-BAKED COOKIE, BUT DURING COOLING A COOKIE'S TRUE TEXTURE DEVELOPS."

DATE-NUT PINWHEELS

HANDS-ON TIME 30 min.
TOTAL TIME 2 hr., 45 min.

- ¾   cup chopped pitted dates
- ½   cup finely chopped walnuts or pecans
- 2   Tbsp. sugar
- 1   tsp. freshly squeezed lemon juice or 2 tsp. orange juice
- 1¾   cups all-purpose flour
- ¼   tsp. baking powder
- ⅛   tsp. baking soda
- ½   cup unsalted butter (1 stick), cut into chunks, at room temperature
- 1   cup packed light brown sugar
- ¼   tsp. fine sea salt
- 1   large egg, at room temperature

1. For date filling, in small saucepan combine dates, nuts, ½ cup water, the sugar, and lemon juice; bring to a boil over medium heat, stirring occasionally. Reduce heat; simmer until the liquid is absorbed and dates and nuts are spreadable. Transfer to a bowl; cool to room temperature.

2. For dough, in a bowl combine the flour, baking powder, and baking soda. In a large mixing bowl beat butter, brown sugar, and salt with an electric mixer on medium speed about 3 minutes or until smooth and creamy, scraping bowl as needed. Add the egg and beat for another minute or until combined. Add dry ingredients all at once, beating on low speed until combined. (You'll have a soft dough that cleans the sides of the bowl.)

3. Turn dough out onto a piece of parchment paper and shape it into a rectangle. Cover with another piece of parchment and roll the dough into a 12×10-inch rectangle. (While rolling, peel paper away from dough often so it doesn't leave creases.) Slide dough, still between paper, onto a baking sheet and refrigerate at least 2 hours or freeze at least 1 hour.

4. Leave cold dough on the counter 10 minutes or until it's supple enough to bend without cracking. Peel off top sheet of parchment from dough. Flip onto a clean sheet of parchment paper. Peel off remaining sheet of parchment. Position dough long side parallel to you. Spread filling to within 1 inch of top and ½ inch of short sides. Starting with long edge closest to you, use the paper to lift and roll the dough into a log, keeping it compact. (The ends will be ragged.) Wrap the log in plastic wrap or waxed paper and refrigerate at least 1 hour.

5. Position racks to divide oven in thirds. Preheat oven to 350°F. Line two baking sheets with parchment paper. Unwrap and place log of cookie dough on a cutting board. Trim ends until you see spirals of filling. Using a thin sharp knife, cut the log into ½-inch slices. (Gaps between the filling and dough fill in as they bake.) Place about 1½ inches apart on baking sheets. Chill remaining log.

6. Bake 15 to 17 minutes (rotate baking sheets top to bottom and front to back after 8 minutes) or until cookies spread, puff, and brown lightly (they should still be soft when gently poked). Cool on baking sheets 2 minutes; carefully transfer to wire rack to cool. Serve cookies warm or at room temperature. Bake the remaining cookie slices on a cool baking sheet. Makes 18 cookies.

EACH COOKIE *188 cal, 8 g fat, 24 mg chol, 55 mg sodium, 29 g carb, 1 g fiber, 2 g pro.*

DOUBLE-GINGER MOLASSES COOKIES

HANDS-ON TIME 1 hr.
TOTAL TIME 3 hr.

- 2¼   cups all-purpose flour
- 2   Tbsp. unsweetened cocoa powder
- 1   to 2 tsp. instant espresso powder (optional)
- 1½   tsp. ground ginger
- 1   tsp. ground cinnamon
- ¼   tsp. ground cloves
- ½   tsp. baking soda
- ½   tsp. fine sea salt
- ¾   cup unsalted butter (1½ sticks), cut into chunks, at room temperature
- ⅓   cup granulated sugar
- ⅓   cup packed light brown sugar
- 1   large egg yolk, at room temperature
- ½   cup unsulfured molasses
- 1½   tsp. vanilla
- ⅓   cup chopped candied ginger or 2 Tbsp. minced fresh ginger mixed with 2 tsp. sugar
- 7   oz. semisweet or bittersweet chocolate, chopped
     Coarse sugar

1. In a bowl combine the flour, cocoa, espresso powder (if desired), spices, baking soda, and salt. In a large mixing bowl beat butter and sugars with an electric mixer on medium-low speed 3 minutes or until combined, scraping sides of bowl as needed. Add the yolk and beat 1 minute. Add molasses and vanilla; beat until smooth. Add the dry ingredients all at once, beating on low

DATE-NUT PINWHEELS

DOUBLE-GINGER MOLASSES COOKIES

speed until flour is almost combined. Stir in candied ginger and chocolate until evenly distributed, being sure to incorporate any dry ingredients at the bottom of the bowl. Shape into a disk and wrap in plastic. Refrigerate at least 2 hours.

2. Position racks to divide oven in thirds. Preheat oven to 350°F. Line 2 baking sheets with parchment paper. Spoon some coarse sugar into a shallow bowl.

3. For each cookie, shape a level medium cookie scoop or rounded tablespoon of dough into a ball and roll in the sugar to coat. Place a couple inches apart on baking sheet. Press to flatten to about ½ inch thickness.

4. Bake 13 minutes (rotate pans top to bottom and front to back after 7 minutes) or until lightly set around the edges but soft in the center. Let stand on baking sheets 15 minutes. Transfer to wire racks to cool. Makes 36 cookies.

EACH COOKIE *135 cal, 6 g fat, 16 mg chol, 52 mg sodium, 21 g carb, 1 g fiber, 1 g pro.*

Mini Double-Ginger Molasses Cookies Prepare cookies as directed, except use greased 1¾-inch muffin cups and use a small scoop to portion the dough. Bake 11 minutes (rotate pan after 6 minutes).

MOROCCAN SEMOLINA COOKIES
Recipe on page 290

RECIPE INDEX

C

METRIC INFORMATION

The charts on this page provide a guide for converting measurements from the U.S. customary system, which is used throughout this book, to the metric system.

PRODUCT DIFFERENCES

Most of the ingredients called for in the recipes in this book are available in most countries. However, some are known by different names. Here are some common U.S. American ingredients and their possible counterparts:

- Sugar (white) is granulated, fine granulated, or castor sugar.
- Powdered sugar is icing sugar.
- All-purpose flour is enriched, bleached, or unbleached white household flour. When self-rising flour is used in place of all-purpose flour in a recipe that calls for leavening, omit the leavening agent (baking soda or baking powder) and salt.
- Light-color corn syrup is golden syrup.
- Cornstarch is cornflour.
- Baking soda is bicarbonate of soda.
- Vanilla or vanilla extract is vanilla essence.
- Green, red, or yellow sweet peppers are capsicums or bell peppers.
- Golden raisins are sultanas.

VOLUME AND WEIGHT

The United States traditionally uses cup measures for liquid and solid ingredients. The chart below shows the approximate imperial and metric equivalents. If you are accustomed to weighing solid ingredients, the following approximate equivalents will be helpful.

- 1 cup butter, castor sugar, or rice = 8 ounces = ½ pound = 250 grams
- 1 cup flour = 4 ounces = ¼ pound = 125 grams
- 1 cup icing sugar = 5 ounces = 150 grams

Canadian and U.S. volume for a cup measure is 8 fluid ounces (237 ml), but the standard metric equivalent is 250 ml.

1 British imperial cup is 10 fluid ounces.

In Australia, 1 tablespoon equals 20 ml, and there are 4 teaspoons in the Australian tablespoon.

Spoon measures are used for small amounts of ingredients. Although the size of the tablespoon varies slightly in different countries, for practical purposes and for recipes in this book, a straight substitution is all that's necessary. Measurements made using cups or spoons always should be level unless stated otherwise.

Common Weight Range Replacements

Imperial / U.S.	Metric
½ ounce	15 g
1 ounce	25 g or 30 g
4 ounces (¼ pound)	115 g or 125 g
8 ounces (½ pound)	225 g or 250 g
16 ounces (1 pound)	450 g or 500 g
1¼ pounds	625 g
1½ pounds	750 g
2 pounds or 2¼ pounds	1,000 g or 1 Kg

Oven Temperature Equivalents

Fahrenheit Setting	Celsius Setting*	Gas Setting
300°F	150°C	Gas Mark 2 (very low)
325°F	160°C	Gas Mark 3 (low)
350°F	180°C	Gas Mark 4 (moderate)
375°F	190°C	Gas Mark 5 (moderate)
400°F	200°C	Gas Mark 6 (hot)
425°F	220°C	Gas Mark 7 (hot)
450°F	230°C	Gas Mark 8 (very hot)
475°F	240°C	Gas Mark 9 (very hot)
500°F	260°C	Gas Mark 10 (extremely hot)
Broil	Broil	Grill

*Electric and gas ovens may be calibrated using celsius. However, for an electric oven, increase celsius setting 10 to 20 degrees when cooking above 160°C. For convection or forced air ovens (gas or electric), lower the temperature setting 25°F/10°C when cooking at all heat levels.

Baking Pan Sizes

Imperial / U.S.	Metric
9×1½-inch round cake pan	22- or 23×4-cm (1.5 L)
9×1½-inch pie plate	22- or 23×4-cm (1 L)
8×8×2-inch square cake pan	20×5-cm (2 L)
9×9×2-inch square cake pan	22- or 23×4.5-cm (2.5 L)
11×7×1½-inch baking pan	28×17×4-cm (2 L)
2-quart rectangular baking pan	30×19×4.5-cm (3 L)
13×9×2-inch baking pan	34×22×4.5-cm (3.5 L)
15×10×1-inch jelly roll pan	40×25×2-cm
9×5×3-inch loaf pan	23×13×8-cm (2 L)
2-quart casserole	2 L

U.S. / Standard Metric Equivalents

⅛ teaspoon = 0.5 ml	
¼ teaspoon = 1 ml	
½ teaspoon = 2 ml	
1 teaspoon = 5 ml	
1 tablespoon = 15 ml	
2 tablespoons = 25 ml	
¼ cup = 2 fluid ounces = 50 ml	
⅓ cup = 3 fluid ounces = 75 ml	
½ cup = 4 fluid ounces = 125 ml	
⅔ cup = 5 fluid ounces = 150 ml	
¾ cup = 6 fluid ounces = 175 ml	
1 cup = 8 fluid ounces = 250 ml	
2 cups = 1 pint = 500 ml	
1 quart = 1 litre	